D0457915

MORE PRAISE FOR

Friendshifts™

THE POWER OF FRIENDSHIP
AND HOW IT SHAPES OUR LIVES

"I compliment Jan Yager on this book. It is very informative in both scientific language as well as layman's terms. There is something for everyone in *Friendshifts*."
—Bill Daniels, Founder and Chairman, Daniels & Associates

"Friends are the glue that holds our lives together. Dr. Yager maps out how to make and nurture these precious alliances."
—Marilyn Ross, author, *Big Ideas for Small Service Businesses*

"In these days of greater distance among people, many yearn for closer relationships. Too often, they don't know where to begin to assuage their loneliness. Simply and straightforwardly, Jan Yager shows them how."
—Harry Levinson, Ph.D., The Levinson Institute

"Reading *Friendshifts* got me to pick up the phone and renew some old friendships. I'd recommend this book to anyone who is evaluating their direction in life and as a great gift for someone who needs a road map to socialization."

—Mitchell P. Davis, Editor, *Yearbook of Experts, Authorities & Spokespersons,* Washington, D.C.

"*Friendshifts* is a very creative, meaningful concept. This book is a very important gift to the community on the extremely important issue of friendship. Many people will receive deep insight into areas they had never thought about or reflected upon previously. This book is terrific!"

—Beverly Cuthbertson-Johnson, Ph.D., Southern Desert Medical Center

"In an age of superficialities and self-centeredness, Jan Yager's book is an in-depth unveiling of friendship's significance and potential in our lives. *Friendshifts* is an informative and intelligent road map for that important journey of discovery."

—John G. Murphy, Ph.D., Executive Director, Friends of Karen

"Engaging and informative. A lovely blend of vivid case material against a backdrop of scientific information."
—Dan Perlman, Ph.D., University of British Columbia

"*Friendshifts* is the perfect title for a wonderful book that helps me realize everything in life, even friendship, changes!"
—Barbara Church-Katten, Associate Director, Center for Career Planning and Placement, Adelphi University

Friendshifts™

Other Books by Jan Yager, Ph.D. (a/k/a J.L. Barkas)

Friendship: A Selected, Annotated Bibliography

Single in America

The Help Book

Victims

Creative Time Management

Business Protocol: How to Survive & Succeed in Business

Making Your Office Work for You

How to Write Like a Professional

The Vegetable Passion:
A History of the Vegetarian State of Mind

Meatless Cooking: Celebrity Style

Friendshifts™

THE POWER OF FRIENDSHIP
AND HOW IT SHAPES OUR LIVES

Jan Yager, Ph.D.

HANNACROIX CREEK BOOKS, INC.   STAMFORD, CT

Copyright © 1997 by Jan Yager, Ph.D.
Printed in the United States of America

Acknowledgment is made to reprint illustrations from "B.C." by permission of Johnny Hart and Creators Syndicate, Inc. and by Tom Cheney, copyright © 1997 by Tom Cheney, reprinted with his permission.

Library of Congress Catalog Card Number: 96-94538

Publisher's Cataloging In Publication
   (Prepared by Quality Books Inc.)

Yager, Jan, 1948-
   Friendshifts : the power of friendship and how it shapes our
lives / Jan Yager.
   p. cm.
   Includes bibliographical references and index.
   ISBN: 1-889262-00-5

   1. Friendship.   I. Title.

BJ1533.F8Y34 1997   177'.6
                               QBI96-20508

Published by:
   HANNACROIX CREEK BOOKS, INC.
   1127 High Ridge Road, #110
   Stamford, Connecticut 06905 U.S.A.
   (203) 321-8674   Fax (203) 968-0193   E-mail: HCBBooks@aol.com

For my husband, Fred; our children; my mother, sister, and devoted friends; and the memory of my father and brother

Author's Note and Disclaimer

Quotes in this book not attributed to a secondary source are from the original research conducted by the author, in the form of either interviews or questionnaires, and are reprinted verbatim and, if necessary, excerpted. If minor editing was required for either sense or clarification, those additions or changes are indicated by brackets.

If anonymity was requested, a fictitious first name has been provided; identifying details have also been changed to maintain that anonymity. However, care has been taken to preserve the integrity of each example.

The purpose of this book is to provide inspiration, information, and opinions on the topic covered. It is sold with the understanding that the publisher and author are not engaged in rendering psychological, medical, sociological, or other professional services.

Despite the author's extensive research, peer reviews of specific chapters or the entire manuscript, as well as professional editing and proofreading of the manuscript, typographical or content mistakes may inadvertently be contained in this book. In addition, information may be out of date because it was unavailable until after this book was completed and printed.

The author and publisher shall have neither liability nor responsibility to any person or entity with regard to any loss or damage caused, or alleged to be caused, directly or indirectly by the opinions or information contained in this book.

Contents

PART 2 *FRIENDSHIFTS*, OR HOW FRIENDSHIP CHANGES THROUGHOUT LIFE

PART 3 HOW TO BE A BETTER FRIEND

PART 4 WORK AND FRIENDSHIP

PART 5 LIFE AND FRIENDSHIP

An ideal friend is somebody who cares about you, really cares about you. Somebody you can say anything you want to, and they're going to say, "It's okay." That's what a friend is.

—52-year-old full-time graduate student and mother of four

PART 1

THAT'S WHAT FRIENDS ARE FOR

Friends are not luxuries—they're necessities.
—The Boys Town Center (booklet), Boys Town, Nebraska

There are two elements that go to the composition of friendship...One is Truth....The other element of friendship is tenderness.

—Ralph Waldo Emerson, "Friendship," *Essays* (1841)

1. THE POWER OF FRIENDSHIP

I'm made up of the people I know and the friends I keep. I'd be nothing without them.

—20-year-old Penn State male freshman

One Sunday afternoon about a year ago, I called my close friend Joyce just to say hello, but she was not home. A few hours later, Joyce returned my call. She started our conversation by sharing with me that she had a job interview the next day. It seemed she was up against 90 others. She was feeling depressed, anxious, and scared. Then she gave me the highest compliment a friend could give to another friend: "Just hearing your voice makes me feel better."

Without even trying, I had helped lower Joyce's stress level. It is just that ability of friends to reduce the stress related to life's tougher events that has led researchers to confirm that friends extend our lives as well as improve the quality of our lives.

Joyce and I find comfort in talking to each other because of our ongoing close friendship as well as our shared history, which began the summer of 1969, when we first met in geology class at Temple University in Philadelphia. From the very start of our relationship, Joyce always laughed at my jokes, bringing out a whimsical side in me that too few others see behind my intense, driven, and studious facade. I shared in Joyce's grief when her mother died too young; I witnessed Joyce's joyful wedding, as she did mine. I was at the surprise shower many years later for her newborn daughter, a blessed event that much sweeter since this pregnancy had not ended in a miscarriage at five months as so many others had.

FRIENDSHIFTS

Although we lived in the same city for just three years—I moved back to New York, then to Connecticut—Joyce and I have kept up our close friendship. *Friendshifts* is a word I have coined for the way our friendships change as we go from one stage in our life to another, or even relocate from one school, job, neighborhood, or community to another. It is a variation on the old adage "Make new friends but keep the old; one is silver, but the other's gold." Whether the need to form new friends is caused by a change in interests, a move to another city, a promotion to another level or into another profession, or the death of old friends or even of a spouse, shifting to new friendships that serve current needs makes it possible to feel connected even if old friends are seen less frequently, if at all.

The variety of roles that we must play throughout our life—as student, worker, spouse, or parent—changes, as does the place that friendship holds in our life. But we still need friends, ranging from casual to close or best friends, and of both sexes. Friendship plays a continual role, although at different stages it will be less or more important to our emotional stability, depending upon the other primary attachments in our life.

When I gave the eulogy for my 83-year-old dearly beloved grandmother, I was saddened to look out at the small cluster of family members in the funeral parlor chapel. I did not see even one of the friends my widowed grandmother had cared about for most of her life, since they had already died or moved far away. But my grandmother also failed to develop new friends, and consequently she was lonelier in her last years than she had to be. She needed to understand the concept of *friendshifts* so her later years could have been fuller; her family was too busy with their own lives, unable to give her the daily intimacy she so desperately needed.

EVERYONE NEEDS A FRIEND

Even if you are lucky enough to be raised in a very responsive and loving family, it is inevitable that you will someday leave home. But friends—old friends whom you have cultivated over the years, or newer ones whom you develop in your new communities—will always be available to you for affirmation and companionship.

Friends can be a source of self-esteem, affection, and good times. In times of despair, friends offer hope: a class of youngsters in California in 1993 shaved their heads so their friend and classmate, who was undergoing treatments for cancer, would not feel self-conscious about his bald appearance. His dozen friends kept their heads shaved until they learned their friend's cancer was in remission.

Friendship. It's something many people take for granted. They are unaware how powerful and positive friendship can be, or they would take it more seriously. The right friends can help you feel worthwhile. The right friends can even help get you elected president. School, work, parenting, and even old age are better and more fun when shared with friends.

I asked 46 college students at St. John's University what factors *must* be present in a close friendship. Almost all agreed that *trust* and *honesty* (44 and 43, respectively) were paramount, followed by *faithfulness, loyalty*, and *being a good listener* (35, 32, and 31), and, finally, *having ideas in common* and *love* (28 and 24). Just one wrote that *attractiveness* counted; only two felt *age* was a factor; only 10 considered *intelligence*, and only 8 deemed *being a good talker* of any significance.

What a glorious relationship friendship proves to be, where *trust, honesty, faithfulness, loyalty, being a good listener, having ideas in common,* and *love* are what count. These are all traits or feelings you can acquire. *Age, attractiveness,* and *intelligence,* largely a question of birth and luck, are considered *unimportant* for a close friendship.

Similarly, you are born to a family; you can choose your friends.

You would probably agree that friendship is crucial for school-age children or for singles who are between romantic relationships. However, friends count for even the happiest couples: friendship affirms and validates in a more distinctive way than even the most positive romantic or blood tie. It is now known that friendship is vital *throughout* life.

"You quickly find out who your good friends are when you are down or when you need them most," writes a 36-year-old married vice president of sales who lives in Cincinnati. "A good friend won't desert you when you are down," this mother of two preteen daughters continues. "Nor will she turn away in jealousy when you succeed."

Another theme of this book is that friendship, like love, requires an investment of time and effort. Even children need guidance in how to develop and maintain friends. Until they are old enough to make arrangements on their own, they need their parents or caretakers to set up play dates for them with their friends. Playing with the kid next door is fine, but it is not enough. They need to cultivate friendships based on likes and dislikes, not just proximity and convenience. They need to be taught how to keep a friendship going even if a friend moves away, or if they have a disagreement.

If you do have a mate or romantic partner, it is ideal to be best friends with your mate as well as lovers. However, even when you attain that ideal, you need platonic friends where shared income, living arrangements, or the roles of spouse or parent are less likely to complicate the relationship.

Furthermore, even if you are fortunate enough to have the most sympathetic opposite-sex relationships—spouse *or* friends—certain gender-specific experiences, such as the onset of menses, the physical act of childbearing, becoming a father, or menopause, can only be shared vicariously. Same-sex friends add a commonality of experience that enriches your life.

Friendship can determine where you live and how you live. A survey by the Roper Organization reported by Diane Crispell in *The Wall Street Journal* discovered that Americans chose *friends* as saying the most about them (39%)—way ahead of their homes (26%), their jobs (12%), or their clothes (12%).

Consider these additional facts about friendship:

- Children with friends do better in school.
- Medical researchers found that those with friends are more likely to survive a heart attack or major surgery and less likely to get respiratory infections or cancer.
- Friends offer a continuous relationship to singles, according them the high status once given only to family.
- A nine-year study of thousands of Californians by Berkman and Syme discovered that those with friends live longer.

WHY FRIENDSHIP HAS BECOME SO POWERFUL

There are reasons friendship is more important than ever before, and will continue to grow in significance:

1. *The trend toward smaller nuclear families is continuing.* I know personally five women and men in their 30s or 40s who have seven to eleven siblings; it is rare for anyone of my generation or younger to have more than five children of their own. Only children, or two, at the most three, are more the norm.

For the only child, friendship offers an opportunity for intimate peer interaction unavailable in the home. "I would die without my friends," says only child and mother Carol Ann Finkelstein, whose parents died within a year of each other in the late 1970s, when Carol was not even 30. "I couldn't function without my friends, even now that I'm married," she adds.

2. *Retirees as well as other nuclear family members are increasingly relocating due to work, educational, or romantic choices.* Because of the relocation to another town, state, or country of working and retirement-age relatives, parents, grandparents, and siblings, family members may not be around in adult years for frequent contact. Although you cannot replace members of your family when someone moves, you can always form new friendships.

3. *The number of working mothers of school-age children continues to rise.* Friendship offers these children an alternative intimate relationship—at school or after-school play—to the maternal one.

4. *Friendship offers the elderly opportunities for close relationships.* As life expectancy increases, so does the likelihood of living a decade or more cut off from the day-to-day interaction offered by a job, or the intimacy provided by a wife or husband who may predecease his or her mate. Friendship may mean feeling wanted and useful in your older years instead of alone and isolated.

5. *Friendship offers intimacy to singles.* For unattached and unmarried, divorced, or widowed singles, friendship will impact on your mental health until you start a family of your own, or if you remain or become single for much or all of your adult years.

6. *Even the best marriages may benefit from the emotional and intellectual stimulation of friendship.* For the married man or woman, friends may offer "another self" to those who need to relate intimately to others outside the all-consuming and sometimes one-dimensional roles of parent, spouse, or worker.

7. *Friends provide each other some of the career continuity once offered by lifetime employers.* As companies downsize and few people have the guarantee of lifetime employment, friends offer continuity to a career or even the inside scoop on available jobs.

FRIENDSHIP TRAINING BEGINS AT HOME

You probably already know that how you relate to others is based on the early patterns you learned in dealing with your mother, father, and siblings. Knowing that fact, and recognizing those patterns, is a crucial first step in changing your current friendship patterns, if you are displeased with them. It will also help you to be a more compassionate and understanding friend if your friends disappoint you. They may be unwittingly reenacting a pattern from *their* childhood that has nothing to do with *you*. For example, a friend who becomes very competitive with you may be doing it because she was always being compared to her two older brothers. You could reject your friend because of her competitiveness, but you would then both lose.

Since the only person you can be assured of changing is yourself, start there. Why does her competitiveness strike such a negative chord in you? Is it really your friend's behavior that is the problem, or your inability to effectively deal with it and with her? Welcome this opportunity to work this conflict out with her and with yourself, or you will find yourself facing the same unresolved conflict over competitiveness with another friend.

FRIENDSHIP OFFERS HELP
TO TROUBLED FAMILIES

Kurt and his younger sister were hit by their father several times a week, beginning when Kurt was four. As Kurt explains in the CBS TV special, *Break the Silence: Kids Against Child Abuse*, "The abuse finally stopped when my sister told some of her friends what had been happening. Her friends told a grown-up who they could trust, who called the child abuse hot line." Kurt and his sister were reunited with their parents after three years in foster care after their father stopped the drinking that precipitated the physical abuse. Both their parents learned how to discipline their children without hitting and causing black eyes or bloody noses.

Whether or not you were born into a nurturing family, your friends could offer what you need. That is one of the themes of this book: that *friends* are an underused source of help for troubled families, especially neglected or abused children, adolescents, and young adults. Friends can offset the low self-esteem and loneliness caused by abusive or dysfunctional families before, or in addition to, intervention by therapists or family services. As then-president George Bush pleaded with America's youth in September 1989, if they had a friend with a drug problem, "I'm asking you not to look the other way."

MY BACKGROUND
AND HOW I RESEARCHED THIS BOOK

I have always been fascinated by human nature, but my formal training began in 1970, when I attended Hahnemann Medical College for a graduate internship in psychiatric art therapy. Over the next decade, I taught college courses, completed a masters degree in criminal justice, and wrote several nonfiction books, including *Victims* (Scribner's, 1978), *The Help Book* (Scribner's, 1979), and *Single in America* (Atheneum, 1980).

My serious interest in friendship began when I was a graduate student and I dated a man who had a very powerful and supportive friendship network with his best friends from high school. Although I have always had girlfriends, it was usually just me and that one other friend. I would usually have numerous unrelated "friendship pairs"; I longed to have a similar female network of "buddies" with whom I too would feel genuinely connected. My only sister's imminent relocation with her husband to Washington, D.C.—for several years, after a decade of living in distant cities, they had been living in an apartment just a block from my Manhattan residence—also caused me to take stock of my friendships. My sister and I had developed an especially open and intimate kinship during those years she lived close by; what girlfriends would be there for me now that my sister would again be far away?

In 1980, as I began to study friendship as the topic for my

doctoral dissertation for my Ph.D. in sociology (City University of New York, 1983), I was initially fascinated to discover differences between male and female friendships. I also wanted to explore why friendships end; I soon realized that to learn why friendships ended, I had to understand friendship beginnings and maintenance.

My dissertation was an in-depth empirical study of the friendship patterns of 27 young, single women living alone on one randomly selected block on the upper East Side of Manhattan. A nine-month analysis and interpretation of those in-depth interviews dispelled several clichés about female friendships, namely that they often involved rivalry over men, were mostly pairs or one-on-one friendships, and were based mainly on sharing confidences.

By contrast, my research discovered that of the closest friendships of the women I interviewed, less than half (41%) were between two women or friendship pairs. The rest were part of a three-way friendship (22%) or a network of four or more friends (37%). The majority of friendships were based on sharing activities and emotional support (85%), with only 7% basing their friendship on sharing confidences. Despite the prevailing myths, only two friendships of the women I interviewed had actually ended because of rivalry over a man. (Some of the findings from my dissertation were discussed by Letty Cottin Pogrebin in *Among Friends,* Eva Margolies in *The Best of Friends, The Worst of Enemies,* and Linda Wolfe in "Friendship in the City," published in *New York* magazine.)

Over the years, I have followed up my dissertation with more than 250 extensive in-person or telephone interviews on friendship with a wide range of married, divorced, and widowed men and women as well as children, teens, workers, and executives. I researched and published a scholarly bibliography with 693 entries, *Friendship: A Selected, Annotated Bibliography* (Garland, 1985), a popular booklet on friendship, and magazine articles for *Modern Bride, McCall's,* and *American Baby.* I also surveyed over 500 students, married men and women, and never-married, divorced, or widowed singles from throughout the United States as well as from Canada, Japan, Switzerland, India, and the United Kingdom, including a survey from 1990 to 1992 of 257 randomly-selected members of the Society for Human Resource Management about work and friendship; since 1994, I have been doing an in-depth study of more than two dozen adult survivors of childhood and adolescent sexual abuse and how those early experiences impacted on their friendship patterns.

WHAT YOU WILL LEARN FROM THIS BOOK

No one is born shy or gregarious. There is no such thing as a friendship "gene." Friendship is a skill you can learn; this book will help you enhance your friendships as you learn—
- sympathetic ways to bring your friends closer
- why some men have twice as many friends at work as do women and why women might want that to change
- the art of self-disclosure—what to reveal, when, and to whom
- how to be for others the kind of friend that you want others to be for you
- how to increase the likelihood of befriending those who share your values (a better predictor of long-lasting friendships than doing things together or being nearby).

I have certainly benefited from all I have learned about friendship. My life is fuller and more rewarding than it has ever been because I put into practice every day the friendship principles I share with you in this book.

*

Marriage is relatively easy to define, but what does it mean to be someone's *friend*? As a relationship, friendship itself has been shifting in the last few decades; today there is an eagerness and quickness to call almost anybody a *friend*. The next chapter explores definitions of *friendship* that should help give you a better grasp of what you mean when you call someone your *friend*.

Friendships are the crown jewels that one owns. 1 stock market might go up and down, but friendsh only grow in their value.

—74-year-old Gladys Bar

2. WHAT IS A FRIEND?

No matter what your house looks like, you let friends in.
—Mary Kent, photographer

Everyone uses *friend*, but what does it mean? *Friend* may describe anyone from a casual friend you meet for a weekly tennis game to a best friend who's "like a sister."

DEFINING *FRIEND*

One way that you might define a *friend* is by those qualities that are sought in a friend, such as commitment, self-disclosure, trust, honesty, and commonality.

Commitment means loyalty and devotion to each other and to your friendship especially when a crisis occurs, whether it is losing a job, poor health, marital problems, or a death in the family. Genuine friends are willing to be there for you; they do not just make hollow offers.

Self-disclosure means the willingness to open up and share your innermost feelings and experiences that are not shared with too many others. (If you are reluctant to self-disclose with your friends, you at least let them open up with you, if they wish.)

Trust reflects the deepest belief by each friend that neither will betray the other. Confidences will not be broken nor will shared turmoil or joys be belittled. "Trust means that I know if I share a confidence with you, you won't blab it to someone else," says psychologist and burn-out expert Herbert Freudenberger. "Trust means I don't forget to come to your birthday party," he adds.

Honesty suggests that you and your friend will be truthful with each other about your experiences, your feelings, and your views.

Commonality is the feeling that you are of a similar mindset, comfortable with each other's points of view and values, or are at ease with any differences between you.

Another way to define *friend* is to say it is someone who is there if you are in need. But today, everyone seems to be more concerned with either job, spouse, or children. Or, if you are single, you are told you should not lean on anyone or anything but instead should be independent and self-sufficient. Besides, the notion of a friend in need is somewhat opportunistic. More than ever before, it seems you need to develop guidelines that are realistic about what to expect from your friends.

A truism about friendship is that it is an optional role. The other necessary roles—of worker, of spouse, or of parent—have to be satisfied first. If friendship interferes with performing those roles, it just might have to be put on hold or eliminated.

THREE TYPES OF FRIENDS:
BEST, CLOSE, AND CASUAL

Still another way to define *friend*, and the way that is used in this book, is by the level of intimacy in the relationship. The three categories of friendship are *best, close*, or *casual* friends. Obviously individual differences have to be taken into account. Someone who is especially cold and withdrawn may label as a close friend someone that a more outgoing person with an enormous capacity for intimacy might call a casual one. By and large, however, best, close, and casual friends are somewhat like the differences among dating, engagement, and marriage, with casual friend at the bottom of the scale, in terms of intimacy, and best friend at the top.

What all these friendships have in common, however, whether you are talking about a best, close, or casual friend, is that the friendship would exist even if the circumstances under which the relationship was formed ended. For example, you leave your job or move, but your co-worker or neighbor is still your friend. Unlike the acquaintances that languish, best, close, or casual friendships are maintained, even if the relationship becomes less convenient.

Friendship offers a deviation from your formal roles of worker or spouse, but *friend* is also a role, with obligations, rules, and privileges of its own. In general, it is unwise to lean too often or too heavily on your friends. If too much emotional support is demanded, there are alternative friendships and other relationships available that may be less draining. (There are, of course, instances when this generality falters, such as the devotion friends offer AIDS sufferers whose families are far away or are emotionally unavailable to them.) However, whether or not you do lean on your friends during a crisis, you should feel that, *if* you wanted to, you *could.*

Best Friends

> In the last year [since we both moved to New York], we've become inseparable. We talk every day on the phone at least once, or twice, or sometimes three times.
> —33-year-old Kate, an unmarried secretary originally from St. Louis

A best friend is in the ancient tradition of what a friend should be and is synonymous with what I call the Great Friend Approach to friendship, as described in the ancient and social science literature. The Great Friend Approach reflected the exalted position a best friendship held in ancient times, when marriages were usually arranged or based on property and procreation rather than affection and choice, as they are today.

This kind of friendship conjures up the strongest fantasies about friendship—someone who is there for you, no matter what, someone who puts you first in his or her life. This person is *the* friend, before all others; it is a relationship that has withstood the tests of time and conflict, major changes such as moving, or status changes, such as marrying or having a child.

As the number of friendships in each category—best, close, or casual—increases, the value of each relationship may decrease, as well as its members' dependence on it. In theory, there can be only one best friend. In practice, men and women will talk about "my two best friends," or "my best friend whom I see all the time and my old best friend, who does not live near me anymore but he will always be my best friend."

That having more than one best friend cancels out calling either one a "best" friend, or diminishes the exclusive status of being labeled best friends, was pointed out by the French philosopher Montaigne, who wrote: "If two called for help at the same time, which one would you run to? If they demanded conflicting services of you, how would you arrange it? If one confided to your silence a thing that would be useful for the other to know, how would you extricate yourself? A single dominant friendship dissolves all other obligations."

For most, a best friendship is antithetical to the demands of modern life, especially for those who spend the majority of their adult years in a marital or romantic relationship with a spouse or romantic partner as their primary intimate relationship. For today's man or woman, committed to a career as well as a spouse and children, or a romantic partner, the Modern Approach to friendship is more prevalent and workable. According to the Modern Approach, friendships are more *casual* or *differentiated.* In that way, there are few, if any, best friends, but several close and many casual ones.

However, some are blessed with life-long best friendships that they manage to maintain in the midst of their wife, mother, and worker roles. For example, Ann Pleshette Murphy, Editor-in-Chief of *Parents* magazine, and mother of two, writes in *Parents* about one of her favorite photographs from the baby shower her mother gave her before her first child was born. It's a photograph of her with her four best friends. She explains: "To my right is Jane, whom my father, an obstetrician, delivered four months before I entered the world." Nicole she befriended in the sandbox at nursery school; they stayed friends for the rest of their school years, including being roommates in college. They still "speak to each other just about everyday." Her third best friend is Eileen, who lived in the apartment directly above hers. Sarah is "another nursery-through-high school friend" who "now lives with her husband just around the corner from us." Pleshette notes that their friendship was a factor in deciding to move to her current neighborhood.

Twenty-six-year-old Barbara is a single woman who is currently not dating anyone. She has one best friend in the Great Friend tradition for 11 years, going back to high school, although they first met in sixth grade. That friendship with Melissa has helped Barbara minimize her loneliness. Barbara and Melissa both moved from Texas four years ago, although Barbara lives in New York City and Melissa lives in Washington, D.C. They still manage to see each other once a month and to talk frequently on the phone.

Barbara says:

> I have very strong friendships. I think being an only child has a *big* influence. When Melissa and I were in high school, we were very close, and she's like a sister. I think I've adopted people as family members, because I don't have sisters and brothers....Our friendship will always be one of our priorities, even though it has its ebbs and its flows. We've battled through enough major things that we make an effort to keep it together, no matter what.

For most everyone, even those fortunate enough to be happily married or to have a "significant other," having at least one best friend who is the quintessential "soul mate" is a common goal. But since, by definition, a best friendship should be *the* one, *numero uno*, a close friendship may be a better choice since it will be easier to maintain. It is also less demanding, especially for married women and men, or involved singles, to have close (rather than best) friendships.

Close Friends

> All five are close friends, in fact, none is the closest. All of them I have known for thirty years and more.
> —72-year-old married Westchester woman

Close friends are faithful, dear, tender, reliable, and intimate. It is close friends, especially outside the workplace—not best or casual ones—who offer you the choice relationship outside of romance or family ties to fulfill your emotional or intellectual needs.

All the necessary elements of friendship are found in close friendships—compatibility, commitment, self-disclosure, trust, and commonality, but without the exclusivity of best friendship that would make it a threat to your other primary loyalties. A 56-year-old married man has two close friends, but he considers his wife to be his best "friend." A 34-year-old married physician filled out my questionnaire with two different colored inks: blue for his closest friend, his wife, his "real answers"; and red for his closest male friend "if my wife were not to be considered."

Di, a Manhattan social worker, has an out-of-town boyfriend and five close friends. Their ages range from 25 to 30, within five years of Di's age (a generality about close friends). Di explains: "My friends are important to me, and I'll make the time to see them. It might not be as much time...but the friendship, the communication [is meaningful to me]."

"Really good friends are the people who know what's going on in your life without you telling them," explains a high energy 38-year-old woman who recently married for the first time. "Friends are distinct from acquaintances in that my friends really have to share my value structure," she adds.

Shared values are more important in predicting the longevity of a friendship than shared interests.

What are the common traits of her close friends? "They're honest, and they'll say what they think," she explains in her strong voice. "Sometimes I might not like what I hear, and I might have to think about it, but I can count on an honest opinion....[Also] a sense of humor. The ability to laugh."Close friendship offers reciprocity and intimacy without the unrealistic demands on your time and emotions that a best friend might demand.

"A close friend is not necessarily somebody you see a lot in a sense that you see or call them every day," explains a 28-year-old woman who moved to New York from California to attend graduate school. "But if you needed them in an emergency, your health was at stake, or you were depressed and wanted them to visit or to talk to, they would come."

Not so with most casual friends.

Casual Friends

I consider Evelyn a friend although I would not want to burden her with any problems, any serious problems, I might have.
— a 36-year-old flight attendant from Holland

A casual friend is the kind of friendship that is becoming synonymous with *friend* for today's busy women or men and for those who feel they have too much to lose by "telling all" in a best or close friendship.

Distinctively a cut above an acquaintance in terms of intimacy and trust—"an acquaintance is a pleasure to see briefly, but the relationship isn't significant," as a 56-year-old married man notes—casual friends take less time to develop or maintain than close or best friendships. In the post-adolescent years, especially if you have strong romantic or family ties, or work commitments, casual friendship may be all you can handle.

The cartoon that follows from "B.C." by Johnny Hart reflects the difference between a casual and a close or best friend:

Reprinted by permission of Johnny Hart and Creators Syndicate, Inc.

As relationships become more intimate, the information shared becomes more personal. That is why, even in the best romantic relationships, interacting with friends, especially casual ones, may benefit a couple.

Casual friendships, because less intimate information is shared, work well in a group or network situation. (Group friendship patterns are discussed more completely in Chapter 5, "Friendship Patterns.") As Edda, a 24-year-old copywriter from Texas who has a network of more than 14 men and women casual friends, comments: "There are some 40 people we all know in New York that we can gossip about pretty good."

Pseudo Friends:
Fair Weather and Foul Weather

Fair weather and foul weather pseudo-friendships are noted here even though they are not really friendships, to help you recognize those relationships for what they really are. Genuine friendships have to be shared or reciprocal, but fair weather and foul weather relationships are one-sided.

Fair weather pseudo-friends require that you are always "up." Limits are set by one friend, not both. You cannot call, or call on, fair weather pseudo-friends when you are in need, although they may feel completely comfortable dumping their current messes on you. Sometimes you first notice this tendency in phone conversations. You listen patiently, perhaps for as long as a half hour to an hour, to their tales of woe, but the minute you start to talk about what is bothering you, they are suddenly out of time and "have to go."

Foul weather pseudo-friends are those who might be there for you at four in the morning, if you are desperate or despondent, but they do not want to listen and rejoice with you when your life is going well. Foul weather pseudo-friends need to feel like a "savior" who is rescuing you. Also, your misery makes them feel better about their own lives; if you are no longer miserable, they feel more threatened, and their jealousy of your fair weather gets in the way of having a positive friendship.

New York psychologist Sharon Hymer describes the foul weather pseudo-friend situation that her patient, an actress, had to work through when her joyful married life became the point of envy of her still-single friends who were also unhappy with their lives. Says Hymer: "Misery loves company. But then when things started to go 'swimmingly' for my patient and her husband, she came in with tears in her eyes. 'These friends are not my friends. They're treating me differently.'"

Foul weather pseudo-friends are those who call themselves friends but may be trying to destroy you, which is not a very friendly thing to do. They need you to have foul weather. While they may consciously try to help you, their help rarely materializes.

*

Returning to a discussion of real rather than pseudo-friendships, the next chapter explores the interdisciplinary literature on friendship, including a further discussion of the Great Friend Approach versus the Modern Friend Approach to friendship.

3. PERSPECTIVES ON FRIENDSHIP

Without friendship life is not worth living.
— Cicero

A review of the literature on friendship reveals that there are two assumptions about it that are indisputable:

- friendship is a voluntary relationship, outside of legal and formal control
- friends are not related by blood.

After that, the agreement ends. For example, friendship has been praised throughout time, by philosophers such as Aristotle, who wrote, "Friendship is a virtue," then by poets such as John Donne, who wrote, "No man is an island," and finally by social scientists and epidemiologists such as Lisa F. Berkman, who have concluded that it is a factor in lowering disease and extending life expectancy.

But is friendship itself vital, or is friendship's value dependent upon how it replaces or enhances other traditional institutions, such as the family, community, or workplace? Sociologists have especially noted that *the value of friendship increases as the closeness of the family declines.* Psychiatrists such as Harry Stack Sullivan have stressed that same-sex friendships are the training ground for developing the skills for future heterosexual romantic intimacy. Other debates about friendship have revolved around whether women are capable of friendship, if there are any gender differences in friendship patterns, and, if so, whether those variations are inborn or due to socialization.

Although the interdisciplinary literature on friendship is extensive, I have discovered that it may all be placed within two distinct perspectives: the Great Friend Approach and the Modern Friend Approach.

THE GREAT FRIEND APPROACH

The first and oldest perspective on friendship, but one that is still perpetuated, I call the Great Friend Approach. This orientation was heralded by the ancient philosophers, like Plato, Aristotle, and Cicero, and later refined by essayists, such as Sir Francis Bacon, Montaigne, Ralph Waldo Emerson, and Henry David Thoreau. It has been carried into the twentieth century by social scientists and popular writers.

According to the Great Friend Approach, friendship is:

- idealized and romanticized
- a twosome (dyad), since there can be only one great friend
- between those of the same sex
- based upon an appreciation of each other's "essence"
- reciprocal
- in competition with marriage and the family.

The two-person nature of the Great Friend Approach is implicit.

So all-encompassing and exclusive a relationship would be hard to sustain in a three-way (triad) or a group (network) setting. Such an idealized and intimate friendship thus cancels out other friends or friendships. The Great Friend relationship is hence as exclusive and as binding emotionally as marriage is legally.

That marriage and friendship are in competition with each other, a tenet of this approach, is reflected in the writings almost a century ago of German scholar Georg Simmel (1858-1918), an influential thinker in the development of sociology, in which he contrasted these relationships. Sociologists Peter Berger and Hansfried Kellner offer a more contemporary rendition of this when they theorize that marriage overrides friendship and reinterprets those competing relations in its own image. The marital union is too intimate and all-encompassing to its participants to let a friend come between the partners.

A theme over the centuries is that the Great Friend knows the friend's true self, other self, or helps to create a third self. Aristotle wrote that a true friend is "another self." Montaigne viewed a great friend as a "second self." For Bacon, it was "another himself." For symbolic interactionist Gerald Suttles, it is a "real self."

Until the twentieth century, only adult men were considered capable of having a great friend. In ancient Greece, for example, women were considered too ignorant and uneducated to be capable of a meaningful friendship. It is possible that Emile Durkheim, in his classic study of suicide rates for different groups, shared that two-thousand-year-old view. He did not even consider what role friendship played in the lower suicide rates of unmarried women (compared to single men and married women).

By the beginning of the twentieth century, however, women were finally acknowledged as being capable of friendship. Simmel wrote that although women were once "at the state of low personality development" so that friendship was impossible, "the modern highly differentiated woman shows a strikingly increased capacity for friendship and an inclination toward it, both with men and with women."

Despite the male view that women were not capable of

friendship, women seem to have had very important "great friends" in days of yore. For example, Nancy Cott, in describing New England women from 1780 to 1835, based on their diaries, shows how female friendships provided an emotional expression often lacking in their marriages. Cott notes: "Wives who had female friends or relatives living with them seemed the most contented of women."

Thus a female version of the Great Friend Approach has emerged. It mirrors all the age-old characteristics of this approach; only the gender has changed. For instance, a popular novel, *Women's Work* by Anne Tolstoi Wallach, is a well-written but stereotypical account of a divorced executive with two grown children who is trying to make it to the top of the advertising world. She does have a great friend but, interestingly enough, the heroine only "gets her man" after the great friend suddenly dies, the victim of heart failure while undergoing facelift surgery, as if "a man" and a "great friend" are mutually exclusive.

THE MODERN FRIEND APPROACH

According to the Modern Friend Approach, friendship is:

- viewed realistically
- as possible for women as for men
- between those of the same or opposite sex
- between two or among three, four, or more
- differentiated, meaning it is based on only one aspect of a person's personality or self
- not necessarily an equal exchange
- not threatening to other intimate relationships.

What I call the Modern Friend Approach, first advanced by sociologist Simmel, directly opposes the Great Friend Approach. Simmel believed that the kind of best friends that characterized the Great Friend Approach was impossible for modern times. Simmel wrote: "Such complete intimacy becomes probably more and more difficult as differentiation among men increases...Modern man, possibly, has too much to hide to sustain a friendship in the ancient sense." (That may account for psychotherapy's increased appeal today, an idea explored in Chapter 13, The Friendship Factor in Everyday Life.)

An unmarried doctoral student in her early 40s typifies Simmel's notion of modern or differentiated friendship:

> I like opera. I like sports. I like a lot of things. I don't find that my friends share all my interests. I may go to plays with some, but with others I may go to the opera. There are others with whom I may go bicycle riding, and still others with whom I may share my problems in school.

Since friendships are more differentiated in the Modern Friend Approach, and not necessarily between two persons, it follows that three-way friendships, more stable but less intimate, are possible.

The social science literature on friendship may all be placed under one theory, Like Attracts Like, and two orientations, the Developmental View and the Sociological Perspective.

Like Attracts Like

The notion in friendship that like attracts like is ancient; now, social scientists are supporting that axiom with experiments, observations, survey research, and data analysis. Thus psychologist Theodore Newcomb's experiments in the 1950s with University of Michigan transfer students confirmed what Aristotle had written in *The Nicomachean Ethics*, that "like attracts like."

Wenda J. Dickens and Daniel Perlman, in their study of friendship over the life cycle, document six key concepts in friendship literature, all which reiterate "like attracts like." Thus, friendships tend to be between those who:

- like each other
- share similar values
- have similar personalities
- live (or work) near each other (proximity)
- are the same age
- are the same sex.

The Like Attracts Like theory also encompasses the exchange theory, expounded by George Homans and Peter Blau, among others, namely that friendships usually are between those who:

- feel the exchange is equal.

The Developmental View

According to the Developmental View, friendship:
- changes from infancy to maturity along with your intellectual, emotional, and social development
- is important because it fosters, supplements, or conflicts with other primary roles
- is different for males and females.

This view incorporates the Great Friend and Modern Friend Approaches and the Like Attracts Like theory, but it adds two other dimensions — life cycle and gender differences.

A systematic application of the Developmental View are friendship stages noted by psychologists Robert L. Selman, Dan Jacquette, Brian J. Bigelow, and John J. La Gaipa, among others.

DEVELOPMENTAL MODELS OF FRIENDSHIP STAGES

SELMAN/JACQUETTE MODEL

Stage 0	Ages 3-7	Momentary Playmateship
Stage 1	Ages 4-9	One-Way Assistance
Stage 2	Ages 6-12	Two-Way Fair-weather Cooperation
Stage 3	Ages 9-15	Intimate, Mutually Shared Relationships
Stage 4	Age 12+	Autonomous Interdependent Friendships

BIGELOW/LA GAIPA MODEL (Ages 8 to 14)

Stage 1	Situational
Stage 2	Contractual
Stage 3	Internal-psychological

Using the Selman model, two adults who meet for the first time might begin their relationship at the child's Stage 0 and, as their relationship evolves and deepens, progress to stage 4.

It might be useful to use Selman's stages to characterize friendships of different levels. For example, *acquaintances* might be Two-Way Fair-weather Cooperation, a *best friend* might be an Intimate, Mutually Shared Relationship, but a *close friend* might be an Autonomous Interdependent Friendship.

However, behind the developmental view of friendship is still the notion that opposite-sex intimacy is the primary goal of life. Friendships are considered preparatory to that goal, especially in childhood, adolescence, and the single years before marriage.

The Sociological Perspective

What makes the sociological perspective so useful, and the backdrop to this book, is how it sees friendship as providing something unique, unavailable anywhere else. As Suttles and other sociologists have noted, according to the sociological perspective:

- Friendship is a unique institution providing intimacy and presentations of self not permitted in any other role settings like work, marriage, or parenting.
- Changes, such as moving up or down the corporate ladder, should not impact old friendships, since friends connect on a deeper basis.
- Friendship's value *throughout* life is emphasized.

A best or close friendship allows deviation from formal roles that makes it self-validating and, conversely, potentially devastating if the relationship ends, since the consequences of ending become more damaging as increased intimacy augments vulnerability.

*

The next chapter examines how and why a particular acquaintance might evolve into a friend.

Friends can't be your family, they can't be your lovers, they can't be your psychiatrists. But they can be your friends, which is plenty.

—Phillip Lopate, *Against Joie de Vivre*

4. FROM ACQUAINTANCE TO FRIEND

The meeting of two personalities is like the contact of two chemical substances; if there is any reaction, both of them are transformed.

—psychiatrist Carl Jung
(quoted in *The Heart of Friendship*
by Muriel James and Louis M. Savary)

An acquaintance develops when you meet someone and interact with him or her; you are more than strangers, but less than friends. Out of your myriad of acquaintances, why do just a handful become your best, close, or even casual friends? This chapter will try to answer that question.

Acquaintances tend to be based on a specific situation and to be convenient relationships; unless the relationship becomes a friendship, when the situation ends, so does the relationship. Fred and Barry served in the Navy in Vietnam together, but they are still "close but long distance friends" 20 years later. Even though they live at opposite ends of the country, their shared writing interests and commitment to preserving their friendship keeps them connected. Herb, a man of 35, has a network of some 10 close friends, all going back to their high school days together. Natalie's newest friends are the mothers of her preschooler's friends; they remain best friends even though their children now go to different schools and have developed other friendships. By contrast, when Sally moved just five blocks away, her relationship with her neighbor Jill ended due to inconvenience—proving it to be an acquaintanceship, not a friendship.

THE STEPS FROM ACQUAINTANCE TO FRIEND

How do you first make the acquaintances that might become best, close, or casual friends? How do you help an acquaintanceship along so it becomes a friendship? First and foremost, *visibility* is vital. By being visible, you are putting yourself into situations where new acquaintances and, subsequently, new friendships are possible. Visibility means you get out and are open to acquaintances that you meet through work, at religious or community organizations (such as volunteering at a shelter for the homeless), at the parent-teacher organization, at the playground, or by joining a new professional group or club, starting a club (such as a weekly investment or gourmet cooking group), or pursuing a hobby or interest.

Becoming visible is the first antidote to the depression that often results from isolation. Especially if you have moved to a new community, or gotten a new job, visibility is crucial to developing acquaintances that might become friends.

Visibility will allow the necessary *access* to those whom you wish to befriend, providing the second ingredient to helping an acquaintanceship evolve into a friendship, namely, *having a shared experience.* In Pat Conroy's best-selling novel, *The Prince of Tides,* the protagonist's mother, Lila Wingo, a poor woman living on the wrong side of the tracks, in her later years manages to become friends with the wife of the man whose money and power she had always envied. How did she accomplish that? It seems the wealthy woman became ill and her own friends shunned her. But Lila Wingo stepped in and took care of her, till her dying day. By nursing the sick woman, Lila Wingo got access to her, and a friendship ensued.

The third ingredient for an acquaintance to become a friend is *to expand your interaction beyond the original basis on which you and your acquaintance first met and interacted.* For example, Stanley P. Heilbronn, a New York-based Merrill Lynch financial consultant, has several close friends who started out as clients. Speaking about one friend who lives in California, Heilbronn explains the evolution from acquaintance/client to friend:

> First I met my client. Then he introduced me to his wife. Then I brought my wife along. Everyone got along with everyone else. We got to meet their children. They got to meet our children. Every time we see them, the relationship expands. It took a few years [to become close friends]. We just went to Santa Fe together, and it wound up being a very pleasant experience. It was strictly a non-business, very social four days.

The fourth ingredient is *time.* According to my research, *it took, on average, three years from the time two people met and became acquaintances until a genuine tried-and-true friendship developed.* The time frame of three years from meeting a new person to becoming tried-and-true friends makes sense; by that time, most acquaintances are no longer convenient. Someone may have graduated, switched schools, gotten a promotion, changed jobs, moved away, gotten married or divorced, or had a child. All those changes are "tests" of your relationship. Interestingly, psychologist Dorothy Tennov, in her study of love entitled *Love and Limerance*, found it took an average of three years for a romantic relationship to be proven a true love or just an infatuation.

Acquaintances that become tried-and-true friendships even before the shared situation that brought the two acquaintances together ends are those relationships where the convenient interaction expands and is tested out in non-utilitarian ones. For example, two business associates go on a fishing trip together or two neighbors reveal information about themselves that is more intimate.

It is because these non-utilitarian encounters can be so revealing that you or your acquaintance may be reluctant to test out your relationship before your shared situation ends: it may be easier to work with an acquaintance who "might" become your friend than to continue to work with someone you have befriended and, then, found disappointing or even reprehensible.

I asked a 35-year-old married writer what he considers the difference between an acquaintance and a close friend. "Longevity, mainly," he answered. He continued: "My friends and I have survived so many changes of life together that it's no longer necessary to explain or describe things to them. In a sense, friends can be taken for granted, acquaintances cultivated."

Acquaintances may be superficial, but they are also safe. Little is risked emotionally or, by the same token, gained compared to the benefits (and risks) of genuine friendship. During the time it takes for an acquaintanceship to become a friendship, you are determining, consciously or unconsciously, whether or not you want to move your relationship along to the next higher level of *friend*.

In the section that follows, you will see what goes into these friendship decisions. The chart on the next page illustrates this process from a shared situation and an acquaintanceship to becoming best, close, or casual friends.

Structural changes, such as relocating to a new community, getting married, being promoted, or becoming widowed are all challenges to acquaintances. If you replace an acquaintance with someone who is more convenient, or an acquaintance does the same with you, and you no longer have any contact with your previous acquaintance, it was probably, in retrospect, a utilitarian acquaintanceship, not a friendship. If your relationship persists after structural changes, even if on a less frequent basis, if you and your *amigo* still care about each other, it probably became a friendship.

MODEL OF FRIENDSHIP
FROM SHARED SITUATION

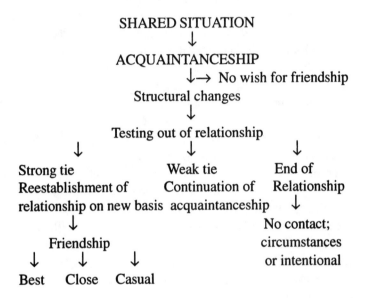

Why a Friend Is Chosen

Why would someone take the emotional risks with a particular person to become a best or close friend or, to less of a degree, since there is less gained but also less risked emotionally, to become even a casual friend? There has to be something about the acquaintanceship that causes you both to feel something valuable will be gained by going further with your relationship.

There is usually a "chemical" reaction—a connection—to each other that makes you feel you want to get to know that person better and to perhaps become his or her friend.

"We met in kindergarten. We had a natural affinity right away. I remember it very clearly even though I was five years old at the time," says Sondra Forsyth, a magazine writer, mother, and former dancer. Forsyth's friendship persisted throughout her school years, surviving an extended separation when her friend relocated to another town, and their lives went in different directions. They reconnected in their later adult years and are still friends today, decades later.

The wish to become friends needs to be shared or the relationship will stop in its tracks.

However, although the wish to become friends must be shared by both acquaintances, *what* you share need not be equal. "All my friends leave it up to me to be the one to pick up the phone," says Debbie, who moved to New York to get into film production, in a somewhat annoyed tone. Connecticut-based time management expert Lucy Hedrick is not bothered by that: "I let go of that in recent years. I know I have friends who meet me halfway and I have friends for whom being with them is as important to me, but I call them every time. I have friends who genuinely seek me out more often than I would think of them. I think you can set yourself up for rejection if you insist on this fifty/fifty deal."

What are the most frequent reasons an acquaintance becomes a friend? Besides having a shared desire to become friends, the most frequent reason is if you think your future friend will offer *companionship—someone to do things with* or *talk to.* The next most common reason is *shared interests,* followed by the belief that your friend will offer you *emotional support.*

As noted before, friends tend to be similar—like attracts like—so acquaintances who are most like you are, by and large, most likely to become your friends.

On an unconscious level, you may choose to turn an acquaintance into a friend because you are reminded of your early parent-child or sibling relationships. That is fine if you experienced nurturing, positive patterns, but not so fine if the patterns were negative or destructive.

The good news is that while friendship may be a repetition of past familial relationships, it may also be an opportunity to work on, and even improve, those early interactions. But until you have an understanding of why you choose certain friends, you will probably repeat, rather than change, those fundamental models. By getting in touch with the deeper motivations behind your friendship choices, however, you may begin to make different selections. Esther, for example, the oldest of six children, unwittingly chooses friends who are always in need of her help, repeating her childhood pattern of taking care of her five younger siblings. Although in her 40s and single, Esther has no wish to marry or to have children. She is already playing the role of caregiver to her needy friends who have drinking, marital, and career problems (as well as her extended family of siblings, in-laws, nieces, and nephews). Interestingly, Esther is unaware of her own pattern of pulling away from a friend as soon as the friend gets her life in order.

If someone had negative early experiences, why would she pick friends to replicate those sentiments?

Perpetuating a pattern is a less emotionally painful option than confronting it and trying to change it.

For example, Esther, by picking friends who have family or romantic relationships that are far worse than hers, avoids reexamining her own less-than-satisfactory intimate relationships.

Friendships primarily based on *emotional support* are, predictably, more intense and uneven than those based on doing things together, talking, or shared interests. Two friends I interviewed who mainly offer each other emotional support said they have even come to physical blows. (Emotional support may, in time, become part of a friendship primarily started for companionship, but it is not the initial motivation for the relationship.)

These emotional support friendships are the most similar to

the Great Friend Approach to friendship and the ideal of yesteryear. Twenty-five-year-old Lisa and Betty's friendship is an example of an acquaintanceship that became a best friendship based on emotional support. Betty and Lisa, who was separated from her husband of three months at the time her friendship with Betty blossomed, talked through the night at Lisa's apartment. They were then both working as waitresses and companions at a Manhattan club that catered to foreign businessmen:

> We ended up going with clients from the nightclub and staying out until 2:30 or 3:30 in the morning. And I remembered that Betty lived in Brooklyn. She's five feet tall and weighs 98 pounds. "You're going to take a train now to Brooklyn at three o'clock in the morning over my dead body," I told her. "You'll stay here."
>
> I barely knew her, but because I've been attacked late at night on the street, if it were within my power, I couldn't let somebody do it. It would make me nervous. "You'll stay on the couch."
>
> We sat up until about six o'clock with me talking nonstop about my entire life. At ten after six, I turned around and I said, "I have had diarrhea of the mouth and you haven't said a fuckin' word. I don't know who you are or where you come from. I've bared my entire soul. Can't you give me just a little something?"
>
> And she very quietly started to say, "I'm married and my husband..." and all this stuff [came pouring out]. So that's how we became friends.
>
> She knows she can count on us [Lisa and their other friend Tina]. We're all very careful to watch what happens with each other and to be supportive because we know this is a lot more solid. Men come and go. Girlfriends hang around a lot longer.

Finding Out Your FCQ
(Friendship Compatibility Quotient)

Sometimes it is simply too risky to decide, on the basis of a phone call or even a lunch or two, if you want to befriend someone. Asking yourself some or all of the questions below about your acquaintance may give you some additional information to work with when you decide if you want to move this relationship from an acquaintance to the coveted and valuable status of *friend*. Ongoing contact, such as getting on the same committee for your professional group, volunteering together, or committing to a weekly tennis or card game, may provide a shared experience and the opportunities to get to know each other to help you make that decision.

Here is a quiz, based on friendship research, to help you decide if a specific acquaintanceship you now have is more likely to lead to a reciprocal and rewarding best, close, or casual friendship.

Friendship Compatibility Quiz

1. Have you gotten verbal or nonverbal signs from your acquaintance that she or he wants to become your friend?

2. Have you the time and the energy to add this friend to the friendships you already have?

3. Right now, is friendship very valuable and important to you?

4. Do you and your acquaintance have fun together?

5. Do you and this potential friend have any similar interests?

6. Do you feel comfortable when you and this acquaintance talk on the phone?

7. Are you aware of any value disparities between you and your acquaintance but those value differences will not pose a problem?

8. If your religion, ethnic group, or racial background are not the same, is this acceptable to both of you?

9. If your socioeconomic class is different, is the difference

unimportant to either of you?

10. Are you in agreement about how often you need to call or see each other?

11. Do you reside or work near each other?

12. Whenever possible, will you return phone calls from your friend within 24 hours?

13. Would you keep a prior date with your acquaintance even if your romantic partner, date, or spouse suddenly asked you for the same time?

14. Do you have the gut feeling of liking this person?

15. Do you think your acquaintance would answer "Yes" to questions 13 and 14?

If you answered *yes* to all of the above questions, you seem committed to this acquaintance and compatible with her or him; there is a good likelihood she or he could become your friend. If you answered *no* to just a few questions, think about what those *no* answers reveal. Are these situations, feelings, or value conflicts you could overlook or work through within yourself or with your acquaintance? Now that you have considered your answers to these questions, you have to consider what your acquaintance might answer to these questions as well.

Helping an Acquaintance Become a Friend

There are definite ways to help advance an acquaintanceship to a friendship. Even if it still takes a "time test" to see if your friendship will last, here are 10 tips to help the process along:

- Show an interest in your acquaintance's life—family, work, hobbies, and personal concerns.
- If an acquaintance asks you to come through, do it. If you say you are too busy, you might never be asked again, and the relationship might never progress. (Avoid saying, "I would, but…")
- Avoid gossiping about your acquaintance.
- Remember your acquaintance's birthday or any other key upcoming anniversaries or special occasions.

- Return phone calls promptly.
- Communicate with each other, and see each other, on a regular basis.
- Create as many opportunities as possible for your relationship to develop outside of the specific context in which you first met.
- Take cues from your acquaintance about what pace will be most comfortable for your relationship.
- Emphasize shared values and interests.
- Avoid taking your evolving friendship for granted or leaning too heavily on it.

According to my research, there is also a very important factor to consider in why an acquaintance may become a friend, namely the *fun factor*. Since there are usually other relationships in your acquaintance's life to turn to for emotional support, information, advice, or help, one of the most sought-after qualities in a friend is the ability to "have fun together." With so many overwhelming responsibilities in life, so many school, work, or family obligations, being able to laugh or have a good time together is a key trait in a friend. When George Burns died at the age of 100, many throughout the world mourned. He, like other comedians, had an exalted status in our society because he could make people laugh. My husband, Fred, told me he interviewed George Burns when Fred was an entertainment writer for the Associated Press. Fred shared with me that throughout the interview, George Burns was always funny. Now, acquaintances need not be professional comedians, but if you feel they will add laughter and joy to your life as your friend, you may find yourself seeking them out more often than those who always make you feel sad, depressed, or negative, or who bring you down.

When an Acquaintance Stops a Friendship

Most everyone learns that dating and courtship are a sorting and sifting process along the road to mating. However, there may be a reluctance to view acquaintanceship as the experience and process that allows the necessary sifting out on the road to possible friendship. For example, 39-year-old Sara, a secretary who is single, relates her ambivalence about encouraging a woman whom she met the week before at a party. The story points out how important it is for both acquaintances to want to develop a friendship. If that mutuality is missing, being visible and following up on an initial meeting are futile. As Sara says: "Last week I went to a dinner. Just women. And one of them called me up and wanted to go out for drinks. I wasn't that interested. I told her I was busy that week and I really didn't know about next week, and she didn't get the hint. 'I'll call you on Monday.' So maybe I'll end up having a drink with her. I didn't understand the phone call. It was quite a surprise to me."

If, like Sara, an acquaintance declines your wish to move your relationship further to a friendship, it may be because your positive feelings are not shared, or it may be a question of time. I remember back in the 1970s, when I was single, I invited a married female criminologist to a cocktail party I was giving. She called to decline, explaining, in an exasperated voice, that she had all the friends she could handle in addition to her professional and personal obligations.

You will probably want to keep going till you find an acquaintance who is ready for a new friend. However, you might also, at some point, consider re-approaching acquaintances who earlier rejected you to see if feelings or situations have changed: taxing jobs may be more manageable; children will have grown up; other friends may have moved away; or a spouse may now have a steady Wednesday night card or squash game so you and your friend could more easily get together.

*

The next chapter looks at the type of friendship formed with an acquaintance, since that may have as much to do with a developing friendship as the personality of its participants.

We were worst enemies. We got in a fight. After that, we had to work together at an ice cream stand at school and that's how we got to know each other. We forgot about being worst enemies and became best friends.

—13-year-old suburban Long Island girl

5. FRIENDSHIP PATTERNS

It's very handy because we all go out together. Or if one of them can't do something with the other, you may call the others. We do have a good network. A jolly little foursome.

—31-year-old Bev, a single pediatric nurse

This chapter explores friendship patterns based on how many persons are in a friendship—two, three, four, or more—as well as such other factors as ethnicity, race, or gender.

WHEN TWO'S ENOUGH COMPANY

Do you want a friendship that is exclusive, intimate, and private? Then a two-person friendship, or friendship pair, the most common type of friendship pattern, is ideal for you.

Why is the friendship pair (dyad) so popular? The friendship pair depends on just its two participants for its existence. Because there are just two, it is more private and intimate, potentially offering the finest opportunity to express emotion and reveal your vulnerability. However, it dissolves if either person lets the relationship lapse.

Because of the exclusivity and intimacy of this smallest of groups, almost all best, and the majority of close, friendships will be one-on-one pairs.

Jonathan Cruzan, Director of Human Resources at Mercy Health System in Janesville, Wisconsin, has a best friendship dating back 30 years. For several years, when he was the vice president of human resources at a bank, his best friend was also his boss. "It's been a mentor relationship," Cruzan explains. Although being best friends with one's boss could be problematical for most people, he and his friend were able to handle it for several reasons. First of all, their friendship preceded their work relationship. Secondly, they have open communication, which has helped them keep their friendship going within and outside the workplace. Cruzan says: "We talked about the friendship long and hard before I came to work for him. The friendship never really was a negative because he's a very strong personality. It didn't bother me to know that he was the boss. Definitely a decision maker. I'm much more laid back. It's never been an ego battle kind of thing."

Another example of a friendship pair is Nan and her best friend, Liz, whom she befriended at a singing event in 1979. Nan and Liz both live in Manhattan; they are both single and in their late 30s. They see each other two to three times a week. At the time Nan befriended Liz, she was going through a crisis with her other best friend, Jane—Jane was angry with Liz for going to a psychic—whom Nan had befriended 12 years before. Although Nan and Jane patched up their differences, Nan maintained her new best friendship with Liz.

THREE'S A NICE CROWD

Threesomes are easier friendships to maintain than pairs, since the group now has its constituents in common; it can survive the loss of any one member. The group of male best friends I met in 1979 that initially sparked my interest in friendship was a threesome of men in their early 30s that dated back to high school. Two of the three friends got together weekly because they lived in the same city; their third friend, who lived in another state, stayed in touch with the other two by phone; they visited each other several times a year.

Forming a threesome is a possible solution for those who find it difficult— emotionally or because of the time involved— to maintain too many unique, and competing, friendship pairs. For instance, if Nan, Liz, and Jane became a friendship threesome, rather than two separate friendship pairs, although exclusivity and secrecy would be lost, it could be easier to maintain the friendships.

However, threesomes can be less stable than pairs; there is a greater possibility of conflict since someone may feel "on the outside." There are no true friendship threesomes; only pairs, plus one. The friendship threesome will always have shifting alliances so that it is, by necessity, an unequal split of affection and attention. Furthermore, the addition of just one person increases the potential number of interrelationships among the friends to six. Because the friendship is no longer a private matter, there may be pressure to maintain the friendships, as ending any intimate relationship, even a friendship, may carry a stigma. For example, when Kevin and John ended their three-year close friendship, they did not have to account to anyone for the end of their relationship, since no one else was involved. Once a third friend is involved, however, if any one friend pulls away from any other friend, it will be almost impossible to conceal that fact. For that reason, three-way companionships may be close or best friendships, especially if all three became friends at the same time.

But when the three-way friendship consists of a preexisting friendship pair, plus one, problems may arise, as the story that follows indicates. Rose, Peggy, and Erika are an example of a close friendship threesome that ultimately failed. Rose was 18 when she befriended Peggy, and 25 when she became friends with Erika. For ten years, Rose maintained two separate close friendship pairs. Within a year of Peggy's attempt to form a threesome with Rose and Erika, Rose ended her close friendship with Peggy. By Rose's account, the faults that Rose always saw in Peggy soon became intolerable once Erika became involved:

> Peggy was a really good friend in a lot of ways....But Peggy's one of these people who's very jealous and very insecure and would be real pleased to tell me, or anybody else, all their faults.
>
> Erika met Peggy and she and Erika became friends. That was one of the things that precipitated it [the friendship ending]. That really infuriated me. Peggy really liked Erika. Here was another person who was more fashionable, had more money....It infuriated Erika because Peggy would see Erika in an outfit and she would go out and buy the same outfit.
>
> Peggy pulled this thing where she would call Erika all the time and ask her to go out and Erika would say, "Well, what about Rose?" and Peggy would say, "You know, Rose's working, she can't make it." Meanwhile, she never asked me....
>
> And then she went on a vacation with Erika....[And] Peggy would start ripping Erika apart to me, and me apart to Erika.

As the above example indicates, with a three-way friendship, *confidentiality* is vital; only share gossip about each other if you have permission.

However, when jealousies, rivalries, or gossiping are missing or dealt with, friendship threesomes can be gratifying and nurturing. Especially for single men and women, friendship threesomes can offer a type of bonding and commonality that a first child provides a husband and wife in marriage. Because the three friends have a shared history, they are able to talk intimately about each other. If they live in the same community, if one friend is busy, they still have someone else for companionship.

WHEN FOUR OR MORE ARE FRIENDS: NETWORKS AND GROUPS

A friendship group or network consists of four or more friends who all know and like each other. It is a pattern that is especially intriguing, since we traditionally think of friendship as a one-on-one twosome relationship. Although there are exceptions, friendship groups tend to consist of casual friendships. However, there may be close or best friendships between two or more group members who are also part of the larger casual friendship network or group.

Friendship groups may start because of a shared school, neighborhood, or work association, but the group survives because it is now based on friendship alone. My sister-in-law Karen travels from Massachusetts to Iowa, where she grew up, to spend a week with her eight close girlfriends from high school. Known as "The Crazy Eight," they have stayed friends for 30 years and try to get together every year or so for at least a week.

Friendship networks may be either closed _cliques_ (like "The Crazy Eight") or open _snowballs._ Cliques are more likely to have close or best friend members; snowballs are more likely to consist of casual friends.

Cliques are networks that exclude others; static, romantic partners or other friends are usually not added. Here are just some examples of cliques I heard about during my research: four male ex-roommates from law school; artists from Ireland; a woman's seven college friends; a network of nine men and women from Fire Island that had lasted five years; a clique of seven mothers of toddlers who initially lived within a few blocks of each other in Manhattan.

In the chapter on work and friendship, you will see how cliques at work have the potential for decreasing productivity by forming "power groups" that interfere with the work that has to be done. However, outside of work settings, especially after the school years, cliques can give a feeling of being part of a friendship family.

Those who have friendship networks invest time and energy in initiating and maintaining those friendship groups. (It is that investment of time—during work and even outside of work—that causes cliques to lower productivity at work.)

A snowball is a friendship group that is open and fluid, with members adding other workers, friends, friends of friends, or romantic partners to the original group. Like a snowball, it picks up additional members as it rolls along. Edda, a copywriter at an advertising agency in New York, is part of a snowball friendship group with Texas connections that began with Carl, then Carl and John, who added Pat, then Edda. Soon it directly expanded to 14 interconnections; within a short period of time it had snowballed to 40 men and women. Edda explains her friendship network's evolution:

> When I came here [from Texas] I knew two people, John and Carl. Through them, I got introduced to Pat, whom they had met when they got up here. I became friends with Pat, who was a classmate of mine in Texas, and I recognized her. Through Pat I met Jill and George. Then a few other people came from Texas who knew each other. It's like people I didn't really know; we all knew who we were, but didn't really know each other well. It's like it was a reference, "Oh, this is Roger, he's a friend of ———. You remember him, he's the one who wrecked Melanie's car."...Robin was also in a class of mine. Turns out she was best friends with the sister of one of my best friends. Jill turns out to be the cousin of a cousin of Carl's. Wendy is going to marry Sam, whose parents just moved to Houston, in the same neighborhood as John's parents.

ETHNIC, RACIAL, AND GENDER FRIENDSHIP PATTERNS

Anthropologist Robert Brain was surprised when he observed the Bangwa of western Africa by friendship's position. Writes Brain in "Somebody Else Should Be Your Best Friend": "To have a best friend was as important as having a wife or a brother—possibly more important....Among the Bangwa, best friends are known as 'twins.'...To celebrate friendship in other parts of western Africa, men throw excrement at each other and comment loudly on the genitals of their respective parents when they meet; this behavior, perhaps unnatural and obscene to us, is a proof of love to friends."

In his popular books *The Silent Language* and *The Dance of Life: The Other Dimension of Time,* anthropologist Edward T. Hall points out the cultural variations in acceptable personal space between strangers, as well as how you perceive time.

The same can be said about friendship patterns: friendship is cultural. What is acceptable friendship behavior in Manhattan may be unheard of in a rural town in Wisconsin; how Asian-Americans define a friend may be distinct from how Asians define one.

Cultural friendship differences among various groups are there for you to discover; it provides information that might help lessen the distance between you and your friends, or your potential friends. For instance, Carl befriended his across-the-hall neighbor, Paul, soon after Paul arrived from Senegal, Africa. They shared an interest in audio equipment; Carl's wife and Paul's girlfriend got along. One evening, about six months into their friendship, Paul called Carl, all excited, because he had just bought a videocassette player and wanted Carl to help hook it up to his television. Carl was exhausted and had already undressed. He promised to help Paul first thing in the morning. But Paul was hurt, and their friendship was never the same. It seems that in Senegal, it is customary to drop everything when a friend asks for your help, even if the request is not an emergency. That was not something Manhattanite Carl was used to doing.

I am reminded of the influence of culture in friendship patterns when I review, and expand on, what I learned about international business protocol for my book, *Business Protocol* (Wiley, 1991). In the chapter, "International Etiquette," I provide a brief survey of business etiquette in 14 countries around the world. Just as national cultural orientations impact on work relationships and how business is conducted, those same culture-specific perspectives modify personal friendship patterns. For example, in my research into business protocol in Japan, it was emphasized that status is far more important in Japan than in the United States. As expert Diana Rowland, author of *Japanese Business Etiquette*, put it, "The Japanese are very hierarchical." It would be a breach of protocol to try to conduct business with someone who was at a different level than you. That helps explain why business cards are even more crucial in Japan than in the United States:they quickly show someone's title and level, avoiding the embarrassment of inappropriate across-class business relationships.

Similarly, the significance of homogeneity in nonwork relationships is reinforced in the friendship survey I received from a 38-year-old free-lance writer in Tokyo who noted: "One need[s] a friend at the same level."

A 38-year-old researcher living in Tokyo wrote that she makes friends "through my work." This is intriguing because Boye Lafayette DeMente points out in his interesting book, *Japanese Etiquette & Ethics in Business*, that although socializing during the workday with co-workers is frowned upon, socializing *after* work is expected. There is even a phrase for it: *hame wo hazusuek,* which means "pulling out all the stops." It would be considered rude in Japan to avoid partaking in such after-hours socializing. A related phrase to this concept is, as DeMente notes, *chotto ippai,* which means, "Let's have a quick drink."

British sociologist Graham Allan, in his extensive studies of friendship patterns in the United Kingdom, points out how these patterns vary, based on class association. For example, in his research note, "Class Variation in Friendship Patterns," published in the *British Journal of Sociology,* Allan shares his observations of middle-class and working-class couples in a suburban Essex village. He discovered that the middle class couples were more likely to expand a friendship beyond a "given sphere of activity," interacting in a variety of situations. They were also more likely to entertain their friends in their homes.

By contrast, the working-class couples he interviewed were more likely to have friendships that were "situation specific." Furthermore, they tended to treat their homes as "the exclusive preserve of the family"; entertaining at home was rare. Allan found the working class more likely to have "mates," which he defines to be more like acquaintances than friends, since the interaction occurs by chance rather than on purpose.

I interviewed Dr. Betty Sung, professor emerita of the City

College of New York, who taught Asian American studies. She said, "Asians in this country are overwhelmingly foreign-born, so it is more comfortable for them to keep friendship within their own ethnic group." She told me of a class assignment where one student surveyed 100 Chinese merchants in Flushing, Queens, on how many non-Chinese friends they socialized with outside of whatever contacts they made through their business. The answer was none.

Professor Sung contrasts the differences she has observed in Asian and American attitudes toward friendship. What some Americans label friendships, Dr. Sung notes, "could more aptly be termed acquaintances. Friendship for the Chinese is a long-lasting strong bond." For example, Professor Sung's husband went to college in China. His classmates still retain ties with each other 50 years after graduation. Professor Sung is American-born and went to college in the United States. She lost touch with her classmates right after leaving the campus.

In contrast to the United States, formal introductions tend to be more important in other countries, such as France and Japan, as the starting point for a new friendship where class and status considerations are more pervasive. In those countries, friendships that start at school are far more likely, and safe, then friendships that evolve out of chance meetings, since being in attendance at the same school indicates that a similar social status and family background are shared. (As the discussion of friendship in the suburbs versus the city that concludes this section points out, "breaking in" in more homogeneous communities in America, and forming new friends, is akin to the greater exclusivity of international friendship patterns.)

J. Barry Gurdin, who has extensively studied friendship patterns in Canada, concludes in *Amitie/Friendship* that ethnicity is "a salient factor in friendship." Gurdin studied 2,371 people randomly selected from a Montreal telephone directory. He notes: "How Montrealers think about and act toward their friends may be strongly influenced by their coming from a 'French-,' 'English-,' or 'Other-''Canadian' background," with the majority of Montrealers choosing their closest friends "from their own ethnic group."

Even taking more time for lunch, as my girlfriend from Venezuela was used to doing, could impact on how quickly a friendship might start and strengthen. I remember when my son, who is now ten, was four and in nursery school in Manhattan. I befriended Elia, who was a few years younger than me. We shared an interest in movies and theater, and there was that "click" that we wanted to become friends. She had been brought up in Venezuela but went to graduate school in Manhattan and stayed on afterward. We became "fast friends" because of shared values and interests, but also because of her Latin American custom of taking a two-to-three-hour lunch. Spending several hours over lunch every week or so, as our children played, helped us get to know each other during that year. (Our friendship did not, however, happen overnight; it wasn't until several months after our first meeting that Elia joined me for lunch, rather than her son's nanny. But I trusted my instinct that Elia was someone I wanted as a friend, so I patiently awaited Elia's involvement in my life.)

In _Among Friends_, Letty Cottin Pogrebin highlights the friendship cultures of Blacks, Latins, Asians, and Jews, among others. On Jewish friendship patterns, Pogrebin quotes sociologist Steven M. Cohen, who found that Jews prefer to have other Jews as friends, although they may not necessarily work or live among other Jews. She quotes a Jewish homemaker, whose comments about having little time for friends after she takes care of her nuclear and extended family sound very similar to the emphasis on family in the Asian perspective. My own experiences and observations of Jewish friendships is that those who have married outside the religion, or who send their children to public schools rather than religious schools or yeshivas, will also be likely to have a wider range of non-Jewish friends.

A business colleague in Basel, Switzerland, commented via e-mail on the differences or similarities in Swiss, German, and American friendship patterns: "It's a general understanding that Americans will make friends much faster and easier than almost all Europeans, but they do forget their friends faster once they're no longer around. But I can only verify this for a few of my American friends, and it, by the way, applies as well to as many European friends!"

He went on to point out a trend toward the "global village" that is influencing international friendship patterns, and friendships, as well: "Friendship, like similar and/or comparable behaviour patterns, moves toward a global level where you won't be able to make any real substantial differences anymore. This goes of course for all the people who have learned to think, and act, globally."

I noticed a decided difference in friendships during the 17 years I lived in Manhattan compared to the half dozen years I have been living in a suburban Fairfield County, Connecticut, community of 110,000. In Manhattan, during my single years, friendships tended to begin from professional activities, work situations, or, occasionally, in the neighborhood. After I married and became a mother, shared parenting experiences were the basis of new friendships. I found being open with my close and best friends was actually encouraged by the size, diversity, anonymity, and informality of Manhattan. "Hey, let's meet for coffee," was a lot easier when you could hold your get-together before or after your other obligations. You could feel safer revealing confidences to a friend, since the bond was to each other rather than to the community. Furthermore, it was unlikely, unless you worked together or lived in the same apartment house, that your friendship networks or other personal or work relationships would overlap.

By contrast, in a smaller community, what you gain—in terms of more physical space per family, a community of thousands instead of millions, a sense of shared identity as residents of a particular town—you also lose in terms of the anonymity that makes revealing confidences a more comfortable thing to do in a big city. Living in a smaller town also requires more self-control and discipline about keeping negative opinions or conflicts to yourself; the ex-friend you chew out might run into you at one of the three main supermarkets in town or at school functions. The prevalence of interaction and interconnecting networks actually causes the "hold your tongue" phenomenon in suburban or rural communities that may be misinterpreted as phoniness. After rushing in once or twice to acquaintanceships that failed to become friendships, or became friendships that ended, an attitude of caution may ensue. That caution born of experience may cause friendships in homogeneous communities to take even longer to evolve, get tested out, and become solid. In smaller, more tightly knit communities, you may be wiser to allow a friendship that you want to end to simply fade away rather than have the kind of dramatic confrontations that characterized so many of the failed friendships of the men and women I interviewed in major cities.

I found a noticeable absence of friendships that crossed racial lines in conducting my research. I surmise this was largely due to the preponderance of school and work settings that were all one race. School and work are the two situations where interracial contact is most likely, since the larger society is currently mostly characterized by residential communities of the same race. So when school children or workers of different races come together and friendships fail to ensue, it is important to avoid jumping to the conclusion that friendships across racial lines are unlikely. Instead, what is being rejected is situations of disparate status or class, not a person's race. I discovered as long as there is an opportunity for mingling in multiracial school, leisure, or work settings where the participants are equal in status, such as same-level executives, professional women, students, or journalists, for example, interracial friendships do develop and flourish.

Unfortunately, the lack of socializing across religious or racial lines is perpetuated as new couples, when house hunting, will often look only in those communities where they will be in the majority or "at least half of the school," as a Jewish mother comments. Some may not require that their religious, ethnic, or racial group be a certain percentage of the school system, but at least that they are welcome. Of course, what defines "welcome"? A man who lives in a rural New England community explains that he and his wife are considering relocating because their adopted daughter is the only Asian-American in the entire elementary school.

Male and Female Friendship Patterns

A man is able to pick up the phone and contact an old friend without needing as many apologies about the lapse of time between communications as would be required for most women's friendships. The friendships of women are usually more nurturing, intimate, and intense than those of men. This tendency evolves from the continual closeness of mothering; her mother is the person the girl models herself after, as compared to the usually more intermittent attention of the father, who traditionally was around less frequently and was trained to be less emotional, to take things more "like a man." Most adults today were socialized in this "old system" of mothers who were generally around more than fathers. Thus, by adulthood, as sociologist Beth B. Hess and other social scientists have noted, there are two distinct friendship patterns: the distant and less intimate but consistent friendships of men; and the more emotional, close, and (sometimes) more explosive ones of women.

In the last decade, the idea that men and women communicate differently has been popularized by Deborah Tannen, Ph.D., and John Gray, Ph.D., among others. Those communication pattern variations factor into the dissimilarities and similarities in male and female friendships. (Tannen discusses this in the section entitled "Contrasting Concepts of Friendship" in *You Just Don't Understand.*)

Mark Fuerst, a free-lance health writer, describes how he talks "more freely emotionally" with his female friend than with his male friend and preferred to discuss his adoption plans with her: "It just seems it's easier to talk to my female friends about difficult issues. It's more locker room talk with the men. It's just harder with the men to break through and get to the emotional level. It happens, but it seems to take longer with men friends. I talk about the same issues, but I open myself up more freely to female friends. It was easy to talk with Lois about wanting to adopt a baby.... She had also gone through a similar situation. When I was talking to Lois about it, there were times when I remember I wanted to talk to my friend Rick about it, but I held back. It took several months before I discussed the issue with him."

As women's work and child-rearing patterns change, you can expect to see a change in friendship patterns as well, changes that are already appearing, as will be noted in Part 4, Work and Friendship. Some older women who have already gained positions of power in the business world reflect those changes. Their friendship patterns more closely resemble a man's in that lapses in contact have become more forgivable. For example, actress and business executive Polly Bergen maintains friendships despite her hectic life. As Bergen told me:

> Due to my work, I have to travel a great deal. I am a devout workaholic. Fortunately for me, my friends understand that months may pass before I phone, but when I do call, it's as if I had just spoken with them the previous day. However, if a friend calls and needs me, I'm there for them, no matter how busy I may be.

Can Women and Men Be Friends?

There are old-fashioned men like my late father, who, all my life, chanted the adage, "Men and women cannot be friends." Swedish playwright August Strindberg (1849-1912) had a similar point of view when he wrote in 1886, "Friendship can only exist between persons with similar interests and points of view. Man and woman by the conventions of society are born with different interests and different points of view." (Translated by Claud Field and quoted in *The Columbia Dictionary of Quotations)*. Or the 40-year-old male Delaware computer programmer who wrote to me, "I have never had a 'friend' of the opposite sex. I heard Thomas Williams (the novelist) once say that he always felt that there should be some chemistry between man and woman that would (to my mind) always leave the relationship under a different heading." And do not tell a woman I used to know that men and women can be friends. She asked her friend to "fill in" for her whenever she had to work late by going out to dinner or to the theater with her husband; a few months later, her friend and her husband ran off together.

In general, however, platonic friendships with members of

the opposite sex are, theoretically, more possible and acceptable than in the past. For most, friendships with those of the opposite sex are in addition to friendships with those of the same sex. Linda Sapadin, a psychologist based in Valley Stream, New York, conducted a survey of 156 men and women contacted through professional work organizations. She found that the men said they appreciated cross-sex friendships because they were more nurturing, intimate, and less competitive than their same-sex friendships. By contrast, in the same areas the women gave their friendships with men a lower rating than their same-sex friendships. Furthermore, the biggest problem with cross-sex friendships, Sapadin discovered, was the "sexual undertone."

But male-female friendships continue to become more common and less subject to gossip. As Susan Margolis writes in her magazine article,"Some of My Best Friends Are Men":

> Friendships between the sexes are important indeed—not just for biding time, nor for quelling loneliness. Not because, in these perilous days, friendship is even safer than safe sex, nor because career women are too tired and involved for new romance. They're important because—in spite of the fact that society is still self-conscious about them—these relationships work.

For a further discussion of gender issues, see Chapter 12, Male and Female Work Friendships.

*

In Part 2, *Friendshifts*, Or How Friendship Changes Throughout Life, you will get an overview of how friendship shifts and changes from infancy through the older years.

No matter how my life changes, my need for friends continues.

—Lois Wyse, *Women Make the Best Friends*

PART 2

FRIENDSHIFTS, OR HOW FRIENDSHIP CHANGES THROUGHOUT LIFE

While raising the kids, pretty much friends came second. We were always busy with soccer or baseball games or [kids'] concerts. Since the kids went away to college, we found we do a lot more with our old friends. In fact, we joined a bowling league in the neighborhood again. We had belonged seventeen years ago. Everybody had just come back. It's a lot of fun. Friends are very important now, otherwise it's much too quiet.

—Jim Mugavero, 48-year-old married high school math teacher

All my immediate family has died, so my friends have become my family.
—Priscilla Orr, 48-year-old single New Jersey poet

6. CHILDHOOD AND THE SINGLE YEARS

What could be finer than to have someone to whom you may speak as freely as to yourself?

— Cicero, "On Friendship"

It is never too early to begin to create the best or close friendships, or even the casual friendships, that will help enrich your adult years. The basic behaviors so necessary to friendship—sharing, caring, showing an interest in someone else, honesty, and avoiding aggressive behavior—are first learned in the sandbox as much as in school, camp, college, or at work.

THE EARLY YEARS

Researchers have discovered that as early as two to three months of age, infants are concerned with the movements of other babies. By five months, they are oriented toward other infants' cries.

Social psychologist-turned-lawyer Zick Rubin, basing his views about infants' peer relationships on his observations of play groups, of his own infant son, and a review of the literature, discovered that initially babies will accept just about anyone as a playmate. Infants interact by exploring their peers as if they were objects, coming into contact with each other because they want to play with the same toys.

But by the end of the first year, friendship starts to serve a specific function for the infant, who is now physically and emotionally weaning away from his or her mother, and able to relate to other babies. By 14 months, babies have distinct playmate preferences. Research has also suggested that as early as two years of age, opposite-sex friendships are less competitive than same-sex ones, and also more emotional and affective; toddler girls embrace and kiss same-age boys, which occurs less often with same-sex toddler boy friendships.

As early as two to three years of age, peer relationships reflect the strength of the mother-child bond. As Rubin notes in *Children's Friendships*: "Those three-year-olds who have the most secure relationships with their mothers also tend to be the most competent in interactions with peers."

I have also noticed a distinct difference in how preschoolers get along with other children based on personality: aggressive children, and those who have a harder time sharing their toys with other children, may be in less demand as playmates. For example, a Palm Springs woman told me her two sons are very different when they have play dates. One is very easy-going and does not have to always have his own way. He just wants to have a good time. Everyone who plays with him has a pleasant time as well.

The older boy is adamant about getting his own way and less willing to take turns or share.

It is no mystery which child is very popular and has lots of friends, and which one is alone more often and has few friends.

Just how important is it for a child to have friends during the early school years? Research has found that children with friends enjoy school more and, consequently, tend to get better grades. Conversely, children who lack friends in elementary school are at greater risk for teen depression. The last two decades have seen a wealth of research being conducted on children's friendships by such sociologists, psychologists, and communication skills experts as Willard W. Hartup, Robert Selman, James Youniss, Steven Asher, Peter Renshaw, Thomas Berndt, Gary Alan Fine, John J. La Gaipa, Brian J. Bigelow, Sherri Oden, and John Gottman, among others. It is now firmly established that having friends is an indication that a child or youth has achieved exemplary social skills. In his journal article, "The Company They Keep: Friendships and Their Developmental Significance," published in *Child Development*, University of Minesota Regents' Professor Willard W. Hartup, Ph.D., also suggests it is time to look at the significance of the friends a child or youth chooses, not just whether or not he or she has friends. Beginning with a dramatic example of a 14-year-old in Minnesota who, in February 1995, along with his best friend, committed a murder, Hartup notes that a child or adolescent with problems will fare worse by teaming up with, or becoming friends with, another antisocial child. He concludes: "Supportive relationships between socially skilled individuals appear to be developmental advantages, whereas coercive and conflict-ridden relationships are developmental disadvantages, especially among antisocial children." In essence, research has to go beyond the criteria of "having or not having friends" and look at just who those friends are and how they contribute to, or undermine, academic, behavioral, moral, or social goals.

An indication of the significance of having a good elementary school experience is reflected in the graduation speech of fifth grader Courtney Byrnes:

> From my first day of kindergarten until this moment, I have had friends here [at elementary school]. They have stuck with me through thick and thin....I remember having a seyance [seance] with some of my friends and almost reaching Elvis!
> Once in 4th grade I got a bad mark on a paper and was getting really upset. But when I called my friend, she listened and made me feel so much better that I told my parents. (They understood of course.) But my friend never told anyone and helped me pull myself together.

...I will miss the teachers, the classes, and most of all I will miss my friends.

I polled six fifth graders about their current best friend. All six told me they met their current best friend in school; three of those best friendships dated back to kindergarten. My father, who was almost 81 when he died, had a best friendship with Dave Schaeffer that continued uninterrupted for 75 years, since kindergarten, even though they attended different high schools and Dave moved across the country 17 years before my father died. Magazine writer Sondra Forsyth discusses the importance of her best friendship, which began in kindergarten, during her formative years:

> My parents were 40 when I was born. I was an only child. My mother was a teacher and very much a career person. Although I had a very lovely childhood, I guess you could say I was lonely. My friend was also an only child, so we became kind of sisters. I was at school in Detroit at the time. We were playmates. We walked to school together. When we got to second grade, they changed the system that year so we had to go up a half grade. We never really fit into that group. They were older. We were little stars in the best reading group. No one really liked us that much, so we became even closer friends. She was a piano student and we were ballet students. She would play, and we made our own little shows. We had our own little fascinating world.

Helping Children Become Better Friends

But when Sondra's family moved away in eighth grade, she lost contact with her best friend. "I had been very sad about it. It had been a very rich relationship," Sondra explains. Then, decades later, her former best friend's mother saw Sondra's byline in a magazine and contacted her. Sondra immediately was in touch with her former best friend, who was now married, living in Africa, and the mother of a four-year-old. They picked up where they left off, rekindling their friendship through letters, phone calls, and once- or twice- yearly visits when her friend returns to the United States.

Sondra used her own experience to help her children hold on to their friendships despite relocations: when Sondra and her children moved to Long Island for a few years, she helped her son and daughter keep up with their Manhattan friends by driving friends out for weekend sleepovers. When they decided to move back to the city, she did the same thing to help her children maintain their suburban friends. The return to city living was a lot easier since her children could return to long-standing friendships.

Maintaining friendships, whether it is because a friend moves to another community, gets a different teacher the year after the classroom-based friendship initially started, or has an argument with his or her friend, are situations that children need to learn to cope with and master. Usually it is up to parents to make that extra effort to organize get-togethers that are now inconvenient. However, you should not force your children to keep up old friendships they no longer value just because you want to maintain a friendship with their former friends' parents. You may still keep those parent-to-parent friendships going on your own time; if it is a genuine friendship, it should persist even though your children no longer consider each other friends.

A difference I have observed in the children of working versus at-home mothers is that at-home mothers usually have more time to arrange play dates for their young children. But if mothers work full time, they can still give their young children the friendship benefits that play dates provide by helping their baby sitters participate in play dates or arranging for occasional weekend get-togethers with peers.

Although ultimately friendship formation, maintenance, or, if necessary, dissolution is up to your child, you can set an example by putting a value on your own friendships outside of your marital "friendship" by phoning your own friends, having regular get-togethers with and without your children, as well as sending holiday cards, acknowledging major events in your friends' lives, and, of course, sending out change-of-address notices after a move.

Parents and teachers should take an active role in helping their children and students become better friends. That will better prepare them to handle interpersonal conflicts by giving children the tools they need to work through those disagreements. Those skills will also help them later on to be better "team players" at work and in their romantic relationships as well.

Parties or reunions may provide an opportunity for your children to renew their old friendships. Some parents complain that the birthday party has gotten out of hand as parents spend hundreds of dollars or even more on parties; there are parents who spend $1,500 on a party for a one-year-old, $350 for a five-year-old's party, or $75 for a nine-year-old's movie and pizza party for four. What really counts is not the amount of money you spend but the fact that your child has regular contact with his or her evolving friendship network.

A question parents often ask about their child's party is: should we invite the entire class? It really depends on how cohesive the class is as a group, your child's age, and whether it is financially or logistically feasible. It is probably more common to invite the entire class in the younger years, from nursery school through first or second grade. However, a friend tells me her son's private school requests that birthday parties include the entire fourth-grade class. But if the class is getting along—everyone seems to like everyone—and you have the space and economic resources, having the entire class could lead to a successful birthday celebration. (It also eliminates leaving anyone out, which could lead to bruised feelings or egos.) However, if there are a lot of additional friends your child wants to include beyond the class, or there are too many children in your child's class who do not get along, a blanket invitation could backfire. In any case, unless the entire class is invited, mail invitations to a child's home rather than distributing them at school. That will hold down the number of hurt feelings.

Since birthday gift giving has for many parents lost some of its meaning and become too materialistic, you might want to encourage your child to create a drawing or write a poem in addition to any store-bought gifts. Use this opportunity to teach your child some protocol by having children sign their name to a card as soon as they are able to—usually by kindergarten or first grade—or even write each thank-you note for the presents they receive by second or third grade. Younger nursery-school children could at least contribute some thoughts about a gift or watch you writing the thank-you notes as a positive example of social etiquette. Perhaps you could ask your child to help you select the thank-you notes, if you purchase store-bought ones, or, if you create them on your home computer, to help you out as you make selections from any of the numerous card-creating software available for children or adults, such as Kid Pix® Studio, Flying Colors™, Print Artist, or The Amazing Writing Machine™, among others.

THE TEEN YEARS

The teen years are an ideal time to continue developing those friendships that may last a lifetime, even if there are shifts in those relationships. Indeed, according to Japanese folk wisdom, the secondary school years are considered the period when it is "easiest to cultivate life-span friendships," writes scholar David W. Plath.

Friendships continued or developed during the adolescent years help a youngster become independent and separate from parents and siblings. A 13-year-old living in Maryland spends "a couple of hours" on the phone each night talking to her friends, who are pivotal right now. She currently sees her sister, who is three years younger, as a competitor rather than a friend. After school, she sometimes has friends over or she goes out with them. Her parents both work—her mother, an executive, often returns home after seven—so her friends offer her attention and companionship that are less available at home during the school and work week.

Adolescents, unlike younger children, do not enter friendships with the previous "take me as I am" attitude. They are now more willing to mold themselves to please a friend to avoid losing that friendship. This can be positive or negative depending upon what behaviors are adopted—dressing more attractively versus taking drugs, for instance.

Actress Beverly Garland emphasizes how important it is for teens to fit in with their friends:

> I said to my little girl, who is now 31, when she was younger,
> something about, "What did people say when you went to school
> and you said you were Beverly Garland's daughter?"
>
> "I never said that you were my mother or you were an
> actress."
>
> "You didn't? I worked all my life to be something. I thought
> you'd be proud of me."
>
> "I don't want people to treat me differently as opposed to
> Beverly 'Blank.'"

Garland's daughter went to public school, where she felt
uncomfortable bragging about or even revealing her mother's
celebrity status. Her son, however, went to private school, where
he handled it differently, telling everyone he had a famous mother.
As Garland explains: "At private school, if you didn't have a Ferrari,
you had a mother who was an actress."

Elizabeth Douvan and Joseph Adelson's comments in *The
Adolescent Experience* reflect how crucial friendships are for the
adolescent: "All in all, it would seem that the adolescent does not
choose friendship, but is driven into it."

Girls of 14 to 16 want best or close friends who offer emotional
support and are able to keep their secrets. Early and middle
adolescent boys use sports, video games, and other activities as the
foundation for their best or close friendships. For example, 15-
year-old Jesse Henkel's best friend is the same age and lives right
next door in suburban Long Island. He says his best friend has
"been there when I need him [or] if I need someone to hang out
with. I lend money to him. He lends money to me. We share the
paper route." They also share "secrets, personal things, stuff like
that."

Echoing Harry Stack Sullivan's view that "chumship" during
adolescence aids the maturing child, who must begin to create a
self outside of the family, Douvan and Adelson write: "The need is
to define personal identity; to accomplish this, the youngster needs
the assurance and mirroring offered by others of the same
disposition," namely, friends.

Those friends could be a lifeline to teenagers whose family is distant, negative, dysfunctional, or even abusive. By providing some of what the teenager is lacking at home, friends may make their childhood more memorable and their school performance better. It is important to help teens-at-risk to seek out friends who are a plus to their lives. This is when the teenager may be at a turning point, when he or she must make some choices that will have dire consequences, such as whether to use drugs, become a gang member, or commit suicide. Being a gang member, even if teens think they are becoming part of a friendship group, is a poor choice. A gang, by definition, according to James Haskins's *Street Gangs: Yesterday and Today*, is an organized group committed to carrying out illegal activities. Yet gangs, especially in poor and underprivileged areas, may be eagerly recruiting new members. Through their names or uniforms, their presence may be obvious and tempting to the teen who feels friendless. Those gangs, although "up to no good"—most are involved in burglaries, robberies, guns, drugs, and terrorizing vulnerable groups, like the elderly—are more obvious than genuine friendship groups, which may be hard to break into, if a clique, or harder to find, if just unrelated friendship pairs.

Teens-at-risk, if parents cannot provide the necessary help with their friendship needs or choices, should be pointed to such organizations as the local chapter of Big Brothers/Big Sisters of America, the YMCA or YWCA, Boys & Girls Clubs of America, or other helpful groups particular to your community for help.

I am also told that for some teens, casual friends from afar, such as pen pals through letters, or cyberspace friends through electronic mail (e-mail), may provide a safer sounding board than even best or close friends who live nearby. However, teens need to exercise the same caution when dealing with these new relationships as they would with any strangers, namely do not give out their home address, phone number, or agree to an in-person meeting. Furthermore, parents also need to be kept informed about any new or on-going cyberspace or pen pal relationships.

In the teen years, with opposite-sex adolescent friendships, the line between friendship and something more often begins to blur.

As the Maryland 13-year-old says: "I like him as a friend. We're friends. And he thinks I like him as a friend, but I think I like him as something more."

Her comments typify how adolescence differs from the preceding stages: the teen, who begins to look for romantic intimacy, now has that as a competing relationship to friendship. Conflicts may start to occur: as one teen said, "If my girlfriend and my friend both want to go out with me on Saturday night, what do I do?"

In late adolescence, as boys and girls begin to transfer some of their energy and time from friends to romance, the skills they developed in initiating and maintaining same-sex friendships may now be applied to romance.

HOW FRIENDSHIP HELPS
THE SINGLE MAN OR WOMAN

Friendship enables single men and women to have intimacy on their own terms. Unlike marriage, friendship does not involve their entire life, a status shift, a change in living arrangements, or a new name. Indeed, the interaction with friends dominates two of the popular TV sitcoms today about singles—*Friends* and *Seinfeld.*

In the countless interviews I have done with singles and marrieds since the late 1970s (for example, for my book *Single in America* and then for my dissertation), it has become clear that friends help the romantically unattached single to feel connected and fulfilled. As a 35-year-old researcher told me: "When I was twenty, I didn't have any close friends, and I was a very lonely person. Now I have four close friends....Whether or not I marry, I feel liked and loved."

In my dissertation sample of urban single women between the ages of 20 and 40, each woman had, on average, one best, four close, and eight casual friends.

"Friendship is very important to me," says 32-year-old Jane, who lives alone and is currently not dating anyone. "Friends are almost like family as far as being there for each other," she adds.

A 19-year-old male college sophomore describes the value of

his closest friend: "We met when we were in fifth grade through another of my friends. Friendship is very important to me. I always confide in my friend. A good friend always understands the way you feel and act. He accepts you as you are."

Forty-two-year-old Jennifer Ash, a vivacious and upbeat writer who lives in Greenwich, Connecticut, since relocating from Los Angeles, has not yet married. She discusses the vital place friends have in her life:

> As an only child, and estranged from most of my family—I reunited with my parents in my mid-30s—it was through the support and encouragement of friends that I fought my way through college, graduate school, and several careers. I left home the day after graduation from high school and began what seemed to be years of wandering, not always marked by physical moves, but certainly within myself. Various older women became my mentors and my friends became my family, providing for me the foundation of love I've need to continue on.

Physician James J. Lynch, in his book *The Broken Heart: The Medical Consequences of Loneliness*, documents how although lack of love is linked to heart disease, friendship may offer the feelings of social support and being connected to offset the greater risks of isolation. Because of those intimate ties, "being single, widowed, or divorced does not automatically bring with it ill health and premature death," Lynch writes.

Forty-year-old Elizabeth, who has never married, and has not been in a romantic relationship of more than a year's duration since her early 20s, has recently reevaluated what kind of friends she wants to be with: "The function friendships serve in my life is changing. My need for a few best friends is very high, and for close friends is medium high. But for casual friends, my need is low. I spend too much time with casual friends, which cuts into the time I have to spend with best friends."

Emma, who had the least number of friends of anyone I interviewed, was a workaholic overachiever; she was mainly connected to her fiancé, who was working in the Far East for a year. She hoped to join him there within a few months and marry soon after that. In the meantime, she expressed a despair and loneliness that having close friends might have helped offset: "Sometimes I wonder if I were to collapse on the street on Friday if no one would know until Monday morning [when I failed to show up for work]."

A 47-year-old freelance editor who has never married, and does not plan to in the future, has 2 male and 10 female close friends. He prefers his friendships with women, explaining, "I'm uncomfortable around men, even my male friends. I keep a distance." By contrast, a 20-year-old male college junior has four close friends, all males. He says, "Friends must have the same interests and goals in life."

Never-married singleness used to encompass those years from late adolescence through the 20s, when most Americans were likely to marry. Weddings of 22-year-olds still occur, but it is also commonplace to find men and women, especially those pursuing careers that require extensive schooling or long apprenticeships, to marry for the first time in their 30s or even 40s. Ash shares just one of the many instances when a close friend helped her through a disappointing romance:

> A few years ago, while I was living in the desert, I dated a man whom I felt had promise. He "said" he wanted marriage and romanced me with dinners, flowers, gifts, helped with my garden....I initially interpreted his lack of any physical contact (hand shakes good night were the extent of things) as a form of restraint, that he genuinely liked me.
>
> When I confronted him, after four months of courtship, he broke it off instantly, coldly stating, "We obviously don't see things in the same way. It's best we don't continue on."
>
> In the midst of my personal tempest and mangled pride, my friend George was there.
>
> "Don't worry, honey," he said. "It happens to everyone..."
>
> George told me he was sending me a gift, one that was very tall and wise and would live for a very long time, and whenever I looked at it I was to be reminded that I was loved.

> Soon after, a large, flat-bed truck arrived. Two men wearing thick gloves used a crane and lots of burlap to hoist an eleven-foot, six-inch saguaro cactus down into the front flower bed. It already weighed over a ton, had yellow flowers on the top, and was at least two hundred years old. Firmly planted, it towered over the other plants with a stately, virile stance. On the tag was written, "Love always, George."

For singles, how well they handle the emotional demands of being single, especially when they are romantically unattached, will often depend on creating and maintaining a supportive friendship network.

As 37-year-old Lois, a media saleswoman, told me: "I don't have any family per se. I don't consider a mother and a brother who live elsewhere as family obligations that one has to adhere to." Lois met her best friend, Cybil, several years before at a Thanksgiving dinner given by a mutual friend. Lois and Cybil see each other daily. Lois says, "She's adorable, very supportive, terrific." Lois is happy with her single life. By contrast, Cybil would like to marry. But for Lois, who has soured on male-female intimacy, Cybil and her other friends are her substitute family.

Twenty-nine-year-old Melanie, an executive secretary at a video production company, has a 28-year-old best friend, who is also single, whom she talks to daily and gets together with once a week, as well as six close friends. She and her best friend first met three years before. They had both been working at the same company but in different departments for a year, "had never really gotten together for some reason" when they "started talking one day." Melanie explains how the friendship developed, and what they give each other:

> I think she said, "Do you want to have lunch this week?" and I said, "Fine." And that's when it started, getting together for lunch, and then for drinks after work. We both have very hard jobs that involve a lot of tension, so after the [work] week, it's great to go out and unwind. A lot of people aren't able to do that—they have other obligations or whatever.... She [also] sort of fascinated me. I felt I wanted to know more about her.

We're very similar in certain areas. We can talk about anything with one another. I don't feel that I will shock her by telling her something or that she will think less of me if I tell her something private. I can tell her anything in confidence and it won't go any further than that.

Single women and men are also developing friendship networks that include married friends as well. They meet for breakfast, lunch, or dinner on a daily, weekly, or monthly basis, or participate in activities, such as tennis, bowling, or theater-going, that they all enjoy. It helps if marrieds or singles, when they get together, respect each other's lifestyles and choices; whether permanent or temporary, no one wants to be reminded how different they are from each other. A 34-year-old never-married physician, for example, says that most of his friends are still single. But when he does get together with his married friends—who are all happily married, with kids—they always ask "Why aren't you married?"

If you avoid this kind of "on-the-spot" questions, networks of singles and marrieds benefit everyone. For example, a 27-year-old single man told me about the breakfast friendship network he participated in for two years. Every morning, at 8 a.m., he and six male and female friends—four are single, two are married—meet, eat, and talk. The daily breakfasts not only offset the possible loneliness caused by being single; they help those who are self-employed or working from home, married or single, minimize the isolation caused by working away from peers. A single woman of 30 prepared 25 dinners for friends in just 11 months. Because she works as a consultant and lacks a regular work network, these dinners help her feel less socially isolated.

A single unmarried graduate student in Manhattan in her 40s talks about the challenges of maintaining a "very close" friendship with her married friend in Boston who has four children:

In fact, the kids call me "Aunt." We have gone through all kinds of things. Every time I'm around the Cape, I usually stop by, or give her a call...stay overnight....When I was in my job, I would pick up the phone and call her rather frequently. But now

I can't do that [since I became a student], and I don't think she and her husband are in the position to make these kinds of calls.

Sociologist and singles expert Peter J. Stein, who interviewed 60 single men and women between the ages of 25 and 45, concluded, "For all of these adults a major source of intimacy came from opposite and same-sex friendships. In the absence of marriage these single adults noted the importance of substitute networks of human relationships that met their needs for intimacy, sharing and continuity."

I am reminded of how important friends were to me during my 20s and 30s, when I was single. I was offered a job in the Midwest but turned it down, explaining to the president of the company, "I have too many ties here to consider moving right now."

"But I thought you were single," he replied, confused.

I continued by explaining to him that if I were married, I could relocate my spouse and children, if need be. But since I was single, my family consisted of several close, unrelated friendships that I had developed over the years. I could not expect any of my friends to move, and I needed those ties to have some sense of emotional consistency to my life.

It is vital to keep adding to a friendship network as friends become unavailable because someone moves or gets totally immersed in a romantic relationship or an all-consuming situation, such as a new job. These *friendshifts* enable you to replenish your network so you always feel connected to at least one close friend.

It was not until a decade later, when my life shifted and I married, and a few years after that, when I relocated almost an hour from my friends, that I learned it is hard to move and leave friends behind even if you have a spouse, even if you and your spouse are the best of friends.

*

The next chapter explores friendships after marriage, including a discussion about friendship after children arrive, as well as friendship for singles who were once married but are now divorced or widowed.

It used to be that I had five days that I could fill up with seeing friends, and now [since I'm married] maybe I have one. So I concentrate very carefully.

—31-year-old publicist married for one year

7. MARRIAGE AND FRIENDSHIP

Part of the motivation of a friendship is just company, someone to be around. You have that in marriage [so] you don't have to put up with people for that part of it, so I think you want something [from friendship] you don't get from marriage. Just a different type of person to do different things [with].

—35-year-old married male writer

Over the Memorial Day weekend, a psychologist was hosting a barbecue for some of his friends and their families. One of the guests was a man in his 50s, who had been the host's friend and colleague for thirty years, along with his second wife and their one-year-old child. As the host was flipping hamburgers on the outdoor grill, his friend came over and said in a hushed voice, "You know, today's my birthday." It seemed his wife, who spent the day frantically running after their one-year-old, had not acknowledged her husband's birthday. The host immediately responded by sending out for a cake, scrounging up some candles, and leading the guests in a rendition of "Happy Birthday." After the festivities were over, the man's wife came up to the host and said, "You know, you must have an incredible memory to remember it was your friend's birthday today." Of course the host had not remembered, but his friend felt more comfortable admitting to his friend, rather than his wife, that he was disappointed that his birthday had been ignored.

THE RICHEST DOWRY:
FRIENDSHIP AND MARRIAGE

"Since you've gotten married, it's harder to see you than it would be to get an audience with the Pope," an infuriated man tells his newly married friend. That angry friend wants his friendship to stay the same in intensity, importance, and frequency as it was when he and his friend were both single; he refuses to acknowledge that marriage is one of the biggest of life's *friendshifts*.

In addition to the time-consuming commitment to a spouse, marriage means taking on another set of family relationships—in-laws, nieces, and nephews—and those role relations cut down on the time, and need, for friends. There is also a spouse's friendship network that will take time to get to know. Thirty-seven-year-old Evelyn, marrying for the first time, spent most of her four-month engagement period getting to know her fiancee's mother and father, three siblings, and close friends. Fortunately her own friends were understanding about the new demands on Evelyn's time.

After marriage, there may be a move to a new residence. Thus, even if you are determined to keep your friends despite a marriage, it will be difficult to live up to that intention as changes occur. In addition to less energy and time for friendship, in the best marriages, spouses will become each other's most intimate friend. "She's my best friend," a 33-year-old man says. He has been married for three years to a 28-year-old who also works as his secretary. "We don't see our friends as much as we used to," he adds. Right now they would rather spend time with each other, or remodeling their house, than with their friends.

But that does not mean that marriage ruins friendship. Quite the opposite; it might help. As a happily married 38-year-old notes: "As your life becomes fuller and you become less needy, you're able to be a better friend. You tend to make and maintain friendships with people who are the same way, whose lives are also fuller. So marriage does change friendship, but often for the better." Today we realize that friendship provides additional sources of intimacy and a reinforcement of self-worth necessary throughout the adult married years.

Deb, a 30-year-old single who moved to Manhattan from Florida, has found that her best friendship with Marge, whom Deb met five years ago when they were both single, has changed because of Marge's marriage. Even though Deb considers Marge's husband a friend as well, Marge's change in marital status and living arrangements has affected their friendship. As Deb explains: "Certain times, because Marge's married, I don't want to impose on them in certain ways, and when I feel they need time alone."

In her senior year of college, Lil's closest friend, Irene, met her future husband. Lil, an attractive book designer in her late 20s, explains how her friendship, which dated back to when they were both eight years old, changed because of her friend's marriage:

> Irene got married and moved to Arkansas. Until after that, I never really thought about our friendship. I just always knew Irene was there. It [the friendship] was a nice secure thing.I found that when my relationship with my ex-boyfriend was in trouble, I'd come home and I'd dream about Irene...because after she met her husband, the friendship was sort of pushed aside. Irene was no longer there. We were no longer as close. We no longer had as much in common as we once had.

Unfortunately, Lil found it difficult to share those feelings of loss with Irene or anyone else; it seemed inconceivable that the loss of a friendship could have such a devastating effect on her. As Lil explains:

> That [our best friendship was waning] was very traumatic to me. I wonder if I'm feeling the same loss [about my romance breaking up] that I felt then [when Irene got married] but I couldn't admit it. Because with a romantic relationship you're able to

admit the loss, but with a friend, somehow it's not quite as acceptable, particularly as adults. I hate it that I don't have Irene anymore, and it's unfair. Why is she abandoning me?

Whether or not your friend's mate gets along with you (and, if you are married, with your spouse) is one of the best determinants of how marriage will impact on your preexisting friendships. Lil says she does not have any rapport with Irene's husband. By contrast, one of the reasons that Diane's closest friend Stephanie's marriage has not adversely affected their friendship is Diane's positive feelings toward Stephanie's husband. As Diane puts it: "I like him as much as I like her."

If a friend is having a problem with a spouse, however, discretion will be needed. As a married educator wrote:

I have one friend who would call me crying because her husband was out all night with another woman. I would try to console her, but I never said anything negative about him. I never liked her husband, and I still don't, but I will never express this to her. She is a friend, and I am obligated to give her moral support. She eventually separated from him for a couple of months. They reconciled and have been together ever since. If I had expressed how I really felt about him, do you think my friend would feel comfortable socializing with her husband and myself? I doubt it.

Marriage may indirectly lead to a friendship's dissolution because of how marriage changes your friend, possibly bringing out annoying qualities in your friend that were less apparent before. As a disgruntled friend explains: "I was interested in my friend *before* [her marriage], with her own interests, and I find it hard to relate to the golfing and skiing that she has become interested in because of her husband. I feel many women give up their own interests and pursue the husband's lifestyle. When this happens, I start to resent the man."

I interviewed Bill when he had been married for four months. Bill was 38 and his bride, Joan, was only 27. Although the age difference has not been a problem for their relationship, it has made getting together with each other's friends awkward at times. Bill tends to be friends with older men and women—he was the youngest of three boys—so his friends are in their 40s. His wife's friends are in their 20s. As Bill explains:

> The age difference sometimes is a problem with friends. When we socialize, the difference can be almost 20 years and that sometimes can be difficult for her. It's not as hard for me. When I'm at a table and I'm hearing concerns I thought about when I was in my late 20s, and vice versa, I'm sure Joan is hearing concerns with my friends who are more toward her mother's generation.

As Deb, Lil, Bill, and other examples have shown, the marriage of a friend has an impact on preexisting friendships. For some, like Gwen, the impact has been a mild one. Gwen even counts her 37-year-old best friend's marriage last year as one of the high points of their 18-year friendship.

Gloria echoes the more prevalent phenomenon when she says, "Most of the time we go out with other couples." Gloria, who has been married for four months, reflects a predictable change. Since the basis of most friendships is "like attracts like," it is expected that couples will tend to socialize with other pairs. As newlywed Bill explains: "I don't really hang out now with as many male friends [as before Joan and I lived together]. It's not like you lose them, you just don't socialize with them as much. I guess we socialize more with Joan's friends....The tendency is to socialize more with couples. Definitely more than with singles."

"It's ironic," Gloria observes, "that my single friends are the ones who have backed off since I got married. I think it's on their part, not mine. They don't want to 'disturb' us, even though Mark and I lived together for six months, and I've always found time for my friends [when we lived together]. Mark's a homebody, and I like to go out and do things more often than he does, so I'd really like to go out with a girlfriend once in a while."

Gloria's mistake is thinking that her friends view living together, or even being engaged, to be just like marriage. Those previous situations do not involve the distinct status and legal changes that characterize marriage. Now Gloria and Mark are a formal, legal unit to be reckoned with. Gloria will probably have to make the overtures to her single friends by asking them if they would like to spend time together, showing them that marriage will not stop her from wanting to get together, even if it is less frequently than before.

Just how dramatic an effect marriage may have on friendship is revealed in the results of a *Psychology Today* friendship poll of 40,000 men and women. In listing the 13 most common reasons that a friendship ended, the fourth and fifth most frequent reasons related to marriage: "One of us got married" and "My friend became involved with (or married) someone I didn't like." (The first, second, and third reasons were, respectively: "One of us moved"; "I felt my friend betrayed me"; and "We discovered that we had very different views on issues that are important to me.")

Couples need to make finding time for friends a key concern in their lives, including new friends they meet together, whose friendships they share. The best way to assure that those get-togethers occur is to have a steady time, once or twice a week, that you and your spouse go out together, as a couple or with friends. Rather than leaving those "connecting" times to chance, make a definite commitment to each other, even blocking out time for your "date" in your weekly planner or, if you have kids, lining up a steady sitter (or mother-in-law or mother). Making a regular appointment to go out also facilitates making plans with your friends.

When she married, journalist Merle Shain made the common mistake of abandoning her friends. As she explains in her bestseller *When Lovers Are Friends*: "If I were to marry again tomorrow, I wouldn't give up one friend. I'd take them all with me as a sort of dowry and tell my new husband that he was getting a rich wife. It takes a long time to understand that there is no relationship which is all-supporting, only those which help you grow stronger in yourself. So a lot of people never realize how important it is to have real friends or how crucial they can be even if you have a mate."

A 24-year-old woman, married for a year, says: "My husband is definitely my best friend just because we share common goals and aspirations. We can laugh together, cry together, and love together. But I have single girlfriends I went to college with, and he has single male friends, and we'll have our friends over to our apartment or, every two or three months, we'll go out alone with one of our friends."

For that couple, however, being each other's best friend is still the main emphasis in their lives. She continues: "Right now, just being apart from each other at work is time enough away from each other." But fortunately, "you and me against the world" has been revised for today's couples so, when it is the right time in your relationship, it is acceptable to think in terms of "you, me, *and* our friends."

Establishing the right to spend time with old friends, as well as to develop new ones, will broaden your experiences. That, in turn, will enable you and your spouse to bring more to your marriage. As a 55-year-old married man, who relocated from New York to Denver, explains about what friendship means to him: "The very nature of 'friendship' is substantially very different at age 20 versus age 55. Even the definition changes. You see, now my definition is not necessarily what we have in common (except 25 years of knowing each other), or whether we agree or disagree, but whether we are concerned about each other, worry about each other, are happy for each other, and so forth. It goes without saying that we also enjoy being with each other, but real friendships survive absences."

In the best of all possible worlds, a couple will like each other's friends. But what if your spouse dislikes your friend? What should you do about it? "I see my friend alone, and I don't talk about her to my husband," explains Arlene. "Sure it would be nice if we could be a happy foursome, but at least this way my friendship can continue, and grow. I can't stand her husband and my husband can't stand my friend." I should add, however, that Arlene's marriage is unique in that she and her husband spend more time apart than together. For them, having separate friends may be just another disconnected activity that keeps them occupied but distant.

What about going away alone with a friend? If your spouse agrees, you may have to grant him the same "right." Accept that consequence, and an occasional trip with a girlfriend without spouses may be relaxing and beneficial. (If you have children, it could also provide an opportunity for your spouse and offspring to spend private time together. Child development experts recommend that each child should have occasional time alone with each parent, with and without other siblings.) Studies have shown that a little absence does make the heart tingle, although too much separation is bad for a marriage. But how much separation is "too much"? Perhaps an evening or even a weekend away with a friend is just what your marriage needs. Certainly having lunch or spending an afternoon with a friend, or an occasional evening out, could prove beneficial, especially if you share certain interests with your friend that your spouse could not care less about, whether it is attending the theater, poetry readings, baseball games, fishing, or just talking about old times or "personal stuff."

NEW PARENTS, REVISED FRIENDSHIPS

Friends are vital for new mothers; they may help prevent you from making excessive emotional demands on your spouse. This is especially true if you are suddenly removed from the work environment that used to nurture and support you, and you have not yet created an alternative satisfying "at-home mother" lifestyle. If your spouse is the only adult contact that you have, your self-esteem, feelings of well-being, and, consequently, your marriage may suffer. One woman, who fell into that trap after her first child was born, explains: "When my kids were little, and before I had friendships with other mothers, when my husband came home at night, I'd jump on him. That's unfair pressure on your husband."

I remember in 1985 when I was pregnant with my first son. My husband and I had spent the first year of our marriage working from home together as he wrote screenplays; I was an assistant professor at a college and a writer. Toward the end of my pregnancy, I went to a networking dinner organized by a Manhattan psychologist. As we went around the room introducing ourselves, one woman shared how, since she had her first child, who was now one, she had become friends with a network of new mothers who were largely responsible for her happiness with her radically new role of "stay-at-home mother."

I protested: "I didn't get married and finally find a man whom I consider my best friend so I could spend a lot of time and energy cultivating new friendships with other women. My husband's going to be there for me after our child is born. He's going to do with me all the things you say you and your friends do together."

Much to my surprise, however, just a week after our first son was born, my husband gave up the uncertain life of a freelancer for full-time employment. Suddenly I was alone with our infant much of the time. Fred's job writing for the morning news shows often involved working weekends or the overnight shift, which meant he had to sleep during the day. And all my old friends were either still single and working full time or had much older school-age children and lived far away. I soon thought of the words that woman had shared so many months before and wished I had already cultivated a few close friendships with other caring new mothers.

It took years for me to finally develop a support network of other mothers, but I have succeeded. Looking back, if I had known how vital friends were going to be to me during the decade I would be raising our two sons while working from not-at-all to part-time from home, I would have used the months of my pregnancy to begin developing new friends. I now know that should have been a pregnancy priority of mine, along with watching what I was eating and getting enough exercise.

Once you become a parent, friendships with others who also have children are likely to become stronger because you now have more in common. There are also the practical benefits of sharing baby-sitting and child-care needs, and even products. "One of my close friends is a woman I met in a dance exercise class that I took when I was pregnant," says my close friend Gail Tuchman, a children's book editor and author whose daughter is now 14. "We stayed in touch after we gave birth, going to the park together with our daughters, who played together."

However, parenthood makes very special demands on friendship; there are emotional as well as practical reasons that the effort is worth it. For example, one mother, whose children are four and one, explains: "I changed pediatricians only after my second baby was born. I had stayed with the first pediatrician for four years even though I felt his personality was a little strange. If I had known some people who had also been his patients, I would have trusted my instincts and gotten a new doctor a lot sooner." Another mother, whose parents died decades before, whose husband's demanding work schedule leaves her alone a lot of the time, and who has not yet returned to the workforce, has found her friendships with other mothers who live nearby and whose children are the same age as her eight-year-old have been like her extended family.

With the increase in single-parent families, however, old friends, whether or not they have children, continue to be important. An unmarried 25-year-old woman, whose infant is in day care so she is able to keep her full-time executive secretary job, was flattered when her girlfriend gave her a baby shower. She thought, because of her unmarried situation, she would be denied such pleasant new mother rituals. She also finds her single friend willing to baby sit occasionally, which provides her with welcome relief. Another unmarried mother, who had her one and only child at 41, found her single friends became a strong support network for her, especially since her own parents were deceased and her two brothers either lived far away or were emotionally unavailable to her. During her pregnancy, her best friend from her extended family of friends became her labor coach; after her baby was born, it was from her friends that she got the emotional support and practical help that a husband, parents, or siblings may offer to other new mothers. For her single, unattached friends, it was a way of being friends as well as compensating for their own childlessness.

Although researchers like Dan Perlman and Norman Shulman

have found that women, after they have children, turn more to their kin than they did during their single years, in today's transient society, that kin may be far away or still involved in their own careers and interests. Friends, by contrast, will probably be close by, going through the same experiences, and more available to a new mother.

Support Groups for New Mothers

A 39-year-old suburban Connecticut mother who left her job as marketing manager of a health food corporation 10 years ago, when her first child was born, joined a support group for new mothers, led by a parent educator, at a nearby mother and child center. "It was my life raft," says Sally, who now leads mother groups once a week. With her work-related routine and relationships behind her, she definitely needed to set up a new network. "I'm in the group almost nine years now. There are 13 of us. Three are close friends. I can call them up if I have a problem. I can let my guard down. The rest are casual friends."

One of the major benefits of the group is that Sally has had a chance to get to know other women who made the same choice she did, to stay home and raise their children. "That validated my choice. I realized I wasn't alone." The weekly support group Sally attends, and the friendships that have grown out of it, have helped her to better cope with this most challenging of roles in her life.

I recently met a new mother who expressed to me a real need that is often not addressed, namely a support group for mothers who are still working, combining a full-time job with new-parent duties. This 37-year-old woman had a three-and-a-half-year-old; her second child was due in just a month. In her suburban community, where she had just moved six months before from Manhattan, it was far more common for women in her situation to give up their jobs. She expressed to me a loneliness because the "stay-at-home" mothers made her feel self-conscious or defensive about her combining full-time work and motherhood. Yet all new mothers need friends, for your own self-esteem and satisfaction, as well as for your child's benefit. That is because until your child is in school, your social life mirrors his or hers. If you are isolated, your child may be socially less developed, and have lower self-esteem, than others who are around peers more often. Furthermore, your child will also miss the validation and fun that getting together with friends provides both generations. Working new mothers, who have little time for socializing with other mothers during the work week, may have to find time on the weekends for such get-togethers. Perhaps taking a class with your infant or young child, or going to the community playground, will at least create opportunities for socializing with other new mothers, ensuring the necessary visibility and access are present so a friendship might ensue.

Some new mothers find that it is not until after the birth of their second child that they feel a need to get involved in a formal group. That is just what happened seven years ago when Paula M. Siegel, a 43-year-old writer, had her second child and found herself seeking out a mothers' group; she joined a group on the Upper West Side of Manhattan that calls itself The Riverside Mothers Group. As Paula explains:

> I did not have a mothers' group with my first child. I'm not a group joiner, and I found plenty of people and friends for him just going to the park. But with my second, I had no time because of the scheduling—of my first-born's school and after-school activities—and I was working part-time as a writer for women's magazines. I felt my second child was getting short shrift in terms of social[izing]; if I didn't carve out specific time for him, he wouldn't have met any kids. So I looked for a mothers' group.
>
> By accident, I ran into Hedy [who was in the group] in a stationery store (she remembers it as being the green grocer). The group was already formed when I entered into it. I was a little concerned about how claustrophobic the mothers' group would be. But it turned out to be wonderful because this was an eclectic group of women with varied interests, very relaxed, open people, very much like myself. A group of non-group joiners. So I felt very comfortable and at home....We were very different in terms of our outlook on a number of issues, like sweets and how we decided to discipline our children, [but]

everybody's point of view was respected.

The Riverside Mothers Group turned out to be a very unique group in that all but one of the mother-members were professional writers; they even co-authored a book entitled *Entertain Me! Creative Ideas for Fun and Games with Your Baby in the First Year*; in 1995, they published their second collaborative effort, *Don't Forget the Rubber Ducky!* However, what originally drew Paula to the group was her need to connect with other new mothers who were going through similar experiences. The fact that they all turned out to be writers who collaborated on parenting books was just "icing on the cake."

In the years since the mothers group' began, there have been numerous shifts in all their lives as three mothers moved to other states, and work became a bigger part of their lives. Even though they no longer have their weekly get-togethers, Paula, who still lives near three of the group's original members, says, "The fondness is still there, and we see each other."

However, friendship *plus* parenthood is often a lot more complicated than peer friendships: new mothers usually see themselves as a package deal—"love me, love my baby." Of course it is possible to form new friendships where one or both mothers are less than enthused about each other's child, but it would be hard for such a situation to intensify, unless you are willing to get together without your children.

The challenge for a new mother is that although it takes time to form genuine friendships, you need them *now*. That desperation usually backfires. As the mother of an 18-month-old says, "I think I'm trying too hard."

As with any developing friendship, emphasize similarities. If you are self-conscious about how little reading you do with your child, for example, you might feel more comfortable meeting in the park, rather than in the other child's room, lined with books and educational materials that might make you feel inadequate. Stay clear of the work-versus-parenthood debate, if you and your potential new friends are at opposite ends of the spectrum about that choice; dwell on the concerns that all new mothers, whether you are out of the workforce for a month, a year, or a decade, have in common, as well as such nonwork sources of interest as the latest movies, current affairs, hobbies, or pets.

The most difficult friends to keep after you have a baby may be your childless friends, whether married or single. A Detroit woman who now has a three-year-old shared with me how difficult it was to be around other parents during the 12 years she and her husband were trying to conceive. Even though she taught piano to school-age children, like most other couples coping with infertility, she found it painful to socialize with pregnant women or to socialize with other couples and their children.

If you have friends worth keeping who find it hard to be around your child, whatever the reason, if that friendship is valuable, find a way to spend time together without your child.

WHEN MARRIAGE ENDS:
DIVORCE, WIDOWHOOD, AND FRIENDS

Just as becoming a parent is one of the major *friendshifts* over a lifetime, becoming single again because of divorce or widowhood also takes its toll on all but the most solid of friendships.

Married couples, by and large, have more in common with, and find it more comfortable to be with, other couples. In the same way, those who are suddenly single because of divorce or widowhood will find themselves pulled toward other singles, especially those who are dealing with the same divorce or widowhood issues. Friendship is crucial for those going through divorce or suddenly widowed, whatever their age. Divorce or widowhood is the disruption of the most fundamental relationship in an adult's life; alternative sources of emotional support are crucial.

Divorce and Friendship

As Mel Krantzler pointed out in *Creative Divorce*, I discussed in *Single in America*, and numerous other popular writers or social scientists have substantiated, divorce is a major shift that impacts on a once-married man or woman as well as their other key relationships, including friendships. As sociologist Robert S. Weiss points out in *Marital Separation:* "The first reaction of friends to the news that an individual's marriage has ended is likely to be solicitude, regret, and desire to help. As time goes on some of these friends remain loyal and supportive, but others withdraw from the separated individual, and he or she from them."

As predicted, it is those friendships that were primarily based on being part of a couple—where the ex-spouse was the primary friend of the spouse of the other couple—that separation or divorce will most likely end. Furthermore, many newly separated couples only become aware that they had fallen into a "couples only" social world when they no longer fit in. As Weiss notes: "The separated discover that, without having quite noticed, they have become a member of a social network restricted to similarly situated married couples. Separation almost devastates this sector of their social life."

Whether or not the separation, and subsequent divorce, ends that friendship will have a lot to do with the basis on which the friendship was initiated and maintained as well as the marital status of that friend. Was it a one-on-one friendship based on shared interests, such as a weekly tennis game, or sharing confidences, over the telephone or over lunch? Was it a one-on-one friendship that began and continues at work? Is your friend also single? Or was it a network of two couples that was really two friends plus their two spouses?

The *friendshifts* after divorce may also be a case of the divorced man or woman intentionally withdrawing from his or her married friends in an effort to seek out new friends who more closely match their current single lifestyle. For example, my cousin Phyllis

Silver Henkel is divorced (since widowed) and in her late 40s. She and her five school-age children live on Long Island. Being a divorced single parent who works full-time has definitely had an effect on Phyllis's friendships, especially those friendships formed during her marriage. Even though she will still see many of her girlfriends whom she met through their children's school or religious school, it is hard or impossible to socialize with them. One factor is time: Phyllis works full-time at a hospital and just does not have the time during the day that she used to spend having breakfast or lunch with friends. She also finds her concerns are so different now, she prefers to spend any free time on the weekends with other divorced single parents whose lives more closely mirror hers. As Phyllis explains:

> I don't really want to be around those friends who are married with children. They have a different lifestyle. I had to desert my old friends from marriage and find new ones because they understand how you're dragged down for so many years. They could understand the pain that I was going through, sympathize with me, and build up my self-esteem. Your married friends are really caught up in their own life, and they don't have time to get into feelings. Basically what helps you at a time like that is support groups. That's where you start all your new friendships. Then you go from there. You build. You go out socially. They become social friends as well. Then you expand. You start having parties. They bring their friends. You become a whole network.

In the late 1970s, I interviewed Brenda, who was then a 37-year-old wealthy, divorced single parent living in San Francisco. When we first met, she was involved in a frustrating romance that was not going anywhere. She was still recovering from her marital breakup. While she was pregnant with their third child, her husband decided he wanted to "run around with other people." They divorced 12 days later.

Brenda soon discovered a certain number of her friendships, especially those stemming from her ex-husband's relationships, ended along with her marriage. Friends that predated her marriage were still there for her, as well as other mothers she had befriended during her marriage through their children.

Determined to land on her feet after her marriage ended, Brenda asked me during our interview: "Should I hold out for 'the magic' or settle for a good old boy who will be nice to grow old with? Hopefully I can have my cake and eat it too."

It would take Brenda 10 years to find a man who could give her all the emotional support and love she needed and deserved. Brenda also had an additional challenge: being a millionaire, she constantly had to deal with wondering if a man loved her for herself or her money, or find someone even wealthier where money was less of an issue. During those post-divorce single years, her three children and friendship are what kept Brenda going. "There are five of us who have lunch every Monday," she told me.

Brenda finally remarried, and that second marriage is going well. Her friendship network helped fulfill Brenda all those single years, enabling her to hold out for the "magic" she was looking for, and to marry for the "right" reasons, not out of loneliness or despair.

Some divorced singles are "divorced, joyously, and not interested in changing the status quo," as a 50-year-old Los Angeles-based freelance writer with one grown son wrote. For her, friends became vital. Her pet peeve? "Many married friends seek me out at their convenience—when their husband's out of town—not realizing they're using me and *I* permit it—because we *are* friends."

Other divorced singles confirmed the oft-heard comment that after their divorce, there is a change in their friendship patterns, usually involving a loss of their ex-spouse's friends. As a 44-year-old divorced self-employed cosmetic manufacturer and mother of three explains: "The friends I did not keep after my divorce were friends my ex-husband made during our marriage." Her divorce ended a best friendship because her "former best friend was so insecure in her marriage she thought her husband would leave her" and follow her ex-friend's example of getting divorced.

Widowhood and Friendship

Friends are even more important for those who are single due to widowhood because, by and large, they will be older, their children will already be grown and living somewhere else, they are more likely to be retired and cut off from work-related contacts, and the likelihood of a remarriage becomes more and more remote. Researchers have shown that just one close friend can relieve the depression and loneliness that often accompanies widowhood. Relationships with grown children, however intimate or frequent, may not compensate for the lack of companionship with others of the same age or sex. Friends provide additional emotional support and validation.

Two women became widows within a few months of each other. One, a childless woman in her early 60s, immediately started going out with her girlfriends and losing weight. The other woman, in her late 60s, had been far more dependent on her husband and her grown daughter, who was too busy to spend time with her mother, who lived an hour away. Within a few weeks of her husband's death, the second woman looked 10 years older. Within a few months, her family had to hire a full-time nurse to take care of her, more for companionship than for health reasons.

The varied ways those two women adjusted to the major life shift, death of a spouse, has to do with their individual personalities; the friendship factor is another pivotal consideration. When he was 80, an acclaimed British journalist, or "Bill," as his friends called him, wrote to me about friendship: "An important difference between a friend and a close friend is that you [and a close friend] can walk for miles together in total silence." After his wife of 35 years died, Bill put more time into his friendships. Those relationships, including a friendship with me that I considered close emotionally even though it was geographically distant, in addition to his intimate relationships with his children and grandchildren, helped Bill feel connected.

It is, however, any kind of friend that a widow needs; there are children and grandchildren for intimacy; there are best or close old friends for a shared history and for feeling valued and worthy. But the widow, who has far more "total silence" than is good for almost anyone, needs contact with others: laughter, companionship, someone to talk to, someone to do things with. Casual friends are needed, for starters. If a close or best friendship develops, most would find that to be fine. However, there are some widows who do not want friends, or, if they want them, they are unable to develop them. These women represent one out of six of the 300 Chicago-area widows that sociologist Helena Lopata interviewed whom she labeled "friendless." Their friendless situation she attributed to one of three reasons: they did not want any nonfamilial relationships; they lacked the social skills to form friendships; or they had such an idealized notion of friendship that they discounted relationships as meaningless that others might have considered solid friendships.

By contrast is my mother, who puts a high value on friendship. Even though she had a best friendship with Charlotte for some 47 years, soon after my father died, she was wisely befriending other widows with whom she would now have more immediate issues in common.

Marcella Semensohn, 75, has two sons, ages 48 and 51; she is also a grandmother. Five years ago, she became a widow after 50 years of marriage. At that time, she was surrounded by loving concerned family. But Marcella knew, in addition, she needed to reach out to friends who also had lost a spouse and could relate to her new single lifestyle. Marcella, who says, "Never underestimate the value of friendship," explains:

> The happiest people are those who have good friends who share your problems...who comfort you and at other times celebrate happy occasions with you. You'll find those who are in the same boat as you, whether a friendship or a grieving group, find a safe harbor in the homogeneity of the participants.
>
> The most satisfying friendships wherever found are not those who shut out reality, but those who face the problems of their current situation with courage and optimism. Life goes on, and we, surrounded by good friends, won't be left behind.

Some friends, who are fortunate enough to have their mates, consider a widow or widower as a fifth wheel. I understand, but don't admire their attitude.

Our group is comprised of nine friends. It is not a formal group, and it doesn't meet at any one specific time. We're all widows (with the exception of one couple). We're the same age, give or take a few years, in about the same economic position, and we share and face similar problems. What makes this group so appealing is the caring and sharing and the wide range of subjects that come up for discussion, from health problems, kids and grandkids (and their accomplishments), favorite restaurants, recipes, "buys of the week," finances, investments, insurance, movies, concerts, and [an] exchange of discount coupons. And of course, we decide where, when , and what to do next time we meet.

Our group is a natural "upper." We face the reality of our situation every day, with the comfort of friends' support. How wonderful!

I love to phone a friend and greet her with "Good morning, good morning. It's great to be alive, good morning, good morning, good morning to you." Another friend would get, "Are you having any fun? Watcha getting out of living? What good is what you've got if you're not having any fun?" and the mood is set for the day.

Some of my newer friendships are members of a "tour" group. We meet about once a month (in addition to other get-togethers) for theater parties, lunch, boat rides, concerts, scenic tours to Connecticut, Pennsylvania, New Jersey, and Westchester. We travel on deluxe buses that even show movies along the way.

In regard to widowhood and friendship, how important friendship is to a bereaved spouse may have as much to do with where she or he is in the life cycle as it does with personality and sociability. For example, a 32-year-old man whose young wife died of cancer, leaving behind three young children, put searching for a new spouse at the top of his list of relationship priorities, as did a 31-year-old widow and mother of two children, ages 4 and 7, whose husband had been murdered during a robbery three years before.

For some older widows and widowers, retirement communities may offer the chance to reconnect with old friends, typically in places with warm climates, like Florida or Arizona, with opportunities to develop new friends at club houses or in the group activities that abound. If there is a preponderance of couples, however, a widowed single may feel out of place. (A possible alternative is to travel with another single woman and share an apartment.) Retirement communities may actually be easier living alternatives for healthy couples in their 60s or 70s; widowed older singles in their 70s, 80s, or 90s, especially if they are in poor health, may need assistance in feeling comfortable around long-standing couples, or in developing new friendships with others, whatever their age or marital status.

Some widows, whatever their age, long for a new man; they consider friends a poor second to romantic love. A Canadian widow and journalist of 59 shared this anecdote: "Rose cried. She's widowed and over 73 years old. I told her that she would have comfort in the apartment building where she is going to live because there are other widows there. That's what made her cry. 'But I'm not used to a world of women,' she moaned."

*

Part 3, How to Be a Better Friend, looks at how to maintain and improve your friendships.

While love and sex are great up-stagers, our sanity and our happiness may rest more firmly on a foundation of friendship.

—Anatole Broyard, "Whistling in the Dark,"
(*New York Times* review of Brain's *Friends and Lovers*)

PART 3

HOW TO BE A
BETTER FRIEND

I cannot have a friendship without having honesty and loyalty. When that starts to decay, friendship does also. Friendship works two ways—it must always be give and take—one must do for the other what they would want done to themselves. If it fails, so does the relationship.

—21-year-old female college senior

"Ok, so he's obnoxious, rude, inconsiderate, possessive, and certifiably insane, but he's my friend, so be nice."

Reprinted with permission of Tom Cheney.

8. HOW TO MAINTAIN AND IMPROVE A FRIENDSHIP

We had an off-and-on period when we had a fight, but we're still friends, no matter what.

—Jesse Henkel, age 15, talking about his next-
door neighbor and lifelong best friend

There is an adage that to *have* a friend, *be* a friend, but what kind of friend should you be? In Dale Carnegie's bestseller of homespun wisdom, *How to Win Friends and Influence People,* he states that the best way to make friends is to get someone to want to be friends with *you.* But how? By being sympathetic, showing empathy, and seeing the other person's point of view, notes Carnegie. Criticism is usually pointless since the criticized friend typically becomes defensive or finds another friend who is more accepting and positive to replace you.

WHAT KIND OF FRIEND ARE *YOU*?

One of the best ways to be a better best, close, or casual friend is through improved *listening skills*. Your friends may want to hear about your triumphs, wows, and everyday goings- on, but they are usually even *more* interested in telling you about what is happening in their lives. The more you sincerely listen to your friends, the more your friends are pulled toward you.

Being *sympathetic* toward your friend's point of view or situation, and showing empathy, is one way to achieve better listening skills. It is too easy to impose your viewpoint—your experiences—rather than to understand where your friend is coming from.

You may unwittingly fall into common communication traps that make you a less-desirable friend. By going over the following examples of statements made by a friend and how you could answer if you want to narrow the distance between you and your friend, you may find ways to improve your friendships.

Friend's statement: "I'm sorry I didn't return your call sooner, but I've been a bit frazzled lately."
Sympathetic statement: "Don't worry about it. It happens to the best of us."
Judgmental response: "Would you have taken three days to return my call if you thought it was a business call?"

Here are additional examples of typical communications with friends. The second statement shows how to pull your friend, especially a best or close friend, closer; the third (or fourth) statement will create more distance:

Friend's complaint: "My boss is on my back to get in even earlier than before. He wants me in by seven-thirty."
Sympathetic reply: "That's incredibly demanding. You don't get home till seven as it is. Do they want you to leave at dawn? When are you supposed to see your family?"

Denying your friend's point of view and taking the opposite side: "You know the higher up you go in most companies, the earlier they expect you to get in. Don't you want to impress your boss and be like the other executives?"

Friend's statement: "My mother's very depressed. There's some shrinkage of the tumor in her lung, but it's still in her liver."
Sympathetic reply: "What a tough thing to be going through. It must be hell for you and your mother and the rest of your family."
Tuning out your friend's statement and not even responding but instead speaking about what's bothering you: "My dad's depressed. They may have to operate."

Friend's statement: "I'm angry that my friend was so cold to me at my party."
Sympathetic response: Just a "yes," a nonverbal hug, or a nod of the head, with or without a simple statement like, "That must have been awful for you."
Imposing a reaction or being critical instead of active listening: "Were you a friend to *her*? Maybe she's getting back at you for coming late to *her* last party?"
Denying your friend's feelings: "Why do you let something like that bother you? Let it run off you like water off a duck's back."

Friend's statement: "I don't know how I'm going to get all my work done in time."
Sympathetic response: "You'll get it done. You always do."
Failing to actively respond to your friend's statement, instead going on to the next unrelated comment: "We're hoping to go to London for a conference this summer."

Friend's statement: "It's three o'clock already."
Sympathetic statement: "You'll get it all done."
Correcting friend in a petty, critical way: "No, it's 3:01."

BUILDING TRUST

Trust is one of the most meaningful traits you can find in a best or close, and even a casual, friend. It means your friend is there for you. It also means if you reveal private thoughts or information or share something confidential, it is not revealed. It means if you expose your vulnerability to your best or close friend, he or she will not betray you by letting others know your weaknesses. Tried-and-true close or best friendships can be as significant as a good parent-child, husband-wife, or sibling relationship because it permits you to step out of your public self and to show, and be accepted for, a private self. But if the self that is revealed is mocked or indiscriminately shared with others, the trust that binds those friends may be shattered.

Meg, using *tolerance* as if it is synonymous for *trust,* describes how trust enters into her best friendship: "I don't know what the word is. *Tolerance*? I mean we don't pull stuff on each other. I really feel I can tell her anything in confidence and it won't go any further than that."

How can you tell if your friend is trustworthy? Do you overhear your friend on the phone telling convenient "white lies" to others? Beware: the white lie used on someone else just might someday be applied toward you. Does your friend cancel appointments or break commitments without enough notice, or without good reasons? Do your friends return phone calls within a reasonable amount of time? Do they return any of the material goods you might lend them—books, clothing, equipment—if you had told them from the getgo that you wanted it back? Be careful about this, however, since I discovered there are some who, for unconscious reasons, cannot part with anything that is loaned to them. It becomes theirs. If you notice this trait in your friend, try to avoid loaning anything so you will not be disappointed and angry when you cannot get back whatever you loaned. It is especially significant to consider this if you plan to loan clothes, or toys to another parent; the child may become so attached to those goods it is too traumatic to yank them away later on.

One way to test out if a new friend can be trusted is to confide an unimportant secret and see if it is kept, or spread around. That will give you a clue as to whether your friend can be trusted with a significant secret at another time. For example, when Helen told her friend Enid a secret only to hear it back a week later from a mutual acquaintance, she was enraged. The demise of their relationship was not caused specifically by spreading the secret but by Enid's response, when confronted: "Don't tell me anything if you expect it to stay a secret." This caused Helen to stop talking to Enid for three months. But she found she missed her and, three months after that, reactivated their friendship, although Helen is careful to follow Enid's advice and not disclose any vital secrets.

Another woman explains how, because of secrets and gossip, she keeps several friends on a casual level: "I have two friends who can't keep secrets and two other friends who are gossips. I wouldn't tell them anything confidential about me. I trust my friends never to reveal my secrets. I'll never talk about one friend to another. The only person I'll talk to about my friends is my sister."

Gossiping about friends may ruin those friendships at some point, especially once the gossip gets back to the talked-about friend. Furthermore, as with overhearing your friend tell someone else a lie, if you gossip about other friends to your friend, your friend may think, "If she's saying that about *her*, what does she say about *me* when my back is turned?"

Honesty goes hand in hand with trust, but you should be suspicious if someone is "too honest." Should you be "honest" and tell your close friend that she should get a divorce, switch careers, or have her teeth fixed? When is honesty cruelty in disguise with the unconscious wish to sabotage your relationship, or hurt your friend's feelings?

Another way to slowly but firmly build trust is to share confidences *as* you share activities, not the other way around. The friendship strengthens and deepens through doing and sharing experiences, not just by talking.

SELF-DISCLOSURES

The way self-disclosures, or confessions, are handled in a friendship will certainly affect the trust friends feel about each other. Although self-disclosures may occur early in a friendship, they usually emerge as friends develop a shared history, and the friendship is moved along from casual to close or best.

Why would someone self-disclose to a close or best friend? To gain acceptance is one motive. But some friends, who unconsciously seek rejection, may actually confess feelings, thoughts, or experiences to trick you into rejecting them. Although they think they want the acceptance of friendship, the risks it presents to their vulnerable psyches cause them to try to provoke an ending.

However, for those who truly seek, and need, acceptance, self-disclosures can afford the stronger feeling of being connected. That is because if the friend is accepted despite the self-disclosure, self-acceptance is further enhanced.

In *The Transparent Self*, Sidney Jourard emphasizes that being able to self-disclose and share one's innermost thoughts, feelings, and experiences is a sign of mental health. Jourard sees disclosing to others as a necessary action to knowing one's own soul. Men, however, notoriously keep their own confidences, or share secrets only with their wives. Women, by contrast, have traditionally been more open. I am still amazed when I realize my husband shared a train ride to Manhattan with his casual friend, whose child was at that point in a coma and dying, and not once did his friend hint anything was wrong with his son. (By contrast, a few days before, unaware of what my casual friend—the wife of the man my husband met on the train—was going through, I had called her just to say hello. Telling me about her son's grave condition was almost the first thing she said to me.) When their son died a week later, at his funeral only his wife and their daughter shared at length their intimate thoughts, feelings, and memories with a room packed with hundreds of mourners. (The rabbi indicated in his eulogy that the father had reached out to him during the trying months of his son's illness; he said they had become friends.)

Alternatives to self-disclosure to a friend are writing in a diary, introspection, therapy, confessing to a member of the clergy, or attending self-help support groups where you disclose to strangers with anonymity, the cornerstone of most groups' foundation.

However, if you or your friend are able to open up to each other, self-disclosure may be one of friendship's most rewarding aspects. It separates friendship from superficial relationships, but it does have its risks. In her book, *Confessions and Psychotherapy,* psychologist Sharon Hymer divides those to whom you self-disclose, the confessors, into three groups: low-risk, moderate-risk, and high-risk confessors. High-risk confessors include friends, parents, and lovers. They are high-risk confessors because "they are three of the most intimate relationships with the greater likelihood that we can be hurt through self-disclosure because it makes us more vulnerable. We have a greater likelihood of being abandoned, ridiculed, censured, even blackmailed."

Moderate-risk confessors are bartenders, hairdressers, and co-workers. Bartenders and hairdressers are moderate risks because they may know some of the same people you know, with the possibility they will blurt out your secrets to them.

Low-risk confessors are strangers you meet during your travels, cab drivers, therapists, rabbis or priests. Cab drivers and strangers, however, are only a Band-Aid kind of confession, notes Hymer, "because you get out the self-disclosure but there is no follow-up and no way of working out the confession. When you tell a friend or a therapist, it's not simply the self-disclosure that's therapeutic but it's working it out in the context of your life."

When self-disclosing in a friendship, it is essential to weigh carefully what you plan to disclose as well as the nature of your friendship with the confessor. Hymer suggests it may be safer to self-disclose very personal secrets, such as sexual orientation, sexual preferences, money matters, illicit affairs, or similar kinds of socially unacceptable behavior to what Hymer calls a functional friend (or what has been called a casual or differentiated friend in this book).

That, however, may still be risky, especially in communities where functional friends or acquaintances may show up in other personal or professional situations, possibly causing embarrassment. It is because of the potential risks to friendship and to other relationships that self-disclosure is never completely "safe." The benefits, in terms of increased intimacy, have to be weighed against the possible drawbacks.

MUTUALITY

Ideally, a friendship is maintained because your needs are being met by the relationship, and there is a shared desire to perpetuate, or even deepen, it. Twenty-nine-year-old Melanie, whose best friendship was first discussed in Chapter Six, Childhood and the Single Years, first met Jennifer when they both worked at the same company. Their best friendship has continued to evolve even after Jennifer got a job at another firm in the same city. Melanie, a striking, tall blonde woman, who is single and living alone, has a four-month-old daughter. Jennifer is the same age, single, and also living alone. Melanie describes how she has become even closer emotionally to Jennifer over the last year, although the baby has changed what they do together: "Even though we don't go out and party a lot anymore, Jennifer will still come over to my house and spend the evening. She'll adjust her schedule to mine now that I have the baby and can't get out whenever I want to."

The reason for initiating a friendship may be that you want someone to do things with, but the most compelling reason for maintaining a friendship is a quality of that friend.

Here are some of the qualities that caused friends to maintain their friendship:
"He's someone I'd like to be like."
"She's a mature, stable person, and that's what I look for in a friend."
"He's someone I trust."

"I like his sense of humor."

"She treats me wonderfully, and all the people around her wonderfully."

"She always seems to have things sorted out."

This change in reasons—from a generalized wish to have a friend, to that friend's specific attributes—is notable because unless that shift occurs, the friendship will end when there are conflicts, or a loss of physical proximity.

What About Gift-Giving or Loaning a Friend Money?

Consider the gift you select, and the person to whom you bestow the gift, very carefully or your positive gesture may backfire. I remember when my older son was turning three and my husband and I were still struggling and watching our pennies. I felt somewhat embarrassed when a wealthy and generous woman I had befriended in Manhattan gave my son a $60 toy for his birthday. Although that building toy was a fantastic, durable, life-long gift that we have enjoyed all these years, I was put in a tough position; I felt unable to reciprocate in kind when it was her daughter's birthday two months later.

When expensive gifts are given, especially if only one friend is comfortable sending such a costly gift, it can confuse the issue. "Do I like her for her personality or her extravagant gifts?" Reciprocity in gift giving will help avoid having a gift backfire.

In conducting research into corporate gift-giving for my book *Business Protocol*, among the 100+ companies throughout the country I surveyed, most suggested a ceiling of $25, if gifts were exchanged at the holidays, to avoid accusations of influence peddling. Perhaps it might be best to have a similar ceiling on gifts exchanged between friends, or for birthday parties. If gifts are more for the thought than the dollar amount—with a comfortable and appropriate ceiling of $10 to $40, depending upon financial circumstances of both friends—gift-giving will still be a gesture of friendship without embarrassing or financially straining anyone.

However, exchanging birthday gifts with friends, particularly once you are older and no one gives you a birthday party anymore—except perhaps those 10-year milestones—can be one of the joys of friendship. Whether it's a $4 coffee mug, a unique paper weight, a tie, soaps, a bookmark, donation to a friend's favorite charity to celebrate a special occasion, it is the symbol of your friendship through the gift, not the gift itself, that counts. If you are really financially strapped, a card—store bought or homemade—or even just a phone call to enhance and mark your friend's special day will endear you to your friend.

But what about loaning a friend money? This is a very controversial area. There are those, like writer Mark Twain, who advise against it, as he wrote in *Pudd'nhead Wilson* in 1894: "The holy passion of Friendship is of so sweet and steady and loyal and enduring a nature that it will last through a whole lifetime, if not asked to lend money."

By contrast, a 50-year-old divorced female doctoral student saw nothing wrong with loaning a friend money, as she had recently done: "I've done that already this year. Just lately, somebody who's losing a house. Someone I've known for ten years and I gave them mortgage payments for the last six months because the bank was going to take over the house. Voluntarily, and with no commitment to return it to me in any way."

Perhaps these two rules will help to minimize the potentially devastating effect loaning money could have on a friendship:

- Only ask for money from a friend if you think you will really be able to return it.
- Only loan money to a friend if you could financially and emotionally withstand the disappointment if, through no fault of your friend's, he or she is unable to quickly or ever pay back the money.

It is also important to remember that if you ask a friend for money, your friend may be more than happy to loan it to you, with no strings or time pressures attached, but it may not be his or her money to lend. A spouse or parent may have to be included in any major money decisions. That is another truism about money lending and friendship if you do not want it to ruin a relationship: if you do ask, be gracious and nonjudgmental if you are turned down. Before you write off that friend for turning you down if you do ask for money, see if that friend will be there for you in other ways that have nothing to do with money, like providing emotional support. Perhaps that friend cannot loan you the three thousand dollars it would take to paint your house so you can put it on the market to sell it, but your friend offers to give you something at least as precious as money, if not more so, namely time, by eagerly agreeing to spend as long as it takes to do the paint job or helping you find someone who will charge less.

Dealing with Jealousy

Sigmund Freud wrote about jealousy in his classic 1922 paper, "Certain Neurotic Mechanisms in Jealousy, Paranoia and Homosexuality," "Jealousy is one of those affective states, like grief, that may be described as normal. If anyone appears to be without it, the inference is justified that it has undergone severe repression and consequently plays all the greater part in his unconscious mental life."

In her book *Jealousy,* Nancy Friday, author of *My Mother/My Self,* writes: "Jealousy is a triangle, involving the feeling of loss to another....By the time we are old enough to take in a world containing more than the mother/child dyad, don't we already have an emotional backlog of loss, a sensitivity to it, depending on what we had with mother? Later jealousy—loss to a sibling, oedipal loss—gets its first fuel from the time when there were just two of us. When love was everything and mother's absence was death."

So if jealousy is "normal," just because a friend is jealous of you, or vice versa, should not automatically rule out that friendship. Even very close friends may be jealous at times. The fact that the jealousy rarely occurs helps define them as friends rather than "everyone else." As the director of human resources development at a manufacturing corporation says, "Understand that everybody is going to have feelings of anger and jealousy, no matter how much they care for you, or they like you. You've got to realize it's their agenda, not your agenda."

Consider where the jealousy is coming from—what in your friend's life is causing the jealous feelings—and try to understand that those jealous feelings say something about your *friend,* not about the *friendship.*

The Challenge of Intimacy

By the same token, you have to be careful not to overreact if you, or a friend, find the intimacy of genuine friendship too much to handle. It could just be your friend's personality: Some are less effusive in how they communicate or share feelings than others. That's as close as they get with anyone.

Closeness also makes you vulnerable. Being close opens you up to the potential for loss and pain. You have to connect before you can separate, as psychologist Dr. David Leeds always says. There are some friends who have never made the necessary early family connections to allow them to now connect, and separate, from friends. You cannot solve that problem for them. They may change, through life experiences or therapy, but in the meantime, if you want to keep your friendship going, you have to accept your friend's emotional limitations.

Sometimes, however, the disappointment that emotional distance brings can just make it too difficult to put the time and energy into a friendship that does not bring the anticipated emotional payoff. You could end the friendship or just put it on the back burner till you are willing to invest in it knowing, full well, your friend lacks the ability to get close at this time or maybe always.

Ironically, if you are befriending someone with an intimacy problem, you may be frustrated to find that as your friendship gets closer, your friend starts backing off. Those friends actually thrive in less demanding or more superficial relationships. The problem is that as your relationship advances from acquaintance to close friend, realizing your friend is incapable of going the distance, it may be hard to go back to a casual friendship, or even an acquaintanceship. If you do choose to continue a friendship with someone who backs off as your friendship gets closer, remember it's their problem, not yours. As with jealousy, depersonalize what is happening so you can preserve your self-esteem. You cannot force someone to get close to you if he or she is unwilling or incapable of doing so. Patience may have its payoff, or you may just continue this friendship at whatever level your friend is capable of, and get what you need from other friends, who are more emotionally open to you, or from other relationships in your life.

Coping with Change

You have seen that structural changes, such as getting a new job, if your friendship began when you worked together, or moving, if you used to live nearby, are all major challenges to friendships. When someone moves, too often a year or two after the move, they will comment, "I just don't have any friends from before." Why did that happen? Too often the reason is that the person who moved left it up to the old friends to contact him or her after the move. But it is a fact of life that it is often up to the person who moved away to reach out to their old friends.

Why? Because it is easier to be the one moving away than it is to be the one left behind. For whatever rational reason the move occurred—a better job, a marriage that necessitated moving to live with the spouse, a dependent child forced to move by her parents, a wish for a different situation for raising a family than the one that worked when single—the one left behind emotionally experiences the change as a rejection. After all, they are still in the old situation. Why wasn't that—the status quo—good enough? Especially if the move is to a bigger and better lifestyle, or a dramatically different one, the person left behind may feel they do not have that much in common anymore. Unfortunately, there is a competitiveness and territoriality that occurs as when those who relocate to California feel they have to bad-mouth their former New York lifestyle, or those who move to a new community justify the expense, inconvenience, and upset of moving by proclaiming they have made the "right" decision.

Change stirs up jealousy.

Change threatens intimacy, as those who allowed themselves to become close now have to deal with feelings of abandonment and separation.

"I don't feel comfortable with the old gang since my promotion," says a man in his late 20s. He is more honest than most that his advancement causes him to prefer new friends at his higher level. Unless he finds a way to integrate his old and new friends, he will be continually moving from friend to friend as he moves up the ladder, without the foundation of long term friends who "knew him when." In that way, he will miss one of the best reasons for maintaining a friendship over time, namely, *having a shared history.*

"Sometimes when a person changes and the other doesn't, one or both feel abandoned and/or angry," writes a married, 36-year-old Albany-based public relations consultant. "If the feelings aren't expressed and worked out, resentment builds, or the situation becomes too painful."

Bring your old friends into your new life as much as possible. Everyone will probably be aware that you all have to find other, more convenient friendships, but that does not diminish what you once had or can still have, on a different frequency basis. Telephone as often as possible, invite them for intimate brunches or dinners, as well as those "big" occasions that make you feel good about your network but at which it is often so hard to talk or connect intimately with each guest. Be willing to go back to your old neighborhood to see your old friends. The invitations should be a two-way street, sharing the burden of the time, effort, and expense of getting together.

Another change that can effect friendships is *weight loss* or *weight gain*. Weight loss may be a challenge to a friendship if one person loses a noticeable amount of weight and the friend, especially if he or she is still overweight, resents it or is jealous. As noted before, however, the jealousy is usually not vicious or malicious when it comes from a friend. It shows that your accomplishment has touched a nerve: what you now have is what your friend values (and wants for himself or herself). Wanting for yourself what someone else has does not mean you wish someone else did not have it.

If you feel jealous about a friend's weight loss, or you feel others are jealous of you, face these feelings. Give it time. Especially if friends have not seen you in a long time—unlike the friends nearby who may have been getting used to the "new"—part of the problem is the newness of the change and the shock of seeing someone you defined in one way, looking quite different. Thin people often dress and carry themselves differently than overweight people. A friend who has lost weight may start wearing flashier clothes—and getting more attention when you walk down the street together—which may be a change for you both.

Gaining a lot of weight may also impact some friendships. For example, if you have friends who measure their attractiveness by the company they keep, having a friend who is now severely overweight may challenge their own sense of self-worth. They may start avoiding you without even knowing why. They may make snide comments because of their own feelings about overweight, which has little to do with your specific weight gain. They may be afraid: if *she* could gain weight, maybe it could happen to me. Bring their reactions out in the open. You can open up a dialogue with your friend by explaining, "I'm not saying this is right or wrong, I just feel as if you're judging me because I've gained weight. Are you aware that you are treating me differently and that it's hard for me to be around you now?"

MAINTAINING CONTACT

How do friends keep in touch, maintaining the contact that is necessary if a friendship is to survive and grow? Close or best friends are most likely to keep in touch by getting together in person. That is a surefire way to keep a friendship evolving. The next most common and beneficial way is through telephone calls; least effective, but still better than no contact at all, is through letters or cards.

Regular get-togethers are the best way for a friendship to stay current and not stuck in the past. Weekly or monthly contact, if possible, is one way to keep your friendship moving along. A weekly tennis or bridge game has as much to do with friendship as it does with the sport or game, although some are shy about admitting it.

Take the lead from children, who seem to prefer for their current closest friends those who are currently in their class, and with whom they have ongoing contact as well as shared, similar experiences. As an adult, however, you may also add to current, close-by friendships those friendships that are less convenient; in that way, you have the *friendshifts* that provide a textured array of new and old friendships.

If physically getting together on a regular weekly, monthly, bimonthly, or annual basis is unreasonable for either you or your friend, supplement visits with phone calls as often as possible.

There are two types of phone friends. The most common kind are those persons you talk to on the phone in addition to regular face-to-face get-togethers. You call to say hello and find out how they are doing, and also to set up your next meeting.

The second type of phone friends use the phone as their primary communication tool.

Most phone friends start off as face-to-face friendships, but because you or your friend relocate to another job, or another neighborhood, calls become the mainstay of your relationship. My very close friend Joyce, for example, who lives in New Jersey now, says, "I call friends who live in Philadelphia [where she used to live], friends I used to see all the time when I lived there." Keeping in touch with old friends has its benefits but, if the calls are long distance, also has its costs: she just received her monthly $100 phone bill.

But, as noted before, those monthly phone bills may be less expensive than they seem since you know that friends help you stay healthier, enjoy life more, and live longer.

If friends live very far away, Joyce will combine phone calls with writing letters. But she is aware that nearby friendships are easier to maintain, since calling long distance causes her to communicate differently: "I'll talk to my friends in the neighborhood or ask them 'How you doing?' I enjoy the local calls more than the long distance ones because I'm more relaxed and not as conscious of the time."

You may also choose to use the phone for friendships you prefer to keep at a physical distance. Furthermore, the phone offers those who are shy an opportunity to be more open and outspoken than they might be in person. Conversely, some who are tongue-tied on the phone may blossom in the flesh, often saying, "I'm not a phone person." A 32-year-old married woman confides her aversion to the phone: "I hate talking on the phone. I just won't make phone calls." Alas, it has reduced the number of her nonwork or non-neighborhood friendships.

Except for the annual holiday card exchange, there were few active friendships continued through letter writing among those I interviewed or surveyed. As Harry Stein pointed out in a column on friendship that he wrote for *Esquire,* the kind of mail delivered by the postal service substantiates this claim: 80% of the mail is business related, 17% is greeting cards. Personal letters seem to account for a tiny amount of delivered mail.

Although writing is a one-sided communication, and it is time consuming, it offers a chance for sharing, connecting, closeness, and communication that friendships, even face-to-face or phone friendships, sometimes lack. Letters offer a relatively inexpensive way of keeping in touch with friends as well as a permanence. Several years ago, William Plummer and Sandra Gurvis in Columbus, Ohio, wrote an article in *People* magazine about a unique "round-robin" letter that had been going on for 58 years. It was started when the 18 women graduated Ohio's Wooster College in 1930 and were committed to maintaining their close friendships. The way the round robin works is that about once a week, one correspondent receives an envelope with notes, clippings, and pictures from each of the correspondents. She takes out her earlier section, adds new materials, and then mails the entire packet on to the next friend on the list. Because of their busy lives, living far apart, and, for some, poor health, in-person get-togethers are rare. The round-robin letter has helped keep their friendship going through all the stages of their adult lives——parenting, marriage, divorce, widowhood, the good times and the crises, ill-health, relocations, and the death of half a dozen of their original friendship group.

A letter friendship that is initiated through the mail may follow the same pattern as if the pen pals first met in person, rather than on paper. It will probably begin as a formal role relation or acquaintanceship, developing into a casual friendship; or, over time, as self-disclosure, trust, and shared experiences increase, it may become something closer and deeper.

It is unfortunate that letter writing is a lost art; although there is an increase in the volume of written communications with the increased popularity of facsimile machines, the bulk of fax transmissions are business related. However, electronic mail, e-mail for short, is changing that. In "Friendships Built on Bytes and Fibers," reporter Clare Collins discusses friendships that have developed from an initial "meeting" on a computer bulletin board or because of the exchange of faxes. For most, in order to develop a friendship from an initial electronic "meeting," like the face-to-face acquaintance process discussed in Chapter 4, the relationship has to move from computer or fax communication to telephone or even a face-to-face get-together. Discussions have to evolve into more intimate ones from purely work-related origins.

The process that Collins described is similar to what happened as Bob Plunkett, a 46-year-old married TV producer who works in Manhattan, developed a meaningful friendship that began in cyberspace. Bob "met" his newest friend four months ago through an on-line bulletin board. It started on a February night, "in the deepest, darkest, dankest part of the winter" when his family was out and he was feeling lonely. Bob found himself on-line "cruising in and out of the clubs and interest groups until something vaguely seemed of interest." In a category that he seems to remember had the general title "Baby Boomers," he started reading the replies to letters that others had written. One reply to someone who expressed distress he found especially "compassionate and sympathetic, sort of a pep talk that had a little more compassion and understanding, not rah rah." Bob spent 25 minutes composing a short letter to the sender and concluded his e-mail by writing, "if you are interested in chit chatting any further, then let me know." Bob describes what followed:

> It turned out to be a 45-year-old college professor in Texas who teaches a lot of history courses and also is a scholar in sixteenth-century-religion, which was kind of interesting since I have spent the last 25 years studying religion. So we've had some discussions on that. We made a psychic connection through cyberspace. There was nothing that he specifically said [in his original letter about religion]; there was something in the tone or tenor of the original message that triggered something for me. He's married and he has a four-year-old son. We've been trading letters for a while. [But] I would never go to Texas. He doesn't want to visit New York. This guy is two thousand miles away, and he knows more about what is going on in my day-to-day life than anybody. In some respects, the distance helps. It gives me a new perspective on a few things....

Bob feels that the speed and convenience of e-mail encourage written communications:

> Here, since it moves so quickly, it starts to make you write more of them....I know the guy is going to get it instantaneously. Unlike the old days where you walked around with a letter in your pocket for weeks because you don't have a stamp [and once you send it] three days later someone might get your letter,

[and] a week later you might look in your mailbox [for a reply]. Here, 10 minutes later you can start to look. At least you instantaneously have a possibility of getting mail. It's very powerful. Suddenly you're sitting there. Nobody wants to talk to you. Nobody wants anything to do with you. You shoot out a piece of electronic mail and everything brightens. Here some guy in Texas might send me a note.

Here are additional tips for maintaining and improving friendships:

• Make getting together with your friends, especially your best or close ones, a key concern, up there along with work, family, relative, hobby, or sports interests.

• Do not let your economic situation determine whether or not you get together with friends. If you are financially strapped, have a potluck dinner at your home, asking each friend to bring part of the meal; or meet somewhere other than your home, so you do not have to cover all the costs of entertaining—at an inexpensive coffee shop or, in nice weather, at a picnic in the park.

• Decide what way of keeping in touch with friends works best for *you*. Financial consultant Stanley Heilbronn has found "one on one" works best for him and his wife; they prefer a dinner out with just one other couple to big parties.

• If your best or close friend—and even a casual one, if you think there is a potential for greater intimacy—invites you to a key event in his or her life, try to get there, even if you have to go without a spouse who is unable to get away. That's what Valerie San Antonio did when her husband's company picnic in Texas turned out to be on the same Sunday as her very close friend's wedding in Connecticut. Her husband took their two young sons and flew to Texas for the weekend (bringing his mother along to help out). Valerie stayed behind and attended the wedding. "My friend's mother made a big fuss over me and my friend was really happy I was there. I'm glad I went," says Valerie, who puts a lot of time and energy into her friendships even though she has seven brothers and sisters.

• Use the holidays to catch up with your friends and to show them they matter to you, whether that means a holiday phone call, a personalized card or letter, or an appropriate gift. (But the holidays should not be the *only* time you remember your friends, or they will begin to doubt just how much of a friend they really are.)

• If you are really pressed for time but still want to maintain contact with your friends, try to combine what you have to do with getting together with a friend. For example, meet over lunch during the workday if you just do not have a minute to spare at night or on the weekends. If you are planning to take in a movie with your spouse, invite another couple along, and talk over a cup of coffee before or after the picture. Ask a friend to join you for your necessary holiday shopping. It will keep your friendship going and might even make the chore more fun. Take an exercise class together. Go on vacation together or, if your friend lives out of town, you might vacation at a point nearby, and rendezvous. That is what I do in the summertime with my close friend Joyce, who lives in New Jersey. We meet at Sesame Place in Pennsylvania, about three hours from my Connecticut home and about an hour away from Joyce's. Not only do we all get together and share some of the traveling, we share experiences that enable our children to actively partake in a friendship that dates back to my senior year of college.

• Make a master list of birthdays and anniversaries, and note those dates on a wall calendar or in your weekly planner, so you will find it easier each year to remember those special dates for your friends.

• If you find yourself wondering when you last saw, or spoke to, some of your best, close, or casual friends, consider keeping a log that records your contact beyond just holiday cards. If you find too many months—even years—going by without getting together, it might help you to get an overview of your friendship contact. Decide how often you would like to talk to, or see, your friends, especially those who live out of town. Try to commit to definite get-togethers.

• Take advantage of as many possibilities for maintaining contact as possible. For example, I have a close friend who lives in the next town; we may see other every month or two, but we also talk by phone, send each other an occasional fax, and recently added e-mail as another way of keeping involved in each other's hectic lives. Since each way of staying connected has its advantages and limitations, its costs and its requirements, having many ways to communicate with your friends multiplies your friendship possibilities.

*

In the next chapter you will learn additional ways to help prevent a friendship from ending, especially a best or close one, and particularly why you should avoid "crossing the line" or "trigger" incidents.

9. HOW TO PREVENT A FRIENDSHIP FROM ENDING

Even the utmost goodwill and harmony and practical kindness are not sufficient for Friendship, for Friends do not live in harmony merely, as some say, but in melody.

—Henry David Thoreau, *A Week on the Concord and Merrimack Rivers*, 1849

An angry word. An insult said without premeditation. A canceled lunch. An ignored phone call. One misunderstanding. I have observed or heard about worthwhile friendships built up over 10 or 20 years ending just because of one wrong. If the friendship *should* end because it is a harmful or destructive one, that's one thing. (You may even *want* to actively end harmful friendships, a subject that is discussed in the next chapter.) In this chapter, you will find out how to try to salvage a positive friendship that is having problems. You will also look at how to avoid crossing the line or trigger incidents that prompt hasty endings.

It is easier to intensify a friendship that has become less

intimate, but there is still some contact, without an abrupt ending, than it is to resurrect one that has dramatically ended.

MAINTAINING YOUR FRIENDSHIPS, DESPITE INCONVENIENCE

Casual friendships end most frequently because of changes that render the once-convenient friendship a royal pain to maintain—unless there's a lot of feeling, caring, and commonality to justify the effort. If you do not let inconvenience end your friendships, you can increase the number of casual friends you maintain by a few each year; dozens over a decade. It is as easy as having a plan to telephone and make time to see casual friends with whom you once worked, went to school, attended camp, met at an organization or club in which you both were interested. By maintaining an ongoing dialogue, whether you are in touch once a week or once every few months, you keep the line of communication open, and the friendship growing, a key way to prevent it from fading or ending.

Another way to prevent a casual friendship from ending is to turn a friendship pair into a threesome or a network. You may then have more power in numbers as a way to more easily keep the friendship flourishing.

Friendshifts permit friendships to be more or less important to us, depending upon where we are in life, as well as what our friend is going through. The friendship persists, but it shifts.

Best or close friendships—and few will have more than one or two best friends, or anywhere from one to half a dozen or so close ones—will require more concerted effort to maintain. Turning those relationships into a threesome or a network might backfire; the friendship survives, but on a less intense or intimate basis, gradually becoming another casual friendship. Telephone calls and getting together, one on one, is probably what your close or best friendships need to be maintained or to become more valuable over time.

Genuine tried-and-true close, best, or casual friendships that have stood the test of time and changed circumstances should continue to be part of your current life, even if the contact is less frequent than before. If they are not, that sends a message about the relationship. As 30-year-old Brenda, a senior editor at a business magazine, put it: "With some [friends] it dissipates with time. You see each other less. You run into them and you say, 'Hmm, I really wish I saw that person more,' but the fact is that you don't, and that says something about the friendship."

EMPHASIZING SIMILAR VALUES

If you do want to maintain a friendship and prevent it from ending, you will increase the likelihood of that by emphasizing similar values. Since a conflict in values will more often end a friendship than a difference in income, attractiveness, interests, or residences, *play up your similarities*. For example, if you know your friend is committed to getting a job, do not keep extolling the virtues of the free-lance life that she is reluctantly leaving behind. Talk about the full-time jobs you have had in the past, or get your friend to talk about the positive benefits of her job change.

Look at a value conflict that could have ended a friendship but did not. Deborah and Christopher had a close platonic friendship. Deborah broke up with her boyfriend and within a few weeks tried to push her friendship with Christopher, who was also single, to become a sexual and romantic one, rather than a platonic one.

Christopher did not want to lose Deborah's friendship, so rather than cutting off the relationship, or hurting Deborah's ego, he put the burden of the situation on himself and made Deborah look good so she could save face, and they could keep their friendship going. How did he do that? By saying things like, "It's not you, it's me. I've seen you as a friend for so long, I can't see you in another role. I wish I could, because you're attractive and sexy and everything a man could want in a woman. It's my loss. I hope we can continue our friendship, which is one of the most important relationships in my life." A potential value conflict over what kind of relationship they would continue to have was turned around so their friendship could survive and grow.

Sometimes, however, this type of resolution is impossible, usually when a third party is involved, namely a new spouse, who instructs a wife or husband that opposite-sex friends or ex-romantic partners are off limits as friends. That is a value conflict that the spouses will have to work out with each other if the friendship is to survive.

WHEN EXPECTATIONS ARE UNMET

"Friendships may end because of an unwillingness of parties to be more flexible in terms of friendship expectations," as a 34-year-old woman living in Virginia and separated from her husband points out. So how do you handle it when your friend tells you that expectations about you or your friendship are unmet? When it is pointed out that you have done something wrong, simply say "I'm sorry." Avoid defending yourself. It is amazing how effectively the simple phrase, "I'm sorry," usually diffuses even the angriest friend's rage. It is such a humble admission. It takes the venom out of the most hurt or vindictive friends.

One of the reasons tried-and-true friendships take three years to evolve is that working through initial conflicts will determine if a friendship has staying power. But have realistic expectations about your friend and your friendship. In my interviews with best and close friends and their former friends, I was surprised at how often their expectations were too unrealistic for anyone short of Supergirl or Clark Kent to have met their needs. If only they could see that the friends they still have, about whom they have lower or no expectations, often offer them less than the ones they have rejected!

The expectations, and what the friends shared, for friendships that failed, were usually all-encompassing. Perhaps too demanding and unrealistic for what friendship can be in these days of competing demands on your emotional self and your time. Less-emotional friendships may be easier to maintain because they make fewer demands, so you and your friend are better able to perform your other work, marital, or parenting roles. What those friendships lack in intensity they make up for in staying power and nonconflictual predictability. For example, a 35-year-old married test pilot, when asked what favors he would feel comfortable asking of his best friend, wrote, "I never ask favors of friends—well, I try not to."

In my research, I discovered the two situations where family, not friends, are more likely to be approached and leaned on are in times of severe sickness, including emotional duress, or if someone needs money. After she broke up with her boyfriend and was emotionally devastated, a single woman echoed the sentiments of most of those I interviewed when she said she decided to go home to her mother to get herself together, rather than impose on a friend.

Recognizing the limitations of friendship may help you make fewer unrealistic demands on your friends and, hence, salvage friendships that might have ended. By the same token, you may then be better equipped to benefit from the unique contributions that friends do make to your life, in contrast to, and in addition to, what your family or spouse may offer.

AVOIDING "CROSSING THE LINE" OR "TRIGGER" INCIDENTS

When a best or close friendship does end, I discovered, it is usually because of a trigger incident or the feeling that someone has "crossed the line." Here are examples of some crossed lines or trigger incidents that ended friendships:

- "When I traveled to see a friend over a holiday (three hours in horrible weather), the friend refused to take the time from studies to go out for dinner or drinks."
- "We were best friends for about eleven years, since four years old. Suddenly she started ignoring me and showed a whole different 'snobby' attitude."
- "Here's two thousand dollars. I'll pay you the other five hundred when I get it."
- "He tried underhandedly to get people in trouble with other people."
- "He became a bastard."

- "She acted so nice and friendly, when in reality, she was two-faced."
- Your friend fails again to give you the emotional support you need.
- You tell your married friend you can't stand his spouse.
- Your friend reveals a confidence to someone else.

Agnes, an executive recruiter, explains how her friendship ended after she learned her close friend crossed the line by living with a boy that Agnes used to have a crush on:

> We were really inseparable for years. But there was this guy I was in love with in high school. She ended up going away to college where he went, and living with him all through college. She didn't tell me about it. I found out about it and that really bothered me. Then she denied it. I mean, they were living together. I called her and said, "Are you seeing him?" and she said, "No, I don't really see him that much." And I thought, "That was really dumb because I know you're living with him."

Esther had a similar crossed line when she discovered her close friend June had been getting together with Esther's friends behind her back. Thirty-five-year-old Bob, a married mathematician living in Detroit, had a close friend in high school for four years, but that friendship ended when his friend crossed the line and became a shoplifter. "The friendship was worth less than staying out of bad trouble, so I slowly terminated it....I don't think I would have cared if he was a shoplifter per se. I just didn't appreciate his placing me in jeopardy without my consent. That was what bothered me more than the act. The act wouldn't have been any different if he had shared an apartment with me and was dealing drugs in the apartment. I would have been just as pissed."

However, crossing the line is a very subjective situation: what you think is "the last straw" may be minor to someone else, who perpetuates a friendship despite a greater violation. As a 19-year-old male college sophomore says, "I stopped a friendship because the person thought that he was better than everyone else, that he was right all the time and everyone else was wrong"; others may be willing to perpetuate a friendship with someone with the very same personality this young man found so objectionable.

HANDLING CONFLICT WITH FRIENDS

There can be no friendship without forgiveness.
—Phillip Lopate, *Against Joie de Vivre*

Conflicts often occur because of changes that impact on the friendship which no one is willing to deal with directly. Instead, there is unresolved hostility, which may make the expense of maintaining the friendship greater than its benefits. Marsha Londe, an Atlanta-based salesperson, explains why reentering the work force after being a stay-at-home mother impacted on her friendships: "I'd come home so exhausted at night that I didn't have the energy or the interest in casual phone calls, and that's what it takes to keep friendships going. In addition to that, I was receiving the social stimulus that I needed through work, and friendships did change."

To prevent endings, it is necessary to deal with how the changes in your life are affecting your friendships. Most friends will be looking for confirmation and affirmation; the changes are causing you to have less time for them, but it's nothing personal.

Friendships that last either have less conflict than those that end or involve friends who know how to effectively handle conflict.

Handled well, conflict may actually be positive. As sociologist Lewis Coser points out in *The Functions of Social Conflict,* conflict clears the air in a relationship and "eliminates the accumulation of blocked and balked hostile dispositions by allowing their free behavioral expression."

Unfortunately, conflict, which often involves temporary stress in the short term but less stress in the long run, is too often avoided at all costs. That cost may turn out to be the friendship.

One way to deal with any problem in your friendship is to confront your friend, eye to eye, and say, "We have a conflict. Let's deal with it. I don't want anything to hurt our friendship because you, and our friendship, are very important to me." Do what the communication experts suggest you do, a technique I use when I work as a group facilitator, an approach parents often use when dealing with a conflict with a child—validate him or her by acknowledging your friend's point of view or position. "Agree to disagree," as they say. Let your friend know you value your friendship, which should help up the stakes in working things out, rather than just cutting the friendship off.

Talk it out. Failing to talk out problems just might end those friendships. As a 19-year-old male college student says: "I would say most of my friendships have ended because of a lack of saying what is felt. If something was bothering me, I didn't say it. I know [now] that if something is bothering a person, that person should say so, without being rude."

Another way to deal with conflict is to *allow a cooling-off period.*

Sometimes a friendship, especially a best or close one, can be saved simply by deciding to step back from the annoying situation and postpone dealing with any irreversible words or actions that might have occurred in the heat of the moment or out of anger. A chilling out time is an adult version of the discipline method of "time out." This cooling-off time—of minutes, hours, days, or weeks, if needed—is a self-imposed time to step back, reassess, calm down, or chill out. It is amazing how much less important most issues, comments, or situations are when put in the perspective that sometimes only *time* provides. It could be an hour, a week, or a month or as long as it takes.

Of course, you must reinitiate contact. Only then should you decide if it is even necessary to bring up whatever it was that enraged you. For example, your friend does not return your calls as quickly as you would like. Perhaps you can work out a system where you indicate you need to be called back right away, versus a "hello" call that could take longer to get to. However, failing to come to terms with the original conflict may result in a second, permanent rupture. If working out the difference is essential to the friendship, calmly bring up the conflict, and deal with it with your friend so that your friend does not feel judged, criticized, or blamed. If you decide what happened was silly or irrelevant, let it ride. Not every problem or issue needs to be discussed continually. But if the initial conflict highlighted value differences, those disparities have to be clarified, explained, or ironed out.

"If we're upset about something, we talk it out," says a married assistant vice president at a title search company in New Jersey. "We don't take it to the point where it's too late to save the friendship."

Salvaging Faded and Fading Friendships

A best or close friendship that becomes less intimate may be more difficult to maintain than a casual one that remains for decades at a more superficial level. That is because the stronger a friendship is, the more like love it becomes, with all the intensity and emotional involvement of a stronger emotion and relationship. We come to be dependent on our best or close friends; if they turn their attention and affection away from us, for work, relationship, or other commitment reasons, it still hurts. However, friendship, unlike romantic love, which rarely tolerates competing liaisons, may have numerous relationships of varying intensities.

The first step toward salvaging a close or best friendship that is fading or faded is to recognize that this friendship requires your attention. Too often friendships, especially long-standing ones, are taken for granted until it is too late. You think your friendship is just fine; you do not put the time and energy into calling or getting together because you are busy and, besides, you feel very secure about that relationship. When you finally do call, however, you find out your close friend is less than warm toward you; you discover you have been replaced by another friend who is more responsive and available to your friend. "Nothing personal."

The second step toward salvaging a fading or faded friendship is to decide, now that you know there is a problem, whether you will confront your friend or let things ride for a while and see what happens. Take a longer view. As the director of human resources at a software corporation told me: "Resist the need to strike back when they do something that hurts you. Get above it. Take a helicopter view of it. If you really care about the friendship, over time they'll come around. But you can't force it. If you try to force it at that point, it just doesn't work. You can't say to someone, 'Get more objective about this.' People have their feelings and you've got to allow them to have those feelings, even if those feelings are negative toward you. You've got to get past that."

Sometimes, however, intervention is necessary; letting things ride translates into a worsening situation. Whatever problems have to be confronted, by working these concerns out with your friend, it might be possible to salvage your friendship. Failing to work things out may further fade your friendship. As 33-year-old Rachel, a married psychotherapist, explains: "Some [friendships] have faded a bit or changed in relative importance. Sometimes situational changes, sometimes a loss of empathy in one or the other of us that made us seek more compatible people. Sometimes allowing a difference to go unmentioned and, thus, letting it grow more impossible to overcome, more of an impediment."

*

The next chapter explores how to handle friendships that, despite your best efforts, do end.

10. HOW TO HANDLE FRIENDSHIPS THAT END

It ended drastically. I could have killed her. It was like an atomic bomb had been dropped.

—Eve, 28-year-old computer programmer

As noted before, casual friendships most often end because of inconvenience. When the shared situation ends, so does the relationship. Unfortunately, it is often hard to know that it was a friendship of convenience until after these tests on the relationship. Dale, for example, describes her realization that the casual friendships she had with Sally and Brenda were not even friendships; it was not until the situation changed that it became clear: "Sally and Brenda both were girlfriends of my boyfriend's friends. So it was that kind of thing. Sally and Brenda are the only two people I've ever had problems with. I tried because of circumstances to be friends with them. I wouldn't ordinarily have been their friends. You can't force something because they're your boyfriend's best friends' girlfriends, and that's what happened there. We fell into this sort of false friendship."

WHY FRIENDSHIPS END

But what about the endings of genuine tried-and-true casual, close, or best friendships, not false ones? As noted before, shifts in circumstances make it harder to maintain casual friendships. A casual friendship that became less important to both men after they no longer worked together was typified by the Freudian slip one man made as they passed each other on the street. Turning to his new co-workers, the man introduced the other man by blurting out, "I'd like you to meet my former friend." Everyone joked about the slip, but it highlighted the change in their relationship since they no longer worked together, a change that was now noted by both men.

You saw in the last chapter how crossing the line or trigger incidents can end even close or best friendships. You also saw how value conflicts and unmet expectations, especially with close or best friendships, cause endings. When Lisa and Linda's best friendship ended, it was for all those reasons. The trigger was Lisa learning that her friend had pocketed the extra money that Lisa had given her for a mutual friend. The value conflict was that her friend could not be trusted, and the unmet expectation was that, after they moved out to California together, Lisa discovered their friendship would not be the way it had always been when they were growing up in Boston. As Lisa puts it: "We lost our virginity together." But after they both dropped out of college and moved to California, Linda changed. Lisa says that when she finally landed a job, she told Linda her good news, but her friend's response was disappointing:

> Linda turned around, looked at me, and said, "I don't want to know anything about you. It's boring." And I stood there and cried because that is my most normal reaction. I didn't get angry until two days later, when I'd gotten over the crying part....But it wasn't just me she did it to....The only consolation I can draw from it is that she did it to two other people as well.

Another example of a value conflict as a reason for ending a long-term close friendship is Sara's friend Leslie, who inherited a lot of money after her parents died in a fire. Sara says that Leslie then "became a racist."

Still another example of a close friendship that ended is Sue: when she was forced to evict her friend from the apartment she had temporarily sublet her because Sue suddenly broke up with her boyfriend and needed her old place to live, she then realized what an opportunist her friend, and former employer, had been all along; her friend refused to voluntarily vacate Sue's apartment.

"Befriend in haste, dissolve at leisure" is a maxim that applies to most failed friendships. Perhaps that is because the testing out that occurs on the road from acquaintance to friend is a necessary step to avoid false or pseudo-friendships. If the friendship is rushed along, too little information about the potential friend will have been processed to avoid value conflicts and unmet expectations. Furthermore, I discovered conducting the research for my dissertation that the reason a friendship was initiated has a great deal to do with whether or not it ends: for those surveyed who had close or best friendships that ended, proximity, or being close by, was the initial reason for starting the friendship (48%). By contrast, for 85% the most frequent reason for initiating a current close friendship that was going well was a friend's expectations for the friendship—companionship, doing things together, someone to talk to, shared interests, or emotional support; for only 7% was proximity the primary reason for initiating the current closest on-going friendship.

It is intriguing that although almost everyone I interviewed was unable to recall the precise moment an acquaintanceship became a friendship, almost all with a failed close or best friendship could pinpoint what specific incident or reason triggered its dissolution. Looking back, most found it hard to recall why they even wanted to become friends in the first place. It reminded me of the statement so often heard around failed marriages: "I don't regret the divorce. I just regret the marriage." Just as those who are pleased with their current close or best friends answer with the vague reason, "We like each other," failed close or best friends have very specific gripes and will also give blow-by-blow explanations of why they now dislike their former friend. For example, Eve, whose comments about her failed close friendship began this chapter, continues her description of a friendship that ended four years before our interview; it began at summer camp when she and her former friend were 19, and had lasted for nine years:

> I had just broken off with my boyfriend, and I was crushed. I called her up because she was with me the night before we broke off. Instead of saying he was lousy, she proceeded to rip me apart for about half an hour. I was in such shock that I didn't even fight because I couldn't believe she was doing this to me when I was so vulnerable. Then I realized that she goes for the jugular because she was wanting to do it all along, but she was waiting for me to reach a low ebb. I have never forgiven her for it.

Often failed close or best friendships are described in emotional and dramatic ways:
"We were partners in crime together."
"We were really inseparable."
"We were sisters."
"I felt like I could tell her anything."
"I needed Emily and she needed me."

If your friendship has ended—because you ended it, your friend terminated it, or it was ended by mutual consent—be kind to yourself as you go through the mourning that typically follows the termination of any significant relationship. As with coping with the death of a loved one, the emotional end of a friendship requires accepting the reality of its end, mourning the end of your friendship as well as the dreams you may have had about the longevity of this relationship, incorporating the pleasant shared history of your friendship or your friend's best traits into your repertoire of memories, and resolving the loss by attaching to new friends or enhancing your commitments to other old friends, relatives, a pet, or even activities such as hobbies, travel, volunteer work, participating in leisure activities, or attending professional meetings.

RECOGNIZING AND DISSOLVING HARMFUL FRIENDSHIPS

However, you may *want* to end a friendship, if it is harmful. Destructive and harmful friendships are all those negative friendships that threaten your own well-being or that of your family members. It could be a friend with such severe psychological problems, such as pathological lying, that his or her trustworthiness is in question, or a delinquent youth that your teenager has befriended. It could be a friend who offers to drive you home from a party even though he is intoxicated, or the friend who uses foul language when he visits you at work so you are afraid your job may be in jeopardy.

Of course, destructive friendships may have started out as positive ones. But a friend could change, for the worse.

The perplexing thing about these harmful friendships, and one reason you may stay in these destructive relationships far longer than you should, is that the destructive friend may be a negative influence in our life but a perfect prince or princess with others. You may observe your critical or jealous friend being supportive with someone else and you wonder, "Maybe it's *me*. Maybe I'm the problem."

When Wayne got his $75,000-a-year job at a consulting firm, it was his best corporate job yet. He had been fired from his last job, mainly because he had not gotten along with the head of the conservative company. Wayne was eager to do well this time. He had two school-age children to support and a wife who had recently returned to graduate school full-time.

Soon after Wayne was hired, he employed a free-lance artist, a single woman, and they became "fast" friends. They had lunch together on a weekly basis. They would talk about work as well as their personal frustrations.

Within six months, Wayne saw to it that his friend came on staff, reporting to him. It seemed innocent enough if those occasional lunches now included dinners and a ride home from a company function.

What Wayne was failing to realize was that his friend had severe emotional problems that began interfering with her work performance. She drank too much and used foul language, even at business functions. She would call in sick frequently and was moody and prone to emotional outbursts. But Wayne overlooked his friend's behavior.

Others, however, noticed. A senior manager warned Wayne's friend she was in danger of losing her job. Without missing a beat, she told Wayne's shocked boss that she and Wayne had been having an affair that predated her employment there. She blamed being distraught over their affair for her poor work performance.

Wayne was fired even though he denied having an affair with his friend. His behavior was considered evidence of his poor judgment; he should have seen how his employee/friend was deteriorating and taken the necessary steps to deal with it and to alert human resources about the situation. Several months later, after a very stressful and demoralizing job hunt in the face of the circumstances surrounding his firing, Wayne finally got a new job. He immediately declared, definitively, "I'm not planning to make any friends here."

Wayne's mistake was misjudging his friend's emotional state. He failed to realize she was more than eccentric; she was deeply troubled.

Just how do you recognize a destructive and harmful friendship? Communication patterns in destructive friendships may be characterized by feeling depleted or tired after the telephone or in-person interaction has occurred, rather than the positive and exhilarating feelings that a healthy friendship should inspire. You may find yourself thinking, "I feel better without talking to him."

The destructive friend may dwell on your past failures, be negative, use information given in trust in manipulative ways, or have little empathy for you. By knowing your vulnerable points, this kind of friend can quickly—with just one phone call—make you absolutely and unbelievably miserable. When communication with a destructive friend ceases, unlike the positive longing to reconnect you will usually feel when a healthy friendship ends, you may find yourself feeling a sense of relief. As a 26-year-old woman from Texas explained to me about why she ended a friendship started in college:

> She was interested in having me as a friend because she just wanted to sap what she wanted out of me....It wasn't a give and take. She wasn't interested in expanding her own perspectives. I haven't spoken with her. I made it very clear that I didn't want to be friends anymore and finally I just stopped answering her letters and tore her address out of my phone book. I just severed communication totally four years ago.

Destructive friends may be overly pleasant while your friendship is forming, during the courtship phase. But once the friendship is underway, they may let down their mask to reveal that they are a destructive or harmful person.

What are other signs that should alert you that you are in a destructive friendship? If Wayne couldn't tell, how can you?
- If it is an opposite-sex friendship, you often "forget" totell your spouse about meetings with your friend.
- Your friend seems to be "taking over" your life, far too quickly and too completely. For example, you have a party and invite all your friends. Your harmful friend has taken everyone else's phone number and by the end of the party is planning meetings with all your friends—without including you.
- Your friend is invading your privacy and overstepping normal boundaries. For instance, your friend calls up your ex-boyfriend and pleads with him to take you back because she has seen how upset the breakup has made you.
- Your friend is untrustworthy or unreliable.
- Your friend fails to return phone calls within a reasonable time and never has a convincing explanation.
- Your friend cancels appointments at the last minute and so often that standing you up it becomes a pattern without

reasonable justification.

    • On more than one occasion, someone else says to you, "I need to talk to you about your friend so-and-so."

    • You find yourself trying to explain away or justify too many actions that "don't feel right" because those actions are cruel, illegal, bizarre, or just plain offensive. For example, your friend bad-mouths others, steals, uses illegal drugs, or acts in other socially unacceptable ways.

    • When you are invited to dinner parties, more than once you're asked, "Please don't bring your friend so-and-so along."

Why Does Someone Get into a Destructive Friendship?

What leads someone to seek out, or befriend, harmful or negative friends? A possible explanation is that an abusive or negative parent-child or sibling relationship at home was a poor training ground; the negative friendships are repetitions of what was going on at home during the formative years.

Ideally, friends offer an opportunity to undo the damage done by the family in the early years by offering the love and acceptance that parents or siblings failed to provide. However, without introspection or the help of a therapist or a support group, the earliest familial experiences might be repeated through destructive friendships. Just as child abuse, untreated, sometimes becomes a cycle—the victim of abuse may grow up to become an abuser—it is necessary to break the cycle of poor family relationships causing the selection of harmful damaging peer relations and hence destructive friendships.

Someone who has a poor self-image and low self-esteem may also unwittingly seek out negative friends to confirm that view.

Others may lack alternative friendships that would enable them to more easily abandon destructive ones. They feel better to have any kind of friend, even if it is a harmful one, than no friend at all.

You have to be realistic about destructive friendships that are harmful and realize that getting out may be the best answer, not working it out.

Since friends sometimes belong to a network, be careful what you disclose to a friend who seems questionable.

Here are other ways to avoid defeat and betrayal in friendship:

- Take time to update your knowledge about a particular friend. The person you befriended 20 years ago may be a very different individual now.
- Trust your instinct if any behavior seems weird, dishonest, distrustful, or unstable.
- Observe carefully: has your friend who plans to drive you home just finished his fifth alcoholic drink at dinner? You should consider that your friend may have a drinking problem; that information will help you protect yourself in certain vulnerable situations so you could continue this friendship without placing yourself in jeopardy.

How to End Harmful Friendships

How you end a destructive friendship, especially a close or best one where feelings are intense and intimate information has probably been exchanged, is very important since you do not want to enrage your former friend. In most instances, you will want this friendship to fade, rather than dramatically end; you will want to wind down your relationship rather than have a direct confrontation to minimize the possibility of someone launching a vendetta against you, or wanting revenge. You may want to avoid having a dramatic ending that could cause you to invest too much emotion and energy in this ended relationship. Carrying a torch for the failed friendship continues to invest your time and energy in a relationship that you probably feel already took too much of your valuable resources. A revised version of the adage, "The best revenge is living well," applies to ended harmful friendships: "The best revenge is having a positive friendship."

You may simply want to "be busy" when this friend asks to get together; after a while, he or she will get the hint. (Be careful, however, that you do not inadvertently use the "busy" technique suggested for ending harmful friendships on your positive ones that you *want* to keep.) Niki, a New York-based attorney, describes a harmful old friendship with someone back in her home town of Philadelphia, that she is intentionally allowing to fade:

> It hasn't failed, but it's in limbo. Not that we had a big fight. I kind of got tired of her being unreliable. I sort of resent her making plans and breaking them. I find it annoying, and it's happened too many times. Then I'd be disappointed because we couldn't go out because she made a date at the last minute. So I stopped calling her. I always called her when I visited my parents, but I haven't called her all summer, and I haven't wanted to call her.

Debbie, who grew up in the Midwest, moved to California, and relocated to New York, tells how her close friendship with Trude just ended one day seven years before, even though they used to see each other every day after school and traveled together. Debbie's story shows that even if you end a friendship without a dramatic confrontation, if the friendship was that important, its ending may still preoccupy you:

> We always talked about "When we get married..." She was a virgin going into her marriage. When we met, she did not know how to kiss a boy, she was that backward.
> Now she had only two close friends: Mary Ann, this one girl from childhood, a millionaire with lots of money, and me.
> Finally, when she was going to get married, she didn't have the guts to tell me that I wasn't going to be in her wedding party. She announced it by saying, "I'd like you to help me pick out Mary Ann's maid of honor dress."
> I could have accepted it if she had told me honestly, cried for a minute. But she chose not to say anything.
> The day of the wedding I was a few minutes late. That was seven years ago. I haven't had contact with her since....It comes back to haunt me in my dreams. It bothers me. So my

conscience keeps telling me, you should call and settle it. It's a shame to invest that much in a friendship with a guy or a girl [and have it end].

Ending destructive friendships may necessitate a three-step plan:

1. Minimize or stop contact.
↓
2. Replace the friendship with a positive one.
↓
3. Be "busy" if your friend tries to initiate contact.

COPING WITH ENDINGS BECAUSE OF DEATH

Other generations had wars and a shorter life expectancy as the reasons they might have had to cope with the premature death of friends. Today, AIDS, car accidents, cancer-related deaths, heart attacks, and even homicide have tragically increased the likelihood that you may lose a friend at a younger age than you might have expected. The older you become, furthermore, the more likely it is that you will have to cope with the death of your friends. In addition, whatever your age, you may have the necessity of being there for a friend who has been touched by the loss of a loved one, whatever the cause of death or the age of their dearly departed.

When a Friend Dies

The death of a friend is a different kind of ending to deal with than endings due to unmet expectations or conflicts. Just as a child often harbors the fantasy that divorced parents will remarry, friends with ruptured relationships have the possibility of reuniting in the future, even if it is a remote one. Not so if a friendship ends because of death.

In some cases, illness may precede the death of a friend. Few are trained in how to cope with a sick or dying friend. Witnessing someone who has the skills to be there for a sick friend can provide a lifelong lesson in compassion, however. As Atlanta-based writer Lynne Alpern testifies, it was just that ability of her friend Dian to be there for a mutual friend throughout an illness and subsequent death that so impressed Lynne more than 20 years before:

> We have the usual assortment of shared trials, tribulations, joyful occasions and much laughter. But what I really learned from observing Dian, early on, was dealing with death. As someone with a high degree of empathy and therefore a low threshold for tragedy, it was difficult for me, then in my 20s, to visit people in the hospital, attend funerals, et cetera. Watching Dian, with grace and compassion, continue to love, visit, and support her friend Gloria, a rabbi's wife whom I did not know, during painful and debilitating months of dying from a brain tumor—when many others "were too upset" to do so—taught me a lot about facing the unfaceable and doing the undoable.

As wrenching and traumatic as it may be to share the weeks, months, or years of decline that a terminally ill friend may endure, it does at least offer you both the opportunity to express your feelings, to reminisce, and to say good-bye. Sara Nelson, in her *Self* magazine article, "The Day AIDS Hit Home," writes about the last six months in the life of her close friend Artie, a gay filmmaker 14 years her senior who "adopted" her when they first met in San Francisco 12 years before, when Nelson was 18. Although Nelson moved East, they maintained their friendship over the next decade through phone contact every couple of months. Then, in one phone call, Nelson got the news: "I just got out of the hospital. I have AIDS." Nelson combines her personal experiences trying to be there for her friend through his last months with expert interviews about coping with a friend who is dying of AIDS. She concludes:

> Artie died a month ago, soon after I ended an I-can't-deal-with-it phase and called him. "How are you?" I asked. "Terrible," he said. "I don't feel like talking." "Okay, I'll call you next week,"

I answered. "Love you." "Me you too."

In their fascinating book, *Final Gifts*, hospice nurses Maggie Callanan and Patricia Kelley point out that the stages of bereavement, as described by physician Elisabeth Kubler-Ross and others, that apply to how you react to the death of a friend—shock, denial, disbelief, apathy alternating with anger, bargaining, and resolution—also applies to how the dying, and their friends (and family), deal with their friend's terminal illness and impending death. The advice they share with friends from their first-hand experiences caring for the dying and their family and friends is that *listening* is what those who are dying need most. Interestingly, all the skills that contribute to being a better friend, as discussed throughout this book but especially in Chapter 8 in the section, "What kind of friend are you?" will serve you and your terminally ill friend well at this stressful and emotionally draining time. Unfortunately, as Callanan and Kelley point out in their book, too often friends are in denial about their friend's terminal illness and avoid visiting their friend because they cannot deal with their friend's condition, or they are afraid of saying the wrong thing. If they do visit, they often think it's best to cheer up their friend with such well-meaning but hollow phrases as, "I'm sure you'll get better soon."

These experienced hospice nurses, however, think the dying need understanding and empathy from their friends to approach death peacefully and comfortably. Their discussion of the phenomenon that they observed in the terminally ill, which they call "Nearing Death Awareness," is outside the scope of this book, but the key ideas that apply to friends are that you need to listen to your dying friend's needs and try to be there for your friend, as much as you can manage, emotionally and time-wise. In the section entitled "Talking About Death" they write:

> Show that you're willing to talk, then let the conversation develop. You might begin with a simple comment: "I'm sorry to hear that you're so ill," or "I really feel sad when I think about what's happening to you." Wait for a response. Listen. There is

no one right thing to say, although it's never wrong to speak of
you love and concern.
      Don't worry about saying or doing the "wrong" thing....
      What's often harder to forgive—whether for the dying person
or in one's self—is the failure to do or say anything....

Losing a close or best friend through death results in the same
kind of loneliness and need for emotional support that is experienced
by those who lose any meaningful intimate relationship. Kubler-
Ross's stages, as applied to terminal illness, as noted on the previous
page, will now come into play upon the actual death of a friend.
How long you remain at any stage, such as shock, denial, or apathy
alternating with anger, or even how many stages you go through,
may have more to do with your psychological makeup, as well as
how many other intimate relationships are now available for
support, as it does with the closeness or value of the friendship that
death just ended.

      It is pivotal that others recognize that you are in mourning for
your departed friend, and that you are entitled to feeling grief and
sadness the same as those who lose a spouse, parent, grandparent,
or any other close relative. Friends grieve just like family members
and relatives. As Montaigne wrote in his essay, "Of Friendship,"
about the death of his best friend, Etienne de la Boetie: "There is
no action or thought in which I do not miss him, as indeed he would
have missed me. For just as he surpassed me infinitely in every
other ability and virtue, so he did in the duty of friendship."

      The unexpected death of a friend may result in the "if onlys,"
regrets, and remorse that you lost the chance to tell your friend
how much he or she meant to you. Back in 1977, I clipped from
The New York Times the Private Lives essay by John Leonard
entitled "On Losing a Friend Your Private World Can Least Afford."
Leonard begins by sharing how, in the face of death, he gets
"stupid." He goes on to share details about his late friend Al
Marlens, a 49-year-old fellow writer and friend who died of a heart
attack while playing tennis, a man who, according to Leonard,
shunned formality: "He owned just one tie, which stayed in a drawer
in the desk of his office, waiting for the publisher of this newspaper

to convoke a solemn lunch," whose "admirable sons...decided to bury him without a tie, in the tennis clothes he was wearing when the universe made a criminal mistake." Faced with the loss of his friend, by writing this emotional essay, Leonard concludes, "this time around I would be stupid in public."

I am reminded of the gathering of her daughter's friends organized by the mother of a high school senior who had been senselessly murdered in Central Park by a young boy who stole her bicycle. At that assemblage, which tried to be a celebration of her daughter's life and friendships, music was played and selections of her daughter's diary were read, sharing her intimate feelings in a way that granted her a kind of immortality.

I heard that story almost 20 years ago from that young woman's mother and sister when I was researching a book on crime victims. I hope that over these two decades at least some of those friends have kept in touch with their murdered friend's family. It is important to remember that your late friend's family has lost more than their beloved; they have also lost their beloved's peer group of devoted friends. Those friends will no longer actively be a part of their family's world as well. You might make the effort to reach out to those family members to keep their world from shrinking more than necessary. It might not be right after the funeral or even during the first year after their loss that you reach out; it might be a year or two, or even a decade, down the road. I remember calling the widow of a writer I considered a friend to express my remorse as soon as I belatedly heard that he had died the week before. I asked if she wanted me to stop by or if there was anything I could do to help. She replied expressing this thought, even if not in these words, "Call me in a year, when no one's remembering me anymore. Right now, I'm overwhelmed with visitors and attention." In *Women Make the Best Friends,* Lois Wyse expresses a similar thought when she writes about how friends are the ones that come through in widowhood: "I know that Liz's friends were on call when her husband became ill. Friends were there through the terrible times. And I'm sure she has a houseful now. But the ones who are still there after the last casserole disappears are the stayers; the others are the goers, off to the next event. Staying is what separates acquaintances from friends."

Friends offer each other a kind of immortality as they name their children after a friend or organize a memorial at the time of death, or even a decade or two later. Writing down your feelings about a friend who has died, in a diary for yourself, in a letter to a mutual friend or to their family as a way of sharing those feelings, or for publication, so others may share those thoughts as well, are all ways of granting your friend an immortality and trying to work through the intense emotions and void conjured up by death.

When Someone Close to You or to Your Friend Dies

Another way that death affects a friendship is when someone close to you or to your friend dies—a parent, sibling, grandparent, child, a miscarriage, or even a cherished pet. Does your friend come through for you? Do you come through for your friend? If you are unable to attend the funeral, do you at least phone, visit, or somehow express your sincere condolences? Some may find it hard to share their feelings in such situations, but friends need to get beyond those excuses and be there for each other. Just how important is it to come through for your friends at these times? As a 33-year-old New Jersey woman writes: "I sincerely believe my friends are more dependable than my relatives. I discovered this when my mother died. I felt the support from my friends and sorority sisters at that time."

For me, coming through for a friend when someone he or she loves has died is my definition of a tried-and-true close or best friend. I guess that's why it is not a coincidence that I have only maintained friendships after the age of 20 based on whether or not they attended, or tried to attend, the funeral of my older brother, who died tragically at the age of 23. The stupidest comment I heard at that time was from a former friend who, in explaining why she was not going to go to the funeral, said, "After all, I didn't know your brother."

When someone close to a friend dies, to my mind, you attend the funeral to support the living, and help them feel your support at this trying time. Of course you might also attend the funeral of a friend's loved one because of the relationship you had with the dearly departed, but that is not a necessary condition for your presence.

That lesson served me well over the years; peers, less experienced in these matters, thanked me for steering them in the direction of coming through for their friends in their darkest hour, such as attending the funeral of a friend whose younger sister, who was in her early 20s, was murdered by her ex-husband when he supposedly came by to get the rest of his things, only to shoot her, and then commit suicide. No one knew our friend's sister; but we were all there at the funeral, at least six of us en force, for our friend.

There are numerous ways you might want your friend to be there for you at your time of need. Some friends you might expect, or want, to have at the wake, viewing, or calling hours, attending the funeral, going to the cemetery, or paying a *Shiva* call, if you are Jewish and you are observing the custom of visiting the bereaved to pay a condolence call for as many as seven or as few as three days after the funeral. But since funerals are rarely planned, there may be some friends who live too far away, are away on trips, are ill themselves, or have their own obligations they are unable to put aside, such as a family member's wedding or graduation; or they are emotionally unable to deal with death or funerals.

But before you discount your friend as uncaring or selfish because she or he failed to come through for you by attending, and sharing, in any or all of the customs surrounding a death, consider whether your friend's explanations and apologies are heartfelt or lip service.

In a nutshell, when someone close to your friend dies, this is not the time to wonder how close you are to your friend, or even to their departed loved ones. This is not the time to be pondering, "Do I really *have* to send a card?" "Should I really go to the funeral?" "Should I spend the money on a basket of fruit or flowers?" "Will they really appreciate this donation to charity in the name of their dear departed?" You may want to do one or all of the above to show support for your friend, or something else entirely.

"Well, she's not my <u>best</u> best friend, or a really close friend, but she is a good friend, if not a great friend."

Reprinted with permission of Tom Cheney.

Furthermore, think about each friend in particular: what is his or her background or personality that might make it hard or easy for him or her to come through for you now? When it comes to dealing with death, you have to be careful to "cut your friend some slack" if you really care about your friend. Some friends, because of their own recent losses, or just because it is hard for most everyone to deal with dying and death, may find it impossible to attend a wake or a funeral or go to the cemetery. Those death rituals just may be too much to expect from some friends. It may not be saying anything about your friendship, or you, but about *them*. For instance, I found when my 80-year-old father passed away after two months of a debilitating illness, some friends found it somewhat harder to share my deep grief if both their own parents had died at relatively young ages, in their late 50s to mid-60s, and they had spent the last decade or more without them. For them, my father's relatively long life was a stark contrast to their own early losses. As a close friend in her late 40s shared with me, "My father's been dead 30 years." Or, as another close friend, whose father had died suddenly of a heart attack just two years before, responded when I told her about the funeral scheduled for the next day, "I'm having a hard time with funerals lately."

A few years before, and if not for all the extensive research and thinking I have been doing about friendship, I might have written off any friend who was a "no show" at my father's funeral (unless those friends had really good reasons). Instead, I tried to, and succeeded at, understanding their behavior from their perspective, and to discover other ways they were each showing their support for me based on their own emotional ability at that time. It is, therefore, valuable to ask yourself at these trying times, and afterwards, "Is my friend's absence at the funeral or less-than-sympathetic behavior toward me in this time of need a one-time thing based on circumstances or their inability to deal with death, or is this just another example of a pattern of disappointments that I have to address?" If this is a one-time aberration, not a pattern of selfishness or lack of concern, you might consider attributing their actions to the overwhelming experience of death. In that way, you could keep the fatalities down to just the recently departed; it is probably in your best interest to avoid adding one or more failed friendships to your list of recent losses. (That death is such a seeming "test" on a friendship may be why some people, consciously or unconsciously, do not even tell even their close friends about a parent's death until after the funeral; in that way, their friends could not have attended the funeral since they did not know about it. Then, whether it is true or not, everyone can believe it when they say, "Oh, I would have gone to the funeral if you had only told me in time.")

In addition, during the initial shock of a loved one's death, and the acute bereavement period, you may want to avoid a definitive decision about who is and is not your friend. Certainly keep track of what friends say or do, but postpone any "crossing the line" or "trigger" incidents or comments until your life returns to a more normal state and you can put everything into perspective.

Rather than shut out any friends who, even if you told them in time, failed to show up at your parent's or loved one's funeral, as hard as it is at your time of grief and sadness, try to think about where they are coming from; what's behind their behavior. Try not to take it personally; as long as you know they would have liked to have been there but emotional or practical forces stopped them, in time you will figure out if this is, indeed, a tried-and-true genuine friendship or a phony one. For now, give your friend the benefit of the doubt. Consider what other ways they are able to show that you, and your friendship, matter to them. It could be as Herculean as attending a funeral, even though you live on the opposite side of the country, or something as simple as sending a card or making a phone call; other ways are sending a meal for the bereaved to eat during the mourning period, donating to a favorite charity, planting a tree in the deceased's memory, writing a poem, visiting after the funeral, sending a plant, flowers, or a basket of fruit, or offering to help address the thank-you notes for the expressions of sympathy.

Therefore, the key to being there for your friends through the death of someone beloved, and the key to them being there for you when you are in need, is denoting that you care, even more than exactly how you show it.

Instead of becoming vindictive because someone disappointed you, consider that they probably missed out more by failing to attend the funeral of your loved one than you lost by their absence, especially if it was an uplifting service, as my father's was, that allowed those present to find some peace and closure in their feelings.

However, just in case you wonder if you should attend a funeral because you doubt having one more person makes a difference, I will share this anecdote: I counted up the number of entries in the sign-in book for my father's funeral. I told my mother that I counted 50 entries, so there were at least 50 people present. The next day, she corrected me, pointing out that she had looked over the book and counted at least 67, if you added up those who attended together.

A phone call, phone message, card, or note can go a long way in demonstrating you care. Phone calls or messages should be brief and to the point unless your bereaved friend wants to talk longer. Try to avoid asking for extensive details about the death, unless they are volunteered. Then, be prepared to listen to your friend as long as necessary. If needed, in advance of your call, rehearse saying something that you would like someone to say to you if the positions were reversed; avoid platitudes, hollow comments, or downright offensive or negative opinions. Try to call at a time you think will be best for your friend; not too early in the morning, or too late at night. Since exhaustion and numbness are common reactions to death, do not take it personally if your friend is unable to talk for very long, or even to talk at all (and another friend or family member is answering the phone and taking messages on their behalf).

Cards or notes, in addition to a phone call, or as the only expression of sympathy, do not have to be long or elaborate, but it should be sent as promptly after you hear the news as possible.

By the same token, the bereaved have to take the time after a reasonable period of grieving—after a minimum of about 30 days—to thank those who express their sympathy, whatever form it takes.

How you show support will depend on a great many factors, but three principles to remember are:

- Do *something* to show your support for your friend.
- Don't ignore the situation.
- Try to think about your friend's needs, acknowledging the situation, even saying directly, "I'm sorry for your loss," and asking, "What can I do to help?"

Coming through for others when they are going through the terminal illness or death of a loved one may not guarantee you are, or will become, better friends, but *failing* to come through may stop that relationship in its tracks.

*

In Part 4, Work and Friendship, you will see that the rules are somewhat different for friendships that start or are maintained at work or in your professional career.

PART 4

WORK AND FRIENDSHIP

Genuine friendship develops not because we think there will be a benefit from it but because of an almost tangible feeling of connection that recognizes an affinity between two people. Friendship's built on mutual interest. Built on personality. Built on common experience. That is why friendships can develop in the workplace very nicely. We have a lot of common experience.

—Nella Barkley, president, Crystal/Barkley Corporation

Primarily all of the six men and women who work for me are good friends. Working with friends adds a whole new dimension of loyalty, commitment, and purpose. In the beginning, they were casual friends, but they have become close friends over the years. It's a lot of years, twelve years. As an aside, you don't know how artificial these friendships are till they no longer work for you.

—Abbie Wilson, multimedia producer

11. HOW FRIENDSHIP ENHANCES YOUR CAREER

People get promoted as much with the approval of the people they work *with* as the people who are their bosses.
— Harold Burson, Chairman,
Burson-Marsteller public relations

In May 1994, when Ogilvy & Mather managed to acquire IBM's multimillion-dollar advertising account, the main reason was the friendships that 46-year-old Rochelle Lazarus had built up over 20 years, according to Laura Bird's article in *The Wall Street Journal.* Bird writes: "For all the crowing about Ogilvy & Mather's global network and advertising prowess, it was largely the quiet efforts of Rochelle Lazarus, president of the agency's North American operations, that helped Ogilvy reel in International Business Machines Corp.'s $400 million-plus advertising account."

Over and over again in the dozens of interviews I did with

executives, entrepreneurs, small business owners, outplacement and human resource professionals, and freelancers in a wide range of industries and company settings, what I heard is how vital friends—casual ones are safest, but carefully managed close or best ones will help—at work and in a profession are in providing a sounding board, and emotional support, giving valuable feedback on performance, sharing information on the inner workings of a company or field, increasing productivity, or even helping get a foot in the door in the first place. Furthermore, approval from friends is a fundamental source of work-related satisfaction.

Success in many careers is based on relationship building, and nothing builds a trusting relationship faster than the elusive and magical relationship known as friendship.

Relied upon and used, not misused, wisely and properly, friendship helps you enjoy your work more; it is also a relationship that may help you succeed faster. J. Oliver Crom, president of Dale Carnegie & Associates, Inc., a corporation with offices in every major American city, Canada, and 70 foreign countries that teaches Dale Carnegie's principles of making friends first advanced in 1936, points out that today it is more important than ever before to work on relationship-building skills in the workplace. Says Crom: "People do not want to be sold a product or a service. They want to deal with people who they think have their interests or who care about them."

Practically everyone would agree that friends are vital during the formative and school years, but there is little known about friendship at work and in the business world, or how friends contribute to a successful career. Part of the reason is what career consultant Nella Barkley calls the "leftover attitude that you should not mix your personal life with your professional life."

Another explanation is that workplace friendships have been less accessible to college-based researchers. To help fill that void, I conducted a study of human resource professionals randomly selected from the database of the Society of Human Resource

Management. I conducted two surveys; 257 men and women responded (140 women, 117 men). The response rates for the two surveys were 29% and 27%, respectively, an excellent response on a mail questionnaire. A wide range of companies and industries were represented in the sample, from hospitals and blood banks to insurance agencies and manufacturing companies ranging in size from a one-person consulting firm to a bank with 8,000 employees in Sioux City, Iowa, or the Kansas City office of an airline with 30,000 workers. In addition to tabulating those 257 friendship and work surveys, I did follow-up telephone interviews lasting 15 minutes to one hour with two dozen men and women from the sample. I also conducted three dozen additional interviews with workers, executives, outplacement experts, and psychologists, in a variety of business settings.

Some professions and jobs have to be more careful about keeping friendship officially out of the workplace to avoid any accusations of influence peddling. Those occupations include civil service jobs; school systems, where job openings and advancement are supposed to be based solely on merit and not favoritism; and the health care professions, where treating everyone the same is one of the ideals of medicine. Human resource professionals also have to be especially careful about workplace friendships since they are privy to confidential information as well as having hiring and firing job functions.

But is friendship *completely* kept out of those settings? Busy doctors may find openings in their filled schedule if a friend has an immediate problem; failing to make the right friends in your department at a college, or with key administrators, may block an assistant professor's advancement. A 57-year-old manager of employee relations at a research and development company in Jacksonville, for example, has 10 close and 20 casual friends at work. His closest friend at work "affords me a sounding board and provides me advice." That friendship hasn't been at all detrimental to his work. By contrast, an employment/training manager at a bank in Chevy Chase, Maryland, writes: "I am well-known throughout the organization, but my friendships are not business-related.

Although I participate in company-sponsored activities, I do not feel a need to look for friendships through work."

When workplace friendships are positive, it can make the workplace and the work better. Workplace friendships make work more fun; they enhance creativity. As Nella Barkley, author, with Eric Sandburg, of *The Crystal-Barkley Guide to Taking Charge of Your Career*, says:

> Last night, two key people and I got together for a bit of dinner while we worked over some brochure copy and a design for the brochure. We were in the restaurant three hours. A waiter came up to us and said, "You look like you're having so much fun, what are you doing?" Over dinner, we got an innovative brochure design. We succeeded in attracting the waiter's attention because we were having so much fun. Creativity flows when you can laugh a little together, spin off each other's ideas, and relax.

But some are afraid to admit that friends play a factor in their professional success; they fear people will think they got where they are just because of their friends, not their talents. Yet in reality, *both* talent and friends are usually needed.

FRIENDS HELP YOU GET JOBS

Just how important are friends in helping someone get a job? Out of the 126 human resource managers in my second survey who answered that question, a whopping 37% got their current job through someone they knew, with the largest category being through their friends or a friend of the family (25%). (Only 3 persons out of 126 got their current job by directly contacting a company.) The second most common way of getting a current job, after friends, was through a newspaper advertisement (24%) followed by an employment agency or headhunter (23%).

One of the reasons so many current jobs are obtained through friends is that companies may encourage job referrals through a networking system. (Nineteen percent wrote that their company has a policy of hiring the friends of employees.) This may help explain why so many jobs never even get to the executive recruiters or newspaper advertisements: friends are recommending friends.

Marie Raperto, president of The Cantor Concern, Inc., in Manhattan, a search firm that specializes in public relations and corporate communications jobs, confirms that more jobs are found through networking—contacting friends and who you know—than any other way. "I think it's a good idea to call friends if you're looking for a job," says Raperto, who has been in the corporate public relations field for more than 16 years. "Any number of job candidates have gone to friends and gotten hired," she adds with conviction.

Larry F. Ginsberg, an attorney practicing in Stamford, Connecticut, typifies the way friendship helps land jobs. Ginsberg says: "We have two very good friends, and they wanted to do wills. They asked me point blank if I'd feel comfortable representing them in a will scenario." Ginsberg said yes, just one of the numerous examples he could point to of how friendship actually translated into business over the more than 18 years he has been practicing law.

Of course you could get your foot in the door, or obtain new clients, without the help of a friend, but a friend certainly greases the way, quickly giving you access to the "inner track" in most situations.

Quite often literary agents want to consider new clients who are recommended to them by other writers or editors. What writer or editor is going to take the time to read a manuscript before he or she has an agent applauding it? A friend. That same friend is the one most likely to provide the necessary referral, and endorsement, for the next step to occur.

"If your agent can't get you in, sometimes a friend will get you in," explains MaryAnne Kasica, a screenwriter who lives in Los Angeles and grew up in Pasaic, New Jersey. "You don't get the job because you know the friend," MaryAnne continues, but you can get "in" because you have a friend. "It's the same as with agents. Agents don't get you jobs. They open the doors. You need someone to unlock the door. The friendship opens the door. What happens once you walk in the door is totally up to you."

The late screenwriter Carl Sautter told me how the editor for a TV series would give out assignments to those friends that he developed during his early years of struggle, when they would all get together for once-a-week meetings to read and critique each others' writing. In addition to hiring each other for actual job openings, they would tell each other the inside scoop on prospective employers.

How important *who you know* is for finding a new job—over all other methods—is confirmed by interviews with executive recruiters, and job seekers, as well as a survey of 351 job hunters polled by placement firm Manchester, Inc., as reported by Albert R. Karr in *The Wall Street Journal.* Of those 351 who were looking for a job, 60% found it through someone they knew—friends, former colleagues, and others in their field. (Only 17% used an employment agency, and only 15% answered or placed a newspaper advertisement.)

"Networking is one step in a business environment that can lead to new friendships," says Irene Cohen, founder of Manhattan-based Cohen Personnel Services. Cohen continues: "It's a way of outreaching away from your immediate environment, which could be very stifling, or you could have changed and you need to grow. It's beginning to meet new people and be exposed to other kinds of cultures. First of all, they have something in common, which makes it a heck of a lot easier to talk."

Friends are a paramount way of finding a first job: in my survey, 24% found their first job through someone they knew, such as through the job candidate's own friend or a friend of the family. For example, the 54-year-old male vice president of human resources for a manufacturing company based in Jersey City, New Jersey, found his first job through a family friend. A 38-year-old female personnel manager of an insurance company in Davenport, Iowa, also found her first job through a family friend. The next most common ways of finding a first job were through newspaper advertisements (21%), college-related services or teachers (20%), and employment agencies (14%), with 12% using their own initiative by knocking on doors, doing mailings to a professional association membership, or directly contacting the company.

"How did you get your job?" I asked a young man soon after he graduated from a college in Washington, D.C.

"A friend's mother told me about the job," he replied.

"Make a friend" is the phrase human resources and executive search consultant John Artise says they used to use when he was a vice president at outplacement firm Drake Beam Morin, Inc. It referred to "going out and building a nurturing relationship with a potential client," says John Artise, who is now a consultant with New York-based Arbor Group, a human resources management consulting and training firm. Artise continues: "You're more likely to be hired as a casual friend to someone. Even more likely than a close friend, where there may be a lot of problems." Artise provides the example of an executive who stayed in a job way too long—14 years—even though he was really wrong for the position, because he and the chief financial officer had been close friends since their school days. When the friend became company president and evaluated his old friend's performance, he realized he had to fire him. But it took him several years to do that; he confided to Artise that if not for their close friendship, he would have fired his friend years before.

Health writer Mark Fuerst explains how a friend opened the door to his first freelance assignment:

In 1976, when I was a young staff writer at *Medical World News,* one of my colleagues, who was a friend, Lois, had gotten an assignment from *Harper's Bazaar* to write an article about eye care. She had done a similar story the year before and she decided she didn't want to do it again. She suggested my name to the editor instead, and I got the assignment. I liked writing it so much that I continued doing freelance assignments on the side for consumers while I continued writing news stories on staff for doctors. I'm thankful for Lois. She was a friend who became one of my best friends. Lois and I are still friends.

Although my research and observations confirm that friends do help friends to get jobs, there are some whose professional experience is contradictory to that conclusion. Executive recruiter David Werner of David Werner International, a firm that deals with searches for only the top-level jobs, says, "It's a myth to think friends can help you in business. The higher the level you are, the less likely you are to find a friend to employ you. Things are so competitive, they don't want to take the risk, in case it backfires."

BEFRIENDING UP, DOWN, AND ALL AROUND

"One of my best friends is someone I originally met in the workplace," says the director of resource development at a software manufacturing company in Cheyenne. She continues: "When you spend eight hours a day somewhere, it's real easy to develop real close friendships." Married, and in her early 30s, she maintains a best friendship with her former co-worker, speaking with her two or three times a week, even though they now have jobs at different companies and live an hour away from each other.

Same-level friendships are safest and easiest to maintain. By being at the same level, you eliminate the potential problems that may occur if one friend has to supervise, criticize, critique, or evaluate the other.

However, even though work or business friendships between equals are easier to maintain and potentially less complicated, they are also less useful to your move up the ladder of your career. If you befriend up, it might be more helpful, but also riskier. It is harder to maintain friendships of unequal status or levels—a manager and a subordinate rather than two co-workers—because of the disparity in status and the potential for supervisory problems. Yet the friendships between a higher-up and an underling provide the greatest opportunity for learning and growth in a company or in a profession. As Charles Peebler, President and CEO of Bozell Jacobs Kenyon & Eckhardt, the parent company for Bozell Worldwide Inc., an advertising company, says: "Certainly befriend at other levels than your own as long as you realize that you have a job to do and I have a job to do, and I will do my job, and I expect you to do your job. That means we do all the things that are required. There has to be some compartmentalization. I'm a person, but I'm also the CEO of a company."

Business executive and business owner Irene Cohen provides these insights into how your level impacts on the potential benefits and pitfalls of friendships at work:

> Friendship can help if it's with a superior who has control over your destiny. It can also backfire, as with any relationship, if you push it too far, or something goes wrong and there's a miscommunication. You've not only jeopardized the friendship, you've jeopardized your income. I really think you deal with friendships in business in keeping with your own personality. If you are the kind of person who keeps friends a long time and you are a good listener, it's probably safer to establish friendships [at work]. But for most people, it's extremely difficult and extremely risky. Not terribly risky with your peers, but terribly risky with your superiors.

What level you are at in a company may even determine how easy it is for you to have friends at work. A personnel manager in Tennessee points out that it is probably easier to have friendships if you are not that high up in an organization: "You are less threatening to other people. There is less friction, and you are more likely to be social in the work environment, truly social."

Thomas Horton, Ph.D., former president of the American Management Association, concurs that friendship aids the workplace. Says Horton: "My own feeling is that friendship is important. It's important to have a friendly, warm, open relationship at work. You can try not to restrict that to your organizational peers, but have friends above and below your organizational line. The sort of chit-chat that goes on is important to developing a feeling of teamwork."

However Harold Burson, chairman of public relations giant Burson-Marsteller, supports the "it's lonely at the top" perspective when he says, "I think it's a lot easier to be very socially active at lower levels of the company than at the upper levels. One of the prices that you pay for being a CEO in a company is you give up a lot of the social relationships within the company. There's a line beyond which you cannot go."

Yet those in the middle, and on the way up, also have to watch their friendships. Befriending someone below you may give out the wrong message to upper management; you project the image of someone more comfortable befriending those with less power. Carefully befriending up may help get you to where you want to go. By befriending someone above you, you can learn about the job responsibilities and challenges at that higher level, giving you an insider's view to the next step in your career. The female vice president and director of human resources at a bank in Cleveland, Ohio, has found that close friendship with another higher-up woman in a different department is beneficial at work. She says: "It has allowed me to understand the culture of the company that acquired us." The friendship is based on mutual respect, liking each other, shared values, and emotional support. She continues, "Work friendships provide an outlet to complain in a safe atmosphere with people who can empathize."

Outplacement consultant Laurence J. Stybel, of Stybel Peabody Lincolnshire in Boston, cautions how befriending two levels up, over your boss's head, could cause trouble with your boss. He relates this anecdote about a client whose problems were caused by such a friendship dynamic: Joe is the marketing director. Bill, who is vice president of marketing, is Joe's boss. Harry, a marketing specialist, is new; his immediate boss is Joe. Harry and Joe do not hit it off, but Harry and Bill, who is two levels above Harry, become friends. As Stybel explains, "Joe sees Harry going into the vice president's office. He shuts the door. He hears laughter. He is taking him under his wing."

Joe finds himself fenced in by a boss and a new employee who are now friends. He "waits for Harry to make a mistake and he fires him," Stybel continues. There is nothing the vice president can do for his fired friend because of the pecking order and culture in that organization. "Pick your friends wisely and understand the politics," Stybel concludes.

A public affairs vice president echoes the cautionary note about befriending up or down when she says, "Let's say a subordinate is a friend. This may cause problems because they probably feel they can take advantage of the situation. 'I can come in a little bit late because she's my friend.'"

By the same token, being discreet is essential with all types of work friendships; avoid discussing intimate concerns at work or revealing confidential information about each other or your family or friends, even in the less-than-private lunchroom or bathroom settings. Not only is it poor business protocol, it could put you or your friend's standing at the firm in jeopardy. Furthermore, it could create ill feeling among peers or other workers who perceive there is favoritism or influence peddling going on.

Furthermore, be careful not to inadvertently misuse the information you are privy to because of your friendship: if you notice your friend/worker is falling asleep at a departmental meeting, avoid disclosing that he was out late last night with you and your other friends if he has been telling everyone that he was up late working on that report that was due today.

It is also important to be careful that your friendship comes first, or you just might be accused of being manipulative and opportunistic. It is a delicate balance: you have to be helped because you are a deserving person who just happens to also be a friend. You cannot ask someone you are *trying* to befriend to do something for you, or your would-be friend might feel used and never become a friend.

Whatever their level, be careful to avoid misusing work friendships. That is what happened to Milton, a middle manager in the health benefits department. When his friend lost her executive secretary job, Milton gladly gave her several short-term assignments. But as the weeks wore on, Milton began to feel used. Just as he was about to say something, she surprised him by demanding that he put in for unemployment insurance for her, something that was not part of the original bargain. Her request put Milton's job in jeopardy, since he failed to go through official channels to hire her. Milton's friend then sued a betrayed Milton and his company, straining their friendship beyond repair.

"According to my resume, you're my best friend... could you elaborate on that?"

Reprinted with permission of Tom Cheney.

Some work environments may be more conducive to friendship than others. For example, real estate agents, who are usually in direct competition with each other, may find it hard to become friends with other agents within the same company or even the same community. To avoid potential problems—competition, indiscretions over privileged information—the president of a consulting firm belongs to a professional organization in New Jersey rather than Philadelphia, where she lives and works. In that way, she feels freer to befriend the women she meets, who are less likely to have regular business contact with her.

FRIENDSHIP AND PRODUCTIVITY

Befriending customers or clients may make it easier and more pleasant for you to do your work and for you to be a success.

Casual Friendship Goes Far at Work

Most agree the ideal type of friendship at work is that of a *casual* friend. It is easier to keep a clear business head when the friendship is only a casual one; the stakes in maintaining it are smaller than for a close or best friendship.

The valuable contributions that casual friends make in the workplace include aiding productivity, fostering a greater sense of teamwork, providing a sounding board, and helping workers feel they are part of a corporate "family."

Casual friends—what outplacement executive Laurence J. Stybel refers to as "chums"—may help you get your job done. As the personnel director at a university in Missouri explains: "I develop casual friendships on the job that help me accomplish goals and utilize the formal organization. It also helps me avoid organization errors. I have survived long service in a highly visible and sensitive position because of awareness of trends in this large organization, and keeping on good terms with all segments of the university. I avoid intrigue and organizational alliances. I try to encourage service and professionalism." He has casual friends at work; close friends are outside of his job. In that way, he has "maintained a reputation for fairness and impartiality."

"People work harder when they feel they're part of a family," writes a divorced executive secretary for a Georgia-based cruise line. "They build on each other's strengths and learn from each other. When you feel like people care about you as an individual, you go out of your way for them." Negatives of having friends at work? She continues: "The only time I see friendships at work being a problem is if the socializing gets out of hand. But I think a mature person would recognize that to be detrimental to getting your job done and would use common sense about it." She should know the importance of friends at work: she is presently working for the friend of a friend.

A 36-year-old single personnel manager endorses work friendships: "Friendships make work more rewarding and enjoyable although friendships at work must be carefully chosen. Problems arise when the friendship aspect overrides professionalism, especially if there is a breach of confidence."

Lucy Hedrick, a Connecticut book author who now works full time as a writer at a consulting firm, is an exception to the "casual is better" rule in that she successfully maintains a close friendship with her literary agent, whom she has known since 1986, that has not interfered with their agent/author working relationship. How? Lucy has always followed a strict protocol about keeping their close friendship and work issues separate. For example, over the years, if she and her agent were at a social dinner party together, if Lucy had a business question she needed answered, she would bring it up privately, perhaps in the kitchen, out of the earshot of other guests "so it didn't occupy dinner table conversation."

For those who are self-employed or who have a succession of jobs, such as independent consultants, actors, artists, writers, or temporary workers, all types of friends—best, close, or casual—who applaud your accomplishments can provide much-needed peer support, recognition, and relationship continuity. As Jane Condon, a 38-year-old Greenwich, Connecticut, stand-up comedian and former journalist says about her best friends:

> I've had these two writer friends since college who are still my best friends. One lives in Soho. The other lives in Sag Harbor on Long Island. So there is a bit of distance. [But] we always stay in touch. The one in New York came to Japan to visit when I lived there for five years. We have this wonderful little custom: when one of us accomplishes something professionally, we have a celebration. We go out to dinner at a fancy restaurant in Manhattan. We are just each other's biggest fans. We're always happy when one of us accomplishes something.

Cliques

Just as casual friends, or a carefully maintained close or best one, may enhance the workplace or a career, cliques may lower productivity and, hence, be destructive in the workplace. In my second survey of 129 human resource professionals, almost half (46%) wrote that cliques were a problem at work:

- Cliques lead to favoritism, which creates morale problems.
- Negative employees are drawn to other negative people.
- Cliques sometimes perceive a problem where none exists, making rumors proliferate without foundation.
- Cliques cause excessive socialization at work, which causes resentment by those outside the clique.
- There may be an unwillingness to share information with those outside the clique.
- New employees may feel like outsiders if there are cliques.
- Managers and subordinates may get too close because of being in the same clique, so that productivity suffers.
- Clique members may receive preferential treatment, causing disharmony and jealousy.
- Cliques can be a powerful negative force that makes implementing new policies very difficult.

Work and Friendship Protocol

Here are some guidelines so friendship aids rather than hinders your workplace environment or career advancement:

1. Keep friendship and work separate as much as possible.
2. Be discreet about your friend's confidences.
3. If you feel your friendship puts you or your friend in a compromised position, discuss it and, if necessary, withdraw from any situations that might involve a conflict of interest.
4. Avoid gossip at work, especially if it involves information you are privileged to know because of your friendship.
5. Be aware of your company's policy about friendship; some

companies have a pro- or an antifraternization policy about friendships at work or with clients or customers. As long as you follow those rules, friendship and work can co-exist. As J. Douglas Phillips, Executive Director of Strategic Planning at Merck & Company, Inc., in New Jersey, says, "I haven't seen friendship at work as a problem."

6. If a friend at work asks you a question that oversteps appropriate privacy lines, refuse to answer, getting out of it as gracefully as possible: change the subject, say you're still making up your mind, suddenly have to place a phone call, go to a meeting, or say directly, "You know I'm not at liberty to discuss that."

7. As CEO Charles Peebler points out, do not misuse a business-related friendship for "leverage."

8. At work, be careful that your body language, voice, or language is not too familiar when talking to your friend.

9. Avoid name-dropping or bragging about your friendships at work or in your profession. It will probably backfire as you appear more opportunist than well connected.

*

The next chapter, Male and Female Work Friendships, explores, among other issues, the finding from this author's Society of Human Resource Management survey of 257 randomly selected members that men had twice as many friends at work as women in comparable positions.

12. MALE AND FEMALE WORK FRIENDSHIPS

Coworker friendships help job satisfaction, teamwork, and productivity.
> —male vice president at a Massachusetts bank, married, age 42

Friendships have no place in business.
> —female personnel manager at a Massachusetts distribution company, single, age 57

According to my survey of 257 human resource managers, on average, women had fewer friends at work and fewer at a higher level than men in comparable jobs. Men had twice as many close, casual, or best friends at work as did the women. I also asked on what they primarily based their closest work friendship. For the men, *shared interests* was the most common reason for establishing their current closest work friendship, followed by *shared values* and *liking each other*. For the women, *emotional support* was the most frequent reason for establishing their closest work friendship, followed by *shared interests.*

What this information about the primary bases for the current closest friendship at work may be telling us is that although men have twice as many work friendships, they are basing those friendships on different criteria. As you know, men define *friend* differently from women and have disparate expectations for friendships. It is possible that women are adhering to the more traditional female view of friendship as a relationship based on confidence sharing whereas men perceive it as a more activity-oriented and friendly exchange.

It is my thesis that women will go further in the workplace when they redefine work and business friendships as something more akin to "hail-fellow-well-met" and friendliness and less like the intimate, gut-spilling, preconceived Great Friend Approach of bygone days. In that way, women could reap the same benefits of work friendships that men attribute to these ties, namely having a sounding board, improved work relationships, and a source of advice and feedback on performance and image.

WORK FRIENDSHIP PATTERNS BY GENDER

As noted in the last chapter, casual friends enhance productivity at work. In my survey, in comparable executive human resource positions, men had 22 casual friends at the office, on average, while women had only 12.

I also asked the men and women in my survey to tell me about the status of their closest friend at work: over half the men (51%) befriended someone at their *same* level at work; only 25% had a closest friend at a *lower* status.

By contrast, 38% of the women had a closest friend at the *same* level; but 48% had a closest friend at work whose status was *lower*.

This is also a key finding, since you know you are judged by the company you keep. By befriending below themselves, women are unwittingly putting themselves in the position of being perceived as less powerful at work.

There was little difference by gender when it came to having a closest friend at work who was a boss; few men or women (3 women and 4 men out of 257 respondents) wrote that their closest work friend was also their boss.

As psychologist, president of the North Carolina-based Center for Creative Leadership, and outplacement expert Robert J. Lee, formerly of Lee Hecht Harrison in Manhattan, points out, it is the "safety of the company climate" that will encourage, or discourage, women from having friends at work. Says Lee:

> In environments that are more androgynous, that are friendlier to women, it's easier for women to have friends. In places which are more hostile or chilly environments, it remains easy for men to have friends, but it becomes increasingly difficult for women to have friends because women are competing with each other for just a few spaces. More successful women don't want to be identified with lower-level women. They also don't want to be burdened with the mentor responsibility. In a receptive environment, women are able to have friends more readily. Secondly, it's a generational issue. Younger women are better able to have friends at work than older women. Younger women expect that they should be able to live lives as human beings and not be constrained in artificial ways to the extent that the former generation was trained to do.

Over and over again, the women in my survey wrote comments like this: "I strive to keep my professional life separate from my personal life" or "I keep personal and work relationships separate."

The 40-year-old female director of human resources at an Arizona-based health care organization writes: "I am very cautious about establishing close friendships at work due to the confidential nature of much of my work....I have often felt a sense of regret at not getting to know someone better at the time of the employee's exit interview!"

A 43-year-old female vice president of finance at a company with 12,000 employees writes: "Because I work in human resources and am the only woman on the senior management team in my affiliate, it is difficult for me to engage in real friendships at work."

By contrast, listen to the men's comments:

"Friends are essential at work," says a 32-year-old male manager of employee relations at a manufacturing company in New Jersey. "You spend 40 to 50% of your waking hours at work with peers. To deny yourself friendships at work based upon a professional code of distance is to have a rather barren life."

"In the helping professions, friendships at work are as essential to success as emotional support and recharging," writes a 52-year-old male president of a consulting firm in Virginia.

Outplacement executive Lee's comments about how the atmosphere at work relates to a woman's ease at having work-related friendships brings up the issue of trust, a basic ingredient in a friendship. In order to have friends, workers must feel that they can trust others. Whether or not someone feels those at work are trustworthy enough to be friends may say as much about the personality and characteristics of that worker as it does about the work situation. As W. Michael Humbert, personnel manager of a school district in the South, told me: "As time goes by, workplaces in general become more nontrusting. I see people as more self-centered and less and less focused on any global principles. There are two people [at work] that I feel I have enough confidence in to label them casual friends. It would be better if I could have more. My method of operating is just not to trust anyone."

As noted before, trust is a basic ingredient in all types of friendship.

As women, particularly working women in executive positions, or men feel they have too much to lose to have friends at work, friendships from past work relationships or from outside of work or business, or a relationship with a marriage partner or a therapist, are becoming more significant as the close or best "friend" with whom work-related confidences can be shared.

Some working women, however, are learning to consider a casual nonconfessional friendship at work as still friendship. As Atlanta-based saleswoman Marsha Londe puts it, "You don't have to spill your guts to be friends."

Can Mentors Be Friends?

Another interesting finding of my survey is that out of 257 companies, only 13% had a formal mentoring program. Mentor programs are ways to help train people to more easily go up the ladder. It is also a possible source of casual, close, or best work friendships, since two of the vital ingredients for a future friendship, access and spending time together, are part of the mentoring relationship.

Actress and businesswoman Polly Bergen says this about mentors: "I never had a single mentor when I formed my cosmetic company. I picked every expert's brains I could, so you could say I had hundreds of mentors."

Most would agree that mentors are pivotal for the fast-track career advancement path at a company or in a profession: professor and doctoral student; well-known producer or director and up-and-coming screenwriter; literary agent and unpublished author; rising young executive guided by a mentor a few decades older.

Sociologist and mentor expert Michael G. Zey, author of *The Mentor Connection*, says that mentoring programs are no longer just targeting women or members of minority groups for participation. However, in practice those are the groups that are most likely to benefit from formal mentoring programs. That is because white males are already in the "social network loops"—the informal mentoring situations— that would help them advance.

Does friendship help the mentor process? Can mentors be friends? Zey offers these comments:

> Friendship is based on chemistry between two people. Although people think that friendship is important for mentoring to be successful, in reality a mentor relationship works because both partners feel they are receiving mutual benefits from the relationship. It doesn't have to be as close as friendship. While it is nice to like your mentor, mentoring is really a hierarchical relationship. There is an imbalance of power—the mentor has

the knowledge and the protégé learns from the mentor. So even if the protégé is friendly with the mentor, he or she still shows a certain level of deference and respect, even *awe*. Because the protégé is never the mentor's equal, the mentor relationship is always one step removed from friendship.

However, Zey has seen some examples of mentoring that led to friendship, such as one married woman who now double dates outside of work with her mentor and his spouse.

Career consultant Nella Barkley notes, "It's complicated to allow a mentor to become a friend, although this is very appropriate in a great number of instances to the extent that you share common interests in addition to your business interests, and mutual interests are the basis of the friendship."

This is also complicated by the man-woman issue. "A number of men mentors have become lovers for the women they mentored," says Barkley. "It is very dangerous to allow that to happen."

WHEN WORK FRIENDSHIP BECOMES ROMANCE

"I met, became friends with, and plan to marry a wonderful man I met at work," explains the personnel manager at a Seattle-based manufacturing firm. "Our company has a policy that husband/wife or girlfriend/boyfriend cannot work together if one is supervisor of the other. [But] we work in different departments so there is no conflict of interest," she adds.

A 1995 survey of member companies by the Society of Human Resource Management, reported by Lisa Genasci of the Associated Press, found that 70% permitted dating within the company, 83% employed married couples, and only 1.5% were opposed to dating or married couples at the company.

Whether friendship at work turns into romance is a positive or a detriment will depend upon numerous factors, such as how well each person can handle the emotions that the romance brings up, as well as whether or not it is an appropriate situation—for example, two single unattached people who are not in supervisory situations. Obviously if the friendship-turned-romance is an illicit affair—one or both parties is married—this may also be a consideration.

A 58-year-old assistant vice president at a Detroit hospital has seen both extremes of a positive and a negative situation when it comes to friendship that turns into romance at work There is a married couple who started out as friends who have stayed on in their respective jobs after marrying, and there are no problems in that situation. But there have also been several incidents of violence in the workplace where friendship turned to romance, and then went sour. A human resources director at an Ohio manufacturing company seems to reinforce the keep-love-and-work-separate rule by saying, "You don't get your honey where you get your money."

But if you decide to continue working after a friendship has become a romance, keep in mind these protocol guidelines:

- Avoid acting like love sick puppies when you are at work, including such obvious romantic gestures as staring into each other's eyes, hand holding, or kissing.
- Avoid calling each other by such demonstrative terms as "honey," "deary," "sweetie," "sweetheart," or a special, intimate nickname you may have for each other.
- Especially if you are at different levels within the company, avoid drawing attention to your romantic relationship to reduce the likelihood of any bad feelings developing because of perceived favoritism.
- Be careful not to let your romance affect your productivity. The managers I interviewed seemed most concerned that a developing romance should not compete for a worker's attention.
- Work friendship that turns to romance implies a risk; if the relationship ends, and being around each other is too stressful for the ex-couple or those around them, someone may have to consider leaving.

OLD BOY NETWORK MEETS NEW GIRL NETWORK

Consider how significant it is that men keep their surname for life, and how that facilitates an old boys' network. Since they always (except for stage names) have the same last name, a man could call a telephone operator anywhere in the world or, traveling through a town, glance at the local directory and search for an old friend from bygone school or work days. Because their name is the same, at least on a practical level, it is easier for men to keep track of and, therefore, maintain friendships throughout their lives.

Women, by contrast, if they change their name when they marry, vanish from their potential old girls' network, or at least are harder to find. (What about starting a centralized roster of married and maiden names that would not reveal any other private information, just the name changes? Think of how quickly women's professional networks and personal friendships would expand.)

Aware of how crucial friends are for succeeding in business, women have been forming a "new girl club" of their own rather than putting all their energy into breaking into the old boy network. In the late '70s, for example, Muriel Fox, an advertising executive, co-founded The Women's Forum of New York, an elite membership organization open to new women by invitation only that offers the networking opportunities that men have always had available to them through their exclusive clubs and executive dining rooms and on the golf courses. Similar businesswomen-only groups have formed since that time in major cities and states throughout the United States including Los Angeles, Pittsburgh, and Philadelphia. All the groups establish some criteria for membership, such as a certain minimum level of annual earnings.

Some women, however, have found the organizational route to networking and friendships in the workplace does not suit their personality. Those women, like men who are not "joiners," prefer to build their careers and their friendships one by one and one on one. For example, Cynthia Wicker Williams, a "40-something" Stamford-based attorney with a civil practice, belongs to the local and state bar associations, but otherwise shies away from membership in organizations. Although Williams thinks organizations can be effective for others, she deals better one on one. Williams explains: "It's more effective, more in line with my personality. I deal better one on one." She prefers a business lunch with just one other person, or getting to know someone by phone if she does not have time for lunch.

Friendships have certainly emerged out of Williams's networking activities. Echoing the time constraints on most married working mothers with school-age children, she explains:

> Who in my group really has time for a lot of friends? I go to work. Go home. Take care of my kids. If not for business networking, that's really the only opportunity I have to make friends. Yes, I have made personal friends through business networking. The answer is, yes, yes, yes. I've met some very nice people. I have certainly met women whom I like personally. We follow up after business meetings with personal gatherings. We get our families together.

Williams, a solo practitioner, has to create opportunities for friendships that are often readily available when you work for a larger company. For instance, when Rhonda Ginsberg was manager of financial, employee benefits, and marketing systems at the corporate headquarters of Waldenbooks, she became part of a girls' network within her company. Ginsberg explains:

> It was needed because there was an old boys' network. It had a lot of old timers in the company. Waldenbooks grew tremendously over a short period of time. There hadn't been too many women in managerial positions. The new girls' network was a group of us in different departments who may have worked together on certain projects. We had lunch together once every month or two to discuss things. It was never official that we were going to help each other, but it evolved that way. By having different areas of the company in there to exchange ideas, we could talk in a way you can't during the normal workday.

Today, as companies downsize, it seems old boy and new girl networks are with friends who are in the same industry, even if at different companies. It is those loyal friends who may be offering you career continuity, or even a new job, today or next year. It is through those friends that you may hear about possible job openings. Those loyalties to a friend are replacing the loyalty to an employer who, in bygone days, especially at places like IBM, AT&T, or Ford, was considered one's boss for life. As Susan Enfield points out in her article "The New Buddy System," especially in industries with excessively high turnover, such as Hollywood's movie jobs, Washington, D.C., political positions, and New York's publishing and TV worlds, "informal networks" have become vital for developing friendships to share employment opportunities and industry trends. As the late screenwriter Carl Sautter once told me, "Our industry is fueled by friends."

Men and women alike, however, have to be careful to avoid imposing too often or too much on work friends, whether those relationships are casual, close, or best. If you make too many demands, or an inappropriate one, even once, you may find your work friends begin to refuse or ignore your phone calls or walk across the street if they catch a glimpse of you, trying to avoid another interaction which they fear might lead to yet another demand. Indeed, that is another benefit of having numerous casual friends at work or in your field; you may spread out any of the favors you might need to ask, never overburdening any one person.

*

Whether your friendship is carried out in the workplace, at school, or in your neighborhood; in person, over the phone, or through letters or e-mail, there are ways to enhance those relationships. In Part 5, Life and Friendship, you will learn those ways.

PART 5

LIFE AND FRIENDSHIP

My mother used to have a wonderful saying that I've adopted, which she would sometimes pull out on holidays. She would drink a toast to us and say, "It's so nice to like the ones you love."
—Nella Barkley, president, Crystal/Barkley Corporation

I consider my brothers and sister friends I take for granted.
> —45-year-old married New Jersey man

I consider my children my friends. We feel very close to each other.
> —72-year-old Westchester married woman

My mom is my best friend. My mom and I have grown closer the older I've gotten.
> —Jeff Coombs, 28-year-old unmarried consultant

13. THE FRIENDSHIP FACTOR IN EVERYDAY LIFE

In my happiest days, my wife is my best friend. In my saddest days, my wife is my best friend. She's the one I can share all my thoughts with.

—my late father, Dr. William Barkas, married 54 years

So far, you have learned how friendships—best, close, or casual—between unrelated peers are initiated, maintained, and improved as well as how friendship, especially casual, aids the workplace and your career. In this final chapter, you will see why it is beneficial to apply those same principles to other key relationships in your life, such as becoming a better friend with your children, parents, or spouse. J. Oliver Crom, president of Dale Carnegie & Associates, Inc., explains how Carnegie's principles of developing friendships and enhancing relationships are applicable in all these settings:

> In a business situation, we have certain skills we use to be successful in our business or professions. If we were to use those same skills in dealing with our family members, we would have much happier, more successful marriages and a better relationship with our children and other family members.
>
> For example, when we're courting, before we get married,

we write little love notes, we buy little gifts, we celebrate every anniversary from the time we met. After marriage, we tend to take these things for granted and we neglect the little things that were so important before. Those people who continue to remember and celebrate life's little joys have happier and more rewarding relationships. When a child takes that first step or speaks that first word, everyone is thrilled. But when the child reaches eight years or fourteen years, he or she is more likely to hear criticism than praise.

FRIENDLY RELATIONS: BEFRIENDING YOUR RELATIVES

I am sure you have heard at least one person say, "My mother is my best friend" or "My brother and I are the best of friends." For those individuals with blood ties—a mother, a father, a sister, a brother, a cousin, a child—that are more like voluntary friendships than obligatory blood ties, the term *friendly relations* applies.

As might be predicted, having friendly relations sometimes rules out a pressing need for close or best friends. Dan and Jerry, for example, are married brothers in their late 30s who have young children. They consider themselves more like best friends than brothers, and have little need for any close or best friends. By contrast, Evelyn, an only child whose parents are deceased, is totally involved with no fewer than eight close friendships, including two close friendships with ex-boyfriends and their spouses.

Discussions about close friendships with siblings were much more likely on the questionnaires completed by my college students at Penn State and St. John's University than of those of the adults I surveyed. An obvious reason might be, especially for the students at St. John's who were still living at home, that their siblings are still in proximity. For instance, a 19-year-old pharmacy major in his sophomore year of college, who has one brother of 21 and one sister of 15, gave this reply to the question, "Who is your closest same-sex friend?" "Brother, cousin."

Ideally, each sibling relationship has the potential to be more like a chosen friend than a relationship that is an accident of fate.

Sometimes the reasons this ideal sibling/friend relationship fails to evolve is a question of disparity in ages. For example, a 22-year-old woman explains why she is closer to her 28-year-old sister than her 35-year-old brother: "My brother is so much older than me and was out of the house when I was young." When the age difference is more than a few years, it may be harder for siblings to be like friends when they are very young; as they get older, however, especially in their adult years, an age difference of five or even ten years is not insurmountable.

Even more challenging to overcome than an age disparity, however, are personality differences or unresolved sibling rivalries. How to deal with those issues could be the subject of an entire book; there are, indeed, several valuable references available, such as *Siblings Without Rivalry* by Adele Faber and Elaine Mazlich.

When siblings get along like the best of friends, however, they offer each other the potential for a textured and powerful friendship; they share one of the most exalted aspects of long-standing friendships, namely a shared history.

Previous studies assumed that singles were least likely to name a relative as their closest relationship; the assumption was that singles were closer to their friends. But a study conducted by Jenny Jong-Gierveld found that 54% of those living alone named a relative as their closest relationship. "My sister is my best friend," says 31-year-old Judy, a bank executive. "I see my sister most often," Judy continues. Her sister, who is also single, lives just a few blocks away on Manhattan's upper East Side. "I spend a lot of time with my sister, which is not always so good. I see her both days during the weekend [and] she sleeps over weekends, and maybe [I also see her] one night during the week. But I'm trying to see other people [friends] since I finished night school."

I discovered few who had networks of close friends consider themselves to be best friends with a family member, especially a mother; friendship networks may be a substitute for such family bonds. For example, Rebecca, a 26-year-old psychiatric social worker from New Jersey, is close to her cousin, father, and stepmother; she also considers her older brother a friend. (She had been very close to her mother until she died at the age of 50 of lung cancer.) Although Rebecca has numerous one-on-one friendships of all levels of intimacy, she lacks a friendship network.

When a family friendship, especially a best friendship, is with a mother or stepmother, father or stepfather, there is the greatest likelihood that a woman or man will lack a best friend. "I'm very close to my mother. I've always considered her, pretty much, my best friend," says Penny, a 25-year-old copywriter who has few friends her own age.

While having friendly family relations with a parent or a sibling may inhibit having a best friend, they usually do not interfere with having close or casual friends. In fact, having such a positive model of relating in the immediate family probably aids having friendships outside the family. Just like "money goes to money," as they say, friends are attracted to those who are happy and fulfilled. What contributes to happiness or feeling fulfilled more than having a family that makes you feel wanted and loved? (I recall Ann Pleshette Murphy's *Parents* magazine column cited in Chapter 2, in which the editor-in-chief wrote about her life-long four best friends; she was reminded of them as she reminisced as she looked at their photograph at her baby shower. Who gave Pleshette the party? Her mother. As Zick Rubin pointed out in his book about children's friendships, it is those children with the strongest mother-child bonds that fare best at friendship.)

Having a cousin who is like a close or best friend is least likely to interfere with having a best friend. Back in the 1940s, cousins' clubs were more common than today. Now, once children are grown up and single or with families of their own, most immediate families are pleased if they get together for Thanksgiving and Christmas, seeing the extended family at weddings, funerals, or milestone anniversaries like the 40th or the 50th. Meetings of cousins—extended families—that, decades ago, may have been monthly or yearly now occur once every ten years, if at all.

Who would not be envious of the circle of 200 relatives of the Tenzer family that Joseph Berger described in his *New York Times* article? Five generations of Tenzers maintain their close family ties that began in 1883 when 14-year-old Michael Tenzer immigrated from Europe. The Tenzer extended family has regular reunions and maintains a family circle, although monthly meetings have been replaced with get-togethers three or four times a year.

BEFRIENDING YOUR CHILDREN

Having a child may be the friendliest relationship of all. Film and television director Bob Rafelson writes about his son Peter in *Fathers & Sons*, a photo essay by Steve Begleiter: "I found a friend for life."

Friendship between parents and children is a very unique type of friendship, however, since, as you have seen, the nature of platonic friendship, and what makes it so comfortable and reaffirming, is that it tends to be between equals. *Friendshifts,* especially as a child becomes an adult, allow a parent-child supervisory relationship to shift to more of a friendship. As Letty Cottin Pegrebin, author of *Getting Over Getting Older*, points out, there are benefits to her, her husband, and their three children from her vantage point of a woman in her 50s with children who are now adults in their late 20s: "Without actually marking the moment of change, the five of us have altered the basic premise on which our relationships are founded. For the first time, we are dealing with each other from a position of mutuality and equivalence, a symmetry of status and sensibilities that does not make me less of a mom, but does make me more of a friend."

The best way to facilitate becoming a friend with your children when they become adults is to spend time with them when they are young, getting to know each other, building a shared history and pleasant memories to be called up for review and reminiscing throughout your lives. The saddest answers in my recent survey of adult survivors of childhood sexual abuse were those who, when asked, "What is your favorite childhood memory?" wrote, "I don't have any."

Establish pleasant family traditions when your children are

young—around the holidays, such as baking cookies or creating greeting cards or simple presents, like bookmarks, together, spending vacations at a particular beach or resort that everyone likes, saying a simple prayer or grace before meals, perhaps even an original one created by one of your children, spending even 20 minutes a day actively listening and sharing with each other, such as playing a game, like a memory game, or putting together a puzzle, or a sports activity, such as bowling, baseball, swimming, bicycle riding, or skiing, depending upon interests, economic situation, abilities, and your child's age level and abilities.

Even television, if it is used in moderation as a shared family activity from time to time, not as a way of tuning out to each other, putting on the TV as a way of giving children something to engage them that does not require parental involvement, can be beneficial. A weekly favorite family show watched together, and discussed, could become "our show," and another way of bonding to each other and to a positive parent-child relationship that will serve you well in your child's adult years. I still recall watching *Sea Hunt* on Saturday afternoons with my dad; he worked a half-day as a dentist on Saturdays throughout my childhood. We had dinner as soon as he returned home, around three o'clock. Then my father would want to relax, but he let me watch TV with him. Even though he would be tired so he rarely spoke at that time, the *ABC Wide World of Sports* that we watched, as well as bowling on Sundays, was "our time" during my childhood, since he did not return from work till 9:30 P.M. every other night of the week.

Consider the exemplary friendship Charlie Matthau, the 31-year-old son of actor Walter Matthau and his wife, Carol, has with his parents. Although an only child, Charlie was never lonely, because his friends included his own parents. Says Charlie: "I've been very blessed. I had a unique situation because my parents were my best friends, and they still are. I would always go and do a lot of adult activities with them. I could interface pretty comfortably with the adult world. I didn't have the burning need to make a lot of friends because I had two friends that were always around. But unlike the stereotype [of the only child], I did not have trouble relating to people my own age."

I asked Charlie what he thinks might account for his enviable friendship with his parents. He replies: "They were very accepting. We'd have fun together. Go to the movies together. Take walks. My father used to take me to all the Dodgers and Lakers games. We've always done things together."

Charlie, a movie producer and director who resides in Los Angeles, thinks the fact that his parents were older—Walter Matthau was 42 when Charlie was born—may actually have helped their relationship. Charlie explains: "Even though you think younger parents can relate to kids better, when you have a certain maturity that helps because you're not working on your own stuff all the time. You can pay attention to your kids." Besides, Charlie adds, his parents were "both very childlike in a lot of ways."

There are others who are opposed to becoming a friend with your child. They consider parents and children to have unequal roles that preclude friendship, although the relationship includes respect, love, education, and shared values. Consider the mentor-protégé relationship. It is also disparate in status and power, yet there are those who are able to enjoy the benefits of a mentor relation that is also a friendship. Similarly, it is possible to have a parent-child relationship, and all that entails, while still adding in all the ideals of friendship, namely trust, keeping confidences, and having fun together.

Children, including adult children, want to be able to tell their parents anything. Sometimes they want a response, or a reaction; sometimes they only want to be able to share their feelings or experiences. Parents need listening skills if they are to enhance their friendship with their own children. Terry, a woman in her early 30s, explains how her mother's need to "fix" all her problems gets in the way of their relationship:

> I tried to tell my mother about the loneliness and pain I felt after my fiance broke our engagement. It was just too much for her. She cut me off and said, "Are we going to see you on Sunday?" That's the way my mother is, and I just have to accept it. She wants to find a cure for everything. If I'm lonely, let's get

together so, at least for a few moments, I won't be lonely. Next time I talk to her I hope I'll have the courage to say, "Mom, I'm just trying to share my loneliness with you. I'm not asking you to cure it. You can't. No one can. Not until I find someone to fill Jerry's place."

Being able to confide in your parent is a goal for most parents and children. A mother suggested I speak with her 13-year-old daughter, because she believed they had the kind of relationship that other girls would envy: her daughter told her everything. Her daughter, however, told me a different story. I asked her, "Would you go to your mother if you had a problem with a boy or something like that?" "I think I'd go to my friend more," she replied. "I think it would be easier to talk to a friend my age."

BEFRIENDING YOUR MOTHER OR FATHER

Sometimes children have to become parents themselves to develop the parent-child friendship they wish they had had all along. For example, Susan Polis Schutz, a successful published poet in her 40s, author of *To My Daughter with Love,* which has sold over 700,000 copies, and numerous other books, who is married and the mother of three, explains how her relationship with her mother has improved over the last two decades. Their current relationship is very different from what it was in the high school years, when Susan says she was self-centered and didn't consider her mother's feelings very much. Nor did she involve her mother in her life. About a decade ago, right before her first child was born, she moved her mother out to Colorado to be nearby. Says Susan: "She was with me when I had my first baby. Before that, we talked on the phone all the time, but only saw each other twice a year." Since becoming a parent herself, Susan appreciates her mother; as she now says, "I really don't know what I'd do without her."

Sometimes the relationship between parent and child can become friendlier only after attitudes are shifted. Lil, whose best friendship with Irene faded after Irene's marriage, now considers her mother her best friend. When Lil's two-year romantic relationship was ending, Lil finally turned to her mother, who drove Lil back to her home in New Jersey. "Sit down and shut up for a few days," Lil says her mother told her, giving Lil the strong response that she had looked for, and not found, from her friends.

A shift in your parent-child relationship may occur when you shift the role you play with your parents. That is what happened to Dorothy: she was so used to burdening her mother with the woes of her singleness that she never thought about what her mother, a 59-year-old office worker, might be worried about. Dorothy listened, and her mother revealed many of her own personal and business problems. "It was then that I saw my mother as a woman who also had problems," Dorothy says. "Maybe she could tell my father those same problems but, finally, after all those years of getting from my mother, I allowed myself to give to her as well. Somehow I felt like I would have to cope better on my own because my mother needed some advice."

As another single woman I interviewed put it: "My mother gave me life. She was the closest person to me. She won't be around forever. I never want to feel that we failed to share our lives as completely as we could."

Becoming closer with your mother or father may help you become more comfortable with intimacy in all the other key relationships in your life.

But what if all your efforts with your mother seem futile, or at least at this point in time are not working? For example, Naomi tried and tried to be honest and have a better relationship with her mother. She even asked her mother to attend a mother-daughter workshop with her, but her mother refused to go. What did she do? "I could always talk frankly with my father, so I decided it was better to strengthen my relationship with him than to just keep fighting with my mother."

As Victoria Secunda writes in her chapter, "Rediscovering Our Fathers," in *Women and Their Fathers: The Sexual and Romantic*

Impact of the First Man in Your Life, the goal of that chapter "is to help daughters to find out what they missed with their fathers so that they can better understand their relationships with men outside the family, whether at work or in love." Secunda writes that there are three steps to working through the father-daughter relationship: remembering, healing, and reconnecting. "The key is to really get to know the actual father—whether or not he is alive or even around—to pull him out of the shadows, apart from Mom, away from the newspaper, and really *see* him.," notes Secunda.

Twenty-seven-year-old Jane, who got married last year, had the opposite problem to Naomi's, described above—her mother, who was divorced, shared her intimacies with her daughter, who found it an uncomfortable situation: "I finally had to tell my mother that I just didn't want to hear about her various boyfriends and live-ins. I was handling the sexual aspects of my marriage, and I thought my mother should be able to handle the intimacies of her own life."

If a married man or woman is too close to his or her mother, it may affect the intimacy of the nuptial ties. But at least those friendly relations did not prevent the marriage from taking place in the first place. As Nancy Friday notes in *My Mother/Myself:* "Very often the new mother-daughter friendship comes at the expense of what should be our prime union—with our husband."

The fact that Margaret's husband was not her best friend, and that she was having marital problems, are truths that she now regrets hiding from her mother. Margaret is 44 and divorced. She considers her mother one of her best friends, yet while Margaret was married, she was unable to tell her mother that her husband was cheating on her. "If I had told my mother 10 years ago, when I first found out," says Margaret, who has three children, "she probably would have told me to leave him right then and there." Instead, Margaret tried to keep her marriage going and only divorced her husband two years ago. "I was so afraid to tell my mother, and to hurt her. My mother, I'm surprised to say, has been completely in favor of my divorce. She tells me what courage I have to start over again. I regret I didn't have the courage to tell her—and divorce him—sooner."

If you are able to accept your mother, or your father, for who they are, and get to know them, instead of wishing for the parent you do not have, you will be closer to gaining a better understanding of who they are, and to self-acceptance as well.

Becoming a better friend with your mother or father, in a very basic way, is the beginning of becoming best friends with yourself.

BECOMING A BETTER FRIEND WITH YOUR SPOUSE

"How important are your friendships?" I asked a 27-year-old woman who worked as a paralegal. "Very important," she replied. "Especially the one with my husband, which we're still developing."

I remember back in the 1980s, a casual single friend gave a holiday party for socializing and networking purposes. She had been madly in love with a man who jilted her after a year-long stormy relationship. She was now involved in a new romance that seemed to be on a more even keel; it was going well, and she was finally happy. I am unsure of the exact words I used to inscribe the book I gave her as a present, but this was the thought behind them: "Romance is friendship plus physical intimacy."

Based on dozens of interviews over the years, with married couples as well as married, and divorced, men and women specifically on the friendship factor in marriage, I have discovered that in the best marriages, husband and wife consider each other their best friends—but not each other's only friends. "David is my best friend," says Joyce, happily married for two decades. "Because I can tell him things I can't tell anybody else," she adds. Again and again, divorced men or women would explain to me the failure of their marriage with these words, "We weren't friends."

Is it possible to put into words what makes a couple happy and best friends? When I was researching my book *Single in America,* and I had not yet personally experienced a happy marriage, I was unsure. I remember traveling to Minneapolis and interviewing a couple whose marriage I had envied from a distance. When I asked each one to tell me what made their marriage work, they stared at me, then there was a long silence, followed by the emphatic statement that it was not something they could put into words.

A few years later, I heard they had divorced. The ex-wife, whom I see from time to time, is now *very* articulate when she shares her glee that she is no longer with her former spouse, although she recognizes that the man she no longer wanted is getting along just fine with his second wife.

Of course, there are times when spouses fail to be best friends with each other because the marriage was based on the "wrong" reasons, or a necessary chemistry was lacking, right from the start. By and large, however, if there was attraction, love, and mutual respect in the beginning, there is the potential for sustaining and even enhancing those feelings, and the relationship, with a little help from each mate.

Here is the poem my aunt Peggy Silver wrote to express her 50-year-long marriage and best friendship with her husband, Irving, a poem she included with the invitations to their golden anniversary celebration:

> *Together——For Fifty Years*
>
> *They met on a blind date Thanksgiving*
> *It took just one month to know*
> *They were clearly meant for each other*
> *That was fifty years ago!*
>
> *Eloping soon after...then becoming*
> *Parents so young...who'd have guessed*
> *Raising Phyllis, Stuart, and Keith through the years*
> *They would be heaven blessed?*
>
> *Surviving the war...and beginning again*
> *There just was no time to waste*
> *And nothing to do but work and work hard*
> *At a marriage done in such haste!*

Now where is that girl of merely eighteen
And that boy of just twenty-three?
His hair is all white and he walks with a cane
And she's tying his shoes...on one knee!

So if your back isn't straight
And your clothes never fit
And some days there's no help from above
Life seems to be so much better
If it's shared by someone you love!

The friendship factor in marriage depends on trusting each other, committing to each other and to your marriage, and spending time together. I interviewed Carol when she was 28 years old; she had been married to Tom, a medical resident, for five years, and they had a two-year-old daughter. Carol found that she and Tom had become so busy they were allowing themselves to lose the friendship factor in their marriage. It was then that she decided it was time to make some radical changes in their lifestyle, in the interest of their marriage. So they moved from Manhattan to a house in New Jersey, with enough space for Carol's widowed mother to move in to help out with baby sitting. "Since we've moved here," says Carol, "Tom and I play more games together. I think sometimes when you're adults, and you're married, you don't play. You do the serious stuff. You go to the opera or you pursue your serious interests. Since we moved here, we play more. We take drives together. Or we'll just sit in the backyard, just by ourselves, which is very nice."

What I have observed is that if husbands and wives gave each other the consideration and affection that they often give to their friends—and even to their pets—they would have happier marriages. Unfortunately, since marriage is an all-encompassing relationship that usually involves living together, and the potential for daily minutiae that the usually intermittent friendship is able to avoid, it takes that much more effort from each mate to keep the marital relationship fun and rewarding. Friends, who will rarely lean on each other for money or turn to each other for daily care in times of sickness—by and large they will go to a spouse, a parent, or an institution, such as a bank or hospital, for help in these situations—and who will often carefully consider what they say to each other since they know they could quite easily be replaced by one or more friends (compared to the legal and social complexities of dissolving a marriage), might consider applying the same "kid gloves" to their marriage. That is not the same thing as being a phony with your spouse or partner; instead it means exercising the same caution and care with the relationship—not taking it for granted—that so many I interviewed told me about how they strive to treat their best and close friends.

Here are additional tips for enhancing the friendship factor in your marriage:

Cultivate activities you and your spouse like to do together, such as sports, cultural, entertainment, culinary, or creative, combining activities that involve talking to each other, such as eating dinner out without the children on a regular basis, taking a walk or jogging together, as well as those that allow a shared experience, such as going to the movies, taking up a sport together, working out at a health club, taking a walk or jogging together, taking a class together, or even collaborating on a project of mutual interest, like painting the house, putting together a bookcase, or renovating a bathroom.

Associate with other happily married couples. Being around couples who like each other and practice good communication skills is certainly more beneficial to your relationship than exposing yourselves, and your marriage, to destructive, negative, or unhappy couples. Of course you do not want to abandon friends just because they are in unhappy relationships; you could consider getting together with your friend individually, rather than having a two-couple experience that might be a drain on all concerned. Similarly, keep up your friendships with single friends; decide in each situation the best way for your marriage to involve your single friends in your personal or couples time.

Avoid excessive criticism of each other, especially in public, as well as of each other's relatives or friends. Be supportive and understanding of each other.

Remember birthdays and anniversaries, even if you have to write them down in your daily planner. Also remember anniversaries that only have meaning to you and your spouse, beyond the typical wedding anniversary, such as the day you met, your first date, the day you proposed, or even a no-occasion surprise card, gift, flowers, original poem or letter, or special gesture to show you care.

Keep secrets and confidentialities.

Share household tasks and obligations, doing them together, if possible. Put a chart on the wall, designating who does what, how often, and when you will switch with each other, if necessary. As a 25-year-old copywriter at a Philadelphia advertising agency, married to a salesman for a year, who has not yet had children, told me: "We do what made sense for both our schedules. I do wash, food shopping, cleaning. We have a maid two times a month. He takes out the garbage and fixes broken things around the house. He's a salesman, so he can make his calls from home and wait around. I do vacations, calling, background information on the area. It's always a trade off. 'I'll do this for you if you'll do this for me.' We're lucky. [There are some married working women] who do 90% and [their husbands] who do [only] 10%."

Once you have children, rather than restricting your activities, in addition to time alone as a couple, include your child in as many outings and events as possible, from tennis to outdoor concerns, from picnics to trips.

Keep in your marriage the same "fun factor" that you strive to keep in your friendships.

Use communication skills that are also recommended to promote befriending your children, parent, sibling, or other relatives, namely using "I" statements to express how someone's behavior makes you feel— "I feel pressured when you tell me to lose 10 pounds"—instead of overreacting with harsh words and insults hurled in retaliation that only push you further away from each other.

Try using a technique I often employ when I conduct a workshop or facilitate a group, role playing—you and your partner reverse roles and speak and talk the way you think the other one would do it—as a way of dramatizing how their behavior makes you feel. Role playing holds up a mirror to someone's interaction; it is a way of acting out someone else's role to enable your partner, who may be trapped in a way of speaking and behaving that he or she cannot see in him- or herself, to get a fresh perspective on his or her actions.

You may also try being more assertive about your needs and feelings, rather than ignoring your frustrations, which allows hostilities to fester or build up, or using tantrums or demands, examples of negative communication patterns. Asserting yourself in an unemotional, calm way reinforces the two-way street aspect of a romantic partnership. (And don't forget to listen to your partner and give him or her time to assert his feelings, fears, wishes, concerns, or thoughts.)

Making time for each other, and giving your romantic relationship a priority place in your life, will take you and your spouse far in enhancing the friendship factor in your romance. Finding effective ways to deal with conflict, rather than letting unresolved issues fester and build up to the point of no return, are other ways that you may become better friends with each other.

PETS AS FRIENDS

Pets offer friendship in place of, or in addition to, peers. Indeed, the care that pets require may just be what is necessary for a child to learn the give and take that most friendships entail. Becoming sensitive to the nonverbal and verbal cues of a pet may enable a child or adult to become a more aware and giving friend.

Bonnie, a single woman in her early 40s who works part-time

while studying to be a graphic designer, has lived in her Boston apartment for the last eight years with her white terrier named Buster. Bonnie says that Buster is most definitely her best friend, especially after her closest friendship of more than 20 years ended a few years back when Bonnie felt her friend stopped liking her. It is the *unconditional* love that Buster offers Bonnie—and that, according to Bonnie, even if it was there, she felt was lacking in her family or any lasting romantic relationship to date—that causes Bonnie to say, "The dog is the best friend I've ever had. Everyone should have a dog if they really want to know what love is about. They can learn something from dogs." This former office manager for a public relations firm continues: "He never talks back and he doesn't make life difficult. He only makes life more pleasant. He's very sweet, affectionate, sensitive. He's always there for me. When I'm sad or crying, he comes over to see what's wrong."

Bonnie also expresses how words, which can often interfere with or end a friendship with a peer, are not an issue in her best friendship with her dog:

> People say things that hurt other people. Most of the time, they don't even mean it. I find when I say things that hurt somebody else, and I don't mean it most of the time, people will just disappear out of my life. Sometimes they come back because they realize they overreacted. But a lot of times, they disappear out of my life.
>
> This will happen with people. It's painful because rather than sit there and try to work something out, and we have the ability to do so, rather than use our power to speak and communicate to our advantage, it becomes a problem for us.
>
> Whereas with dogs, the only way you communicate is that they will do everything to please you, as long as you are nice to them. They don't ask for anything really back, and it's so nice. It makes me want to give more. If people could be like that to each other, it could be wonderful. They're not, so I vote for dogs.

By giving love to an animal, getting love in return, and

becoming sensitive to "reading" your pet's needs, there is that much more love to give to others, pet, peer, and romantic partner alike, as illustrated in Tom Cheney's cartoon, reprinted below, with permission.

"Before we get in any deeper, I need to know how you feel about dogs."

Befriending animals as a way of helping troubled children and teens has been the cornerstone of an innovative residential treatment and education center, Green Chimneys Children's Services, in Brewster, New York, a 150-acre farm 60 miles from New York City. Founded in 1947 by Dr. Samuel B. Ross, Jr., an educator, more than 150 troubled boys and girls, ages 6 to 15, live on the farm and actively take part in the care of more than 200 animals. Dr. Ross has seen countless examples of miraculous improvements in the children; the therapy they receive certainly helps, but it is through their friendships with dogs, rabbits, and horses that they learn to get along better. As Dr. Ross explains:

All children need to be connected to something. At the time [they initially come here], they have difficulty being connected to their families, to their neighborhoods, or to their schoolmates. They develop a feeling of depression, sadness, and loneliness. One of the things we have found is that children who have been reluctant to reach out to peers or adults seemingly will reach out to animals and make the connection first. And from that connection, they will establish a relationship with a peer, and a relationship with adults.

Interestingly, this week we saw a young man who had been here when he was about 10 or 11. He was a troubled youngster who was having problems relating to his family, to school, and to his neighborhood. Now he is an accountant. He's 28. He has done very well. He was just awarded a certificate of merit for tackling a mugger who was trying to overpower a policeman. He saved a policeman's life. I asked him, "What did Chimneys do for you?" He said, "Here I made a connection with a lamb, and I can remember when my lamb gave birth, and it was an exciting time for me."

Children take on a nurturing role, become a nurturer, and establish that kind of relationship. It helps to interrupt the type of behavior and [abusive] environment they might have had before. We've had children who were seemingly having a great bravado, but it was just to keep people away from them. But they're a soft touch when it comes to animals.

THE THERAPIST AS A SAFE "FRIEND"

Whether or not you think of your relatives or spouse as friends, or whether or not you even have friends, there may be a time when you, or someone you know, needs some professional help to sort out work or personal issues. Psychotherapists—psychologists, psychiatrists, therapists, or mental health social workers—offer an objectivity and skill that even the best of friends might be unable to provide. In "Freud's Fragmented Legacy," Dava Sobel describes a woman's search for help through several therapists and techniques. After finally spending two years in successful therapy with "a Jungian trained in Zurich," the patient shares the benefits of those weekly therapeutic interactions, noting, "I tell people that it's worth the expense not just for the support but the objectivity of the therapist. A friend just doesn't do."

The Function of Therapy

In the section on self-disclosure, you looked at the ideal of confidentiality in friendship. There is a benefit to sharing your innermost secrets or thoughts with a friend, but there are also risks, of exposure or rejection, of a confession affecting your friendship.

By contrast, a therapist is trained to hear your confession—to share your secrets—without passing judgment.

You might confess to a friend thinking you will gain acceptance, only to now fear what your friend will do with your secret or, if the friendship ends, what might be done with that information.

Such a fear would not occur with a trustworthy therapist.

Hopefully, if therapy is working for both patient and therapist, a bond is forming that will motivate them to go through the painful process of shedding past traumas and understanding what in the past is causing problems in the present. A successful therapy will enhance friendships by allowing patients to stop misusing friends as a dumping ground for emotional baggage. Friendship needs to be a give and take; those who are upset or in trouble emotionally tend to take more than they can give.

But therapists, who may be friendly, cannot be friends. Milton Haynes, a Manhattan-based social worker (and former journalist), explains how therapy compares to friendship:

> As a therapist, I can say that the unique therapist/client relationship is a peculiarly delicate one. We all know the damage that a friend or therapist can do when trust that is invested is betrayed in any way. A really good therapist is trained to avoid *any* contamination of that kind, and hopefully, the therapist will maintain some kind of supervision therapy, or peer review, to avoid unconsciously sabotaging his or her clients' therapy.
>
> The dictionary I consulted describes friendship as "One attached to another by esteem, respect and affection; an

intimate." I certainly esteem and respect any individual who walks through the door and offers up his or her life for examination and change, who is willing to lay out before both of us his innermost conflicts, sins, fantasies, and fears. It takes tremendous courage....The "affection" part of the dictionary definition is the tricky one for therapist and patient. Feelings of affection on the part of the therapist can distort the therapy. You don't want your surgeon or lawyer to be affectionate, but you do want them to be excellent and appropriately detached in their handling of your case or your body.

*

Chapter 14, Summing Up, the next and final chapter of *Friendshifts*, explores more reasons and ways to make time for your friends, further considerations about how male and female friendships have changed and may continue to evolve, and 14 top ways of how to make friends and keep them for life.

Friend is kind of a loose word. It's probably like beauty, in the eye of the beholder. I would say that as I grow older, I think I need friends less, or certainly not in profusion. It's probably like pruning a tree; you become more selective.

—50-year-old male divorced and remarried journalist

14. SUMMING UP

Friendship is important because if you don't have any friends, nothing is any good.

—6-year-old Jeffrey Yager

Few would deny a child the time to play or to get together with friends. Too often adults, however, torn between the obligations of earning a living and family obligations, will say, "I don't have time to get together with my friends." But there are lots of ways to fit friendship into a busy life as long as you make friendship a primary concern in your life.

As your life gets busier or more compartmentalized, it is too easy to discount how essential friendship is for you, whatever your age or marital status. However, the time and effort you put forth because of friendship will most likely be rewarded and returned ten-fold.

As you know, and this book and all the research confirms, we all need friends of all types, ranging from best or close ones to casual friends. We especially need at least one close or best friend, someone who sticks around through thick and thin, with whom we have a shared history, who takes the time to listen no matter how hectic their own life might be.

MAKING FRIENDSHIP A PRIORITY

Friends can be just plain fun; they can also reduce the emotional devastation that could be associated with such life events as job loss or dissatisfaction, divorce, or death of a spouse. Friendship also helps to reduce excessive dependency on your spouse or relatives.

Friends Can Be Good Medicine, the title of a booklet put out by the California Department of Mental Health, is also a proven medical and psychological fact, as epidemiologist Lisa F. Berkman, Ph.D., and others have concluded from their extensive research into longevity and survival rates after heart attacks.

But friends can only be good medicine if you take the time to keep them involved in your life.

Last year, I was impressed by someone I met because she showed me by her actions how much she values someone who might become a friend. I was meeting Mitzi Lyman partly because my sister told me that Mitzi, her friend for the last nine years, had moved from Washington, D.C., to Connecticut last summer. She lived in Westport, where I was considering moving, and I wanted to talk to her about her house hunting. I also wanted to meet in case a friendship might ensue.

Our meeting was set for a Thursday morning at 10. The night before, there was a ferocious wind, hail, and rainstorm. I called around nine o'clock and told Mitzi, "If the weather's bad tomorrow morning, we'll have to reschedule." I think my call was partly because of the weather, and partly because of my anxiety about meeting someone new.

Despite my panic, and with fairly good weather on my side, I drove to Mitzi's home, about half an hour away. Upon arriving, I was surprised to learn that Mitzi had had quite a morning. Because her car was in the repair shop, she ended up having to send her older daughter to school in a taxi, and she took another taxi with her younger daughter after she also missed her school bus. Although there were certainly enough reasons to have canceled, Mitzi did not disappoint me.

"Another function of friendship," writes friendship expert Steve Duck, Ph.D., in *Friends, For Life,* "then, another reason why we need friends, is to keep us emotionally stable and to help us see where we stand *vis-a-vis* other people and whether we are 'doing OK.'"

"Friends are the glue that keep you together when tragedy strikes," explains my close friend Marcia Hoffenberg, a married working mother of twins who has had her share of losses.

During the nontragic times, however, friends are still fundamental—for your self-esteem, support, and a good time. Now Marcia makes time for her friends "in between play dates, work appointments, and cleaning the house." When Marcia and I were both single, we lived in different parts of Manhattan and made the time, almost weekly, to work out together at a health club, talking as we cycled. We are now both married with families, living and working in different states. We do not talk to or see other as much as we would like to, or as often as we used to, but our friendship persists through our shared commitment that it is worth our time and concern.

My close friend Mary Tierney, who is married, has monthly luncheons at a Manhattan restaurant with her friends. Mary explains how the luncheons began after her first date with the man she would marry, who was having luncheons for his male friends:

> Twelve years ago they started—right after our first date. I started it because I wanted to see him again and knew that women were not invited to the male first Friday luncheon. So in the same restaurant, I got together a great group of women to meet at the same time and sit at the opposite side of the room. (Women had been invited to the male luncheons for tea *after.*) I also wanted the painter Alice Neel to size him up for me. For a few years, it met only annually. Then we started to meet monthly, and many great things happened as a result: friendships, work-related networking (though it is not in any way

that function). At this stage, some of the men are asking that we join the two groups. I continue to say no to that!

As Karen Lobovits, a Massachusetts art therapist with a busy practice, who is the mother of three grown children and the grandmother of an infant, told me: "I need time each week to do something that's fun." Since her divorce a few years ago, friends have become even more important. Karen and another friend bought canoes last year, and they go on canoe trips. She also goes horseback riding and even went to a weekend workshop in Rye, New York, with a group of girlfriends who share her interest in meditation, yoga, and the healing professions.

It is not just getting together with friends that takes time, and needs to be a priority concern; phone calls take time; writing, and returning, letters, whether through the mail or through cyberspace, e-mail, takes time. You can imagine how hurt I was years back, when I was single and so much of the continuity in my personal life came from my in-person or correspondence friends, when a well-known novelist, who had been the one to initiate a correspondence with me several years before as a long-distance casual friendship ensued, suddenly wrote to me: "As to your steady correspondence, sorry, I can't handle it. I've been much too busy to handle your past letters and will be too busy to handle future ones." He continued: "I will answer this one though, so I can tell you the above....Keep writing, everything, except questions to me." Over the years, I realized it was my imminent visit to his hometown that was the "trigger" incident to ending our casual friendship; I had just become too demanding of his time at that point in his life.

Friends Could Provide What Is Lacking at Home

As noted at the beginning of this book, friendship is an untapped source of help for dysfunctional families—in childhood and adult years—and in that way, friendship might compensate for what is missing at home. In most cases, keeping the family very separate and independent of any government or other outside intervention, even that of friends, is a good thing. But when there are problems within the family, the right intervention could be crucial to preventing immediate and long-term trauma and victimization. Victim advocate John Walsh, for example, in an excellent public service announcement about preventing or dealing with childhood sexual abuse, advises children: If the problem is with someone outside your family, tell your mother or your father; if it's because of a family member, tell your teacher or a trusted family friend. In that way, trusted family friends might provide help and objectivity those caught up in the abusive situations may be lacking.

It is also especially vital that those who had poor early relationships—with parents or siblings—find friends who *repair* those painful early memories, rather than repeat them. Bridgett is a 58-year-old married woman with three grown children. She works as a secretary for her husband; they live in Montana. Bridgett and her sister were sexually abused by their father, beginning at the age of nine, after their mother left home. "Between Mom and Stepmom#1 and again before Stepmom #2," since their room was rented out, Bridgett and her sister had to deal with sleeping with their father and his "busy hands." "He continually embarrassed us by exposing himself when we had friends over," Bridgett adds.

Bridgett, who left home at the age of 16, explains that, looking back, she went along with the abuse when she was a child "for love. I didn't know it was abuse. It was just Dad being loving." But her two closest friends, whom she had known since the seventh and eighth grades, helped Bridgett to see that what was going on in her family was abnormal; her friends provided positive models for the way it could be:

> I learned what went on at home wasn't the way things should be. One friend's divorced mom ran a loving family in a tiny apartment. The other friend was more like a "Donna Reed" family. I learned from both that my life was not normal.

Mel is a 29-year-old single man who lives in New Mexico and works as a deliveryman. For 10 years of his childhood, he and his sister lived with their mother, her female lover, and her lover's four children. For five years, beginning when he was nine, the oldest boy sexually abused Mel as well as Mel's mentally disabled younger sister. Mel has survived a suicide attempt three years ago; he is in therapy sorting out the abuse, his intimacy problems with women, his anger, his need to isolate, and his low self-esteem. His best friendship with Paul, whom he met in high school, has helped him through his depressions. "Paul has always been there when I needed somebody to talk to!!" Mel says.

Lillian is a 44-year-old New Jersey woman who, when she was 12, was sexually abused several times by her 18-year-old brother. She explains what it was like during her formative years—"an alcoholic/workaholic father who was seldom there and an emotionally absent mother who was there but very frigid with any verbal or physical displays of love (such as hugs, etc.)"—and what friends have given her that is helping her recover from her childhood:

> When I got married three years ago, Joan (also my maid of honor) would not let me dwell on my mother. My mother had been such a bitch I "disinvited" her to the wedding. Joan's emotional strength allowed me to enjoy the day. Also her [Joan's] wedding gift allowed me to get a golden retriever we could not afford to ship from out of state. (We are both show dog people.)

Friendship offers you a chance to find and select meaningful relationships that you feel were lacking in your childhood. As Lillian explains:

> To have friends you have to be a friend. That's what I've tried to do—treat others as I've wanted to be treated in my family but never was. This translates [into] being thoughtful, perceptive and kind.

But if you find you are picking friends who are just too much like your rejecting and negative family members, consider seeking professional help to break out of the traumatic patterns you are constantly reliving through your equally negative friends. Everyone deserves and is capable of warm, nurturing, fun, and fulfilling friendships. But if you are used to being criticized, disappointed, abandoned, or betrayed, it might prove as difficult and scary to find and experience the opposite positive situations because it is unfamiliar to you. The familiar, although negative and consciously what you say you do not want, on a deeper level may be providing a comfort zone since it is what you are used to.

If you stick with those unpleasant feelings long enough, however, change is possible. Those feelings are actually tied to the unknown, even though the unknown is good for you. Change, even change for the better, sometimes involves anxiety and resistance to it. But if you can stay with the discomfort caused by trying to change your friendship patterns—from negative to positive—on your own, or with professional help, you might be able to work through these pulls back and pushes forward so that you can finally develop the supportive, positive, and reliable friendships you have only dreamt about.

HOW TO MAKE FRIENDS AND KEEP THEM FOR LIFE

Here are 14 additional tips for making friends and keeping them for life that summarize some of the ideas you have learned in this book, as well as extending those concepts into other areas:

1. Behind friendship is the nice or likability factor. A key way to have friends is to be likable and interested in others.

2. Be concerned with your friend, not just yourself. When my son was in nursery school, as I drove my son and his friend to our home, I remember asking my son's friend what he'd like to play once they got to our house. "Whatever Jeff wants to do," the popular and likable boy replied.

3. Be positive and upbeat.

4. Avoid misusing friends as therapists or banks.

5. Friends may be nursemaids if necessary. But, in time, that role may take the place of the friendship one.

6. Listen carefully, sympathetically, and with empathy.

7. Maintain a sincere interest in your friends' concerns.

8. Try to keep the friendship as comfortable as possible, taking your cues from your friends' needs and abilities. If a friend can only handle seeing you once a month, avoid pushing for weekly or daily meetings or phone calls, or you risk sabotaging the entire relationship.

9. Keep confidences.

10. Share your knowledge and experiences with your friends, since friends have the chance to teach you about everything from salamanders to coping with ill parents while still letting you know your perspective may also be valid.

11. Respect your friends' boundaries. I remember how embarrassed my close friend Nona was a few years back when a boyfriend gave her a surprise party. He did not know all her friends, but by contacting a few who knew others, he ultimately reached out to her entire network, without her knowledge. The result? Assembled in one room were all her diverse friends, from artists to stockbrokers, as well as several ex-boyfriends. Some of these people—and all the ex-boyfriends—she would have preferred to keep separated from each other.

12. Of course you are allowed to be busy, but if your friend wants to get together, being busy too often and for too extended a period may result in fading or ending those friendships. If you are busy now, or in the foreseeable future, try to still agree on a specific plan for getting together with your friend and commit to it. In that way, your friend will have evidence that you are truly still committed to your friendship.

13. Keep your view of your friends up-to-date; avoid outdated and unrealistic perceptions based on outdated information.

14. If you are pressed for time, combine getting together with your friend with another task you have to do, such as sharing lunch during the business day, going away on vacation together, shopping, going to the movies, volunteering to serve on the same community or professional committee, or another activity such as walking, tennis, golf, or taking a class together.

Referring to the key ideas in Carnegie's 1936 classic, *How to Win Friends and Influence People*, J. Oliver Crom, president of Dale Carnegie & Associates, Inc., explains, "The fundamental principles are the same, but the language that we use today to express them may have changed." Here are four of Carnegie's friendship guidelines from Carnegie's book that will help you get along better with those you care about:

- Avoid criticizing others "because it wounds a man's precious pride, hurts his sense of importance, and arouses his resentment."
- "Give honest, sincere appreciation."
- "Arouse in the other person an eager want."
- Smile.

Friendship Is Magical

It is fitting to include in this Summing Up a reminder that friendship is still a most curious and complicated relationship based on feelings, more than any other relationship in your life, such as the marital one, which is feelings complicated by legal, monetary, or economic and social contracts; or blood relations, which are defined by birth. Friendship exists only because of shared feelings. Allan Bloom points out in his eloquent and provocative treatise, published posthumously in 1993, *Love & Friendship*, that even French essayist Montaigne recognizes the emotional and gut-level basis of friendship. Bloom first quotes Montaigne: "If you press me to tell why I loved him, I feel that this cannot be expressed, except by answering: Because it was he, because it was I." Then Bloom goes on to explain: "He [Montaigne] and his somewhat older friend were lost in each other and...overcame the distinction between self and other, or I and thou."

Perhaps that is one of the reasons friendship is so magical and so potentially rewarding: it allows connections that permit a window into the soul of another. Some connections, although still miraculous because an emotional link between you and another did occur, are more expected than others: friendships between those who are the same sex and age, who live nearby, and who share similar backgrounds, values, or interests. Then there are other friendships that defy all logic and reason because there are more dissimilarities than similarities. I think of my friendship with Bill, a British journalist and crime victim advocate almost 50 years my senior. Although some might label our friendship a casual one, especially since distance and decades separated us, Bill touched a chord in me and I always felt emotionally connected to him. Through our letters, beginning in the late 1970s, I have a record of what was going on in our lives. Especially during my single years, Bill was someone I turned to to express feelings and ideas that I was afraid might overwhelm my nearby friends, and to get his older, wiser, and foreign perspective. (My long distance but meaningful friendship with Bill seems to be a precursor of today's friendships that have started through e-mail and the Internet, a technological advance that enables almost instant linkage between kindred spirits who may be communicating with each other from the far corners of the world.) I even have the letter I wrote in 1983, the one I did not mail, in which I apologized to Bill because reading my letters and writing back to me seemed to be interfering with his own writing projects.

In 1985, I asked Bill to share with me his thoughts about our long-distance friendship, which he did, in his uniquely detailed and eloquent way, concluding, "And I have Dr. Johnson's liking for what he called 'the endearing elegance of female friendship.' I believe a lot of men do, and are betrayed by it into overestimating themselves. This I feel you would never do, and you will find there's no shaking me off until the world shakes me off; which I suppose it is bound to do soon."

I had always planned to get to England to meet Bill in person. Each year, I would share with Bill my excuses: I was lacking the money, the time, or both.

Soon after receiving my card for his 91st birthday, Bill wrote back: "Me, I'm not too bad. I very much dislike old age, I find; but am encouraged to go on with it because I understand that it's better than the alternative."

Over the years, I grew to take for granted my correspondence friendship with Bill, the man who once wrote to me, "I've adopted you as a quasi-daughter."

Finally, in May of 1995, I wrote Bill an excited, enthusiastic letter that my long-awaited trip to Europe was about to occur: in just a month and a half, we would all finally meet.

On June 10th, I received a fax in reply to my letter; it was from Bill's son, sharing with me the sad news that Bill had died a year before, at the age of 92. He had been in failing health for some time, finally succumbing to cancer. I felt numb, then I cried as if a close friend I had gone to school with had died. I was surprised to realize it had been at least two years since I had last written to Bill. In the midst of my busy life, I had lost track of time, and of Bill.

Even in his death, my friend Bill had taught me a valuable lesson about putting off getting together with a treasured friend. I knew that Bill, who shared with me how he loved paradoxes, would have been the one with whom I would have most wanted to share this paradox, and that was an impossibility. I wrote back to Bill's son John: "I feel very sad that I will never now be able to meet your father in person. I am moved to tears that I will never now be able to shake his hand and see his face....I have lost a brilliant pen pal and a long distance [but not distant] friend."

Friends Are Not Mind Readers

You have to be careful to avoid assuming your friends are "mind readers" about what your emotional needs are at any given time, or that they are even aware of what you might be going through. Sometimes they may be unaware of what you are going through, or that it is has such an effect on you. If they did, they might reach out. For instance, when I had a miscarriage a few years ago, I felt as if only one close friend and one cousin was there for me; I felt my larger network of close and casual friends and relatives had deserted me. On top of my sadness that a much-hoped-for baby died from unknown causes at 10 weeks of gestation, I felt rage at how I felt few of my friends came through for me. It took me two years down the road to realize I had never even told them what I was going through. It was only those few friends with whom I was in fairly regular contact who knew of my despair and grief.

I took that lesson to heart when my father became seriously ill. This time, instead of blaming my friends for not being there for me, I took the time to write a note and send it, along with a poem I had written about what I was going through, to my close friends with whom I was not in constant communication. Almost instantaneously upon receiving my letter my close friend from high school, Judy, called me, leaving a message on my phone machine that echoed these words: "I had no idea what you have been going through…"

When my father passed away a few weeks later, I continued my hard-won lesson that friends are not mind readers and reached out. Unlike when I had my miscarriage, this time *every single one* of my close friends reached out to me because I made it clear I needed their support. This time, even though my loss was still overwhelming, I was able to more quickly regain my emotional equilibrium because my friends (as well as my husband, children, and relatives) helped me to feel connected, cared for, and loved.

Friends Need to Be Able to Find Each Other

Another aspect of taking the initiative to keep your friends involved in your life is to make sure your friends are able to find you, if you move or change your name. You might want to have the name, address, and phone number of at least one, perhaps two or three people who are relatives or friends of your friend. For example, if you are still in contact with your friends from "the old neighborhood" you grew up in, your school days, or a shared job situation, you might also want to have the address of your friend's parents, siblings, or another one or two friends so you could more easily find your friend if she or he does move and fails to notify you of those changes. This will probably only be true for casual friends, or close friends who do not live nearby; best friends and most close friends, hopefully, will notify you of any changes, such as relocating and any name changes, that might make it hard to find your friend. (Mail is usually no longer forwarded from an old address after one year.)

As noted in an earlier chapter, women especially have to consider the implications for maintaining lifelong friendships of changing their name after marriage. Outplacement expert Larry Stybel notes how much easier it is to locate male friends: "In these Internet days and CD-ROM days, it makes it easy for old friends to look you up and for you to look up old friends. For example, I have the CD-ROM which contains the white pages of the United States. I can look up virtually any living U.S. male who has a listed phone. For women, it is harder."

A registry of maiden names—it would simply state what those names were, no other identifying information—might be a useful way for women to have the same lifetime access to prior friends as do men. (There are some, however, who may caution that a maiden name registry is opening up a Pandora's box, as some women may want their maiden or other married names to be kept secret.)

Whether or not a registry of maiden names is put in place, you have to find a way that works for you to inform your old friends of any name changes in your life. Perhaps, if such dual listings are permissible, you might consider listing yourself under both your maiden and married names. It is actually easier for a woman to inform her old friends of a name change due to marriage, through announcements in local, trade, or national newspapers or publications, as it is to gain the same changed name recognition in the event of a divorce (and a return to her maiden name).

How Friendship Is Changing

The biggest changes in friendship I have observed since I began my research in the late 1970s are that as women moved higher up in the workplace, they began to distrust work friendships more, just as men began to open up and trust friendship more, at work and outside of it. Perhaps during the next decade, you will see women's professional or work-based friendships continue to have the activity orientation that used to characterize the "locker room" male friendships, but with a little more of the old-fashioned female friendship qualities of emotional support and confidence sharing to make it meaningful to you, at and outside of work.

One of the key reasons, I have discovered, that taking time off from work to raise a family is so difficult for most women, in addition to the obvious decline in income and status related to a job and career, is the lack of social contact and work-related friendships that occurs when a woman opts out of the workforce, even temporarily. For most women, work replaced school as the place where they met their friends in post-college or graduate school years. If she leaves work, because of a maternity leave, or for many years while her children are young, it may be harder to form new friendships. Like the older retiree or laid-off worker, gone are the convenient friendships at the workplace (as well as the other more tangible benefits of a job). Outside the work (or, when you are younger, the school) situation, such as in the community, you may feel more vulnerable since you no longer have the shared work environment where you could allow a friendship to more gradually, and naturally, evolve. Without the ongoing shared situation of work or school for being together, a bond may form too quickly, based on too little of the necessary preliminary information that you and your acquaintance might need to predict if your friendship will be mutually beneficial.

Today's men and women are trying harder to fit the range of meaningful relationships into their lives, including spouse, children, and friends. They differ from men and women of previous generations, who overemphasized one group at the expense of the others. There are some, however, who stubbornly cling to their old ways. "I don't have time for friends," Mildred told me when all but two of her six children had left home. "Other than my children, my husband, and my job, I don't have time for friendship."

Two years later, on Labor Day, Mildred called: "I'm all alone in this big house," she moaned. Her husband was working, and all her children were away at their weekend house in the Poconos.

"They invited me along, but I had too much to do."

Despite her apparent loneliness, Mildred said she was too busy to have lunch with me.

Two years later, however, Mildred faced up to the changes in her life, sold her house, moved back to her old neighborhood in Manhattan, reconnecting with friends from her youth. It was a good thing, too, since Mildred soon retired from her job and had even more free time.

Indeed, changes in our society have caused the definition of *friendship* that I originally conceived in the 1980s—an optional role that you should avoid leaning on too heavily in the areas usually reserved for family—has to be revised, in selected instances, with a new post-'90s spin. As psychologist Herbert Freudenberger explains:

> What I find is that many individuals who have a friend who is ill with AIDS are beginning to be called upon to function in a way never called upon [before]. To provide food. To go shopping. To write letters or to make phone calls to family. To clean the house. To do many things in friendship. This is a friend, not a lover. Certainly this kind of illness has promoted friendship and extending of oneself far more than people thought they could.

At this time friendship provides psychological benefits as well as very practical ones: Look at how successful the "Friends don't let friends drive drunk" campaign, co-sponsored by the Ad Council and the U.S. Department of Transportation, has been in reducing drunk driving-related injuries and deaths. As my friend Toni Pietrantuono says, "I saved a few friends' lives. I was the designated driver. If there was drinking at a party, I would leave and come back later to drive the others home."

Today's men are approaching friendship differently as they work at finding time to develop a friendship with their children far more than the typical father of earlier generations. That time for children has to come from somewhere. For some, there may be one less night out "with the boys" or no nights out at all. As men add friendship with their children to the demands of being best friends with their wife as well as giving so much time and energy to their careers, hopefully they will find a way to do it all so they can continue to have their valuable friendships with peers.

As psychologist Linda Sapadin, who has studied male and female friendship patterns, told me: "Many people find that when you have young children, you have friends based around common interests. These friendships may change as people get into other life stages or move away. Many of these friendships tend to dissolve. Since time and energy is always limited, there's no room for developing additional friendships if you keep holding on to the old. Some of the old has to be let go."

Friendshifts are inevitable; as our lives change, so do our friendships. Moving a friendship to a different level of intensity or frequency, or even letting it fade away, does not diminish what that relationship once gave you. But avoid letting a cherished friendship fade simply because of neglect or poor time management. Since friendship is a voluntary relationship, if you fail to return your friends' calls, or be there when you are needed, before long they will find other friends to replace you.

"Not too many of my friendships have ended," a 19-year-old college sophomore writes. "Some friends I haven't seen in awhile, but I still feel that the friendship is still there."

She then added a simple concept that was the cornerstone of a 1970s bestseller, *How to Be Your Own Best Friend*, namely, "Before everyone else, I think it is mainly important to be your own best friend. If you like yourself, others will like you."

That is a fundamental concept to reinforce in a book about friendship: *if you like yourself, you will more easily find others who want to be with you as well.*

One of the many ways to feel significant within yourself is to go the distance for others; to come through even when it puts you out; to help your friend, or your mother, spouse, or sibling, when it is tough for you, when it involves a sacrifice of your time, energy, and personal needs and goals, when it is downright inconvenient, difficult, or even expensive to do so. Those are the times you will be most remembered for or, if others do not take note, those are the times that you will feel, from your deepest sense of self, that you are behaving like the kind of person you want others to be for you.

It is just this fusion of the Great Friend Approach of olden days and the Modern Friend Approach of the new contemporary day that offers you the supreme opportunity to have a tapestry of friends enhancing all aspects of your life. We have come far from the differentiated friendships of the Modern Friend Approach that German sociologist Simmel predicted at the beginning of the twentieth century was all that modern men were capable of achieving. It is true that, in the ideal marriages of today, male and female intimacy replaces the same-sex camaraderie that typified the Great Friend friendships of ancient times. But you have also seen that even in the most exemplary marriages, other friends besides your spouse will be beneficial: casual friends to do things with, close or best friends to share same-sex kindred experiences. Then, because of inevitable shifts in life, friendship may be a life raft if, because of divorce, widowhood, job loss, or family relocations, you find yourself separated temporarily or permanently from the key relationships and experiences that sustained you. Communication may be too swift to comfortably "spill your guts" to each and every friend you acquire; you may have to take longer to selectively choose which friends you will bare your soul to, if any at all. But if you are careful, without being overly cautious or distant, you have the potential for a full and fulfilling life consisting of a multitude of romantic, platonic, and familial relationships.

Friendshifts: you have the potential to benefit from the winning and powerful combination of the exalted status of friendship from the Great Friend Approach of the old world with the advantages of the new Modern Friend Approach: improved status of women; enhanced emotional capacity of men; a heightened awareness of the value of friendship from infancy through the older years; faster communication through e-mail, a fax, overnight mail deliveries, and video conferencing; the globalization and barrier removals to friendship because of the Internet; easier ways of keeping in touch and getting together; a newer age that sees friendship as a valuable

Resources

A Sample of Membership Organizations For Reaching Out*

In addition to getting together with the friends you already have, you may want to develop new best, close, or casual friendships. For some, you may find that initially meeting in an informal way, on your own or through another mutual friend or acquaintance, is the way that works best for you to meet new acquaintances who might become friends. For others, becoming involved in formal community, cultural, volunteer, or professional/ work-related organizations provides an opportunity to meet and connect through shared interests. Here is a sample of some of the membership associations and organizations, listed alphabetically, that address specialized concerns or volunteerism in general; some have state affiliates or local chapters.

*The listings that follow are for informational purposes only; listing does not constitute a recommendation. Furthermore, since addresses may change at any time, these listings should be considered a general guide rather than a definitive reference. The author welcomes learning about any inaccuracies in these listings to facilitate correcting future revisions as well as hearing from other organizations or associations that would like to be considered for possible inclusion in a revised edition or another publication.

American Society for Deaf Children
2848 Arden Way
#210
Sacramento, CA 95825-1373

American Friends Service Committee
c/o Quaker Information Center
1501 Cherry Street
Philadelphia, PA 19102

American Self-Help Clearinghouse
c/o Northwest Convenant Medical Center
25 Pocono Road
Denville, NJ 07834

Big Brothers/Big Sisters of America
230 North 13th Street
Philadelphia, PA 19107

Boys & Girls Clubs of America
1230 West Peachtree Street, N.W.
Atlanta, GA 30309

Boys Town
c/o The Boys Town Press
13603 Flannagan Boulevard
Boys Town, NE 68010

Camp Fire Boys and Girls®
4601 Madison Avenue
Kansas City, MO 64112-1278

The Compassionate Friends
P.O. Box 3696
Oak Brook, IL 60522-3696

Foster Grandparents Program
c/o Corporation for National Service
1201 New York Avenue
Washington, D.C. 20520

Gray Panthers
2025 Pennsylvania Avenue, N.W.
Suite 821
Washington, D.C. 20006

Internet Society
12020 Sunride Valley Drive
Suite 210
Reston, VA 22091

Mothers Against Drunk Drivers (MADD)
511 E. John Carpenter Freeway
No. 700
Irving, TX 75062

National Organization for Victim Assistance
1757 Park Road, N.W.
Washington, D.C. 20010

The National PTA
3330 North Wabash Avenue
Suite 2100
Chicago, Illinois 60611-3690

National Self-Help Clearinghouse
c/o CUNY (City University of New York)
Graduate School & University Center
25 West 43rd Street
Room 620
New York, NY 10036

Overeaters Anonymous
P.O. Box 44020
Rio Rancho, NM 87194

Pen Pals for Grieving Parents
c/o Maribeth Wilder Doerr
P.O. Box 8738
Reno, NV 89507-8738

Widowed Persons Service
601 E Street, N.W.
Washington, D.C. 20049

Where to Find Professional Help

If shyness, low self-esteem, insecurity, or social phobia stops you or someone you care about from developing friendships, help is available from a range of trained counselors—psychotherapists, psychiatric social workers, psychologists, clinical sociological practitioners, family therapists, or psychiatrists. In addition to asking a family physician or friend for a referral, recommendations to member professionals may be available from the local chapter of these national professional associations:

American Academy of Child and Adolescent Psychiatry
Public Information Coordinator
3615 Wisconsin Avenue, N.W.
Washington, D.C. 20016

American Association of Marriage & Family Therapy
1133 15th Street, N.W.
Suite 300
Washington, D.C. 20005-2710

American Psychiatric Association
1400 K Street, N.W.
Washington, D.C. 20005

American Psychological Association
750 First Street, N.E.
Washington, D.C. 20002

National Association of Social Workers
750 First Street, N.E.
Washington, D.C. 20002

Professional Associations

Researchers who have an interest in studying friendship and other personal relationships have at least these two interdisciplinary international membership organizations:

The International Network on Personal Relationships (INPR)
c/o The University of Iowa
Department of Communication Studies
Iowa City, IA 52242

The International Society for the Study of Personal Relationships
    (ISSPR)
c/o University of Louisville
Kent School of Social Work
Louisville, KY 40292

For Further Resources

The American Self-Help Clearinghouse (listed above) publishes *The Self-Help Sourcebook: Finding & Forming Mutual Aid Self-Help Groups*, regularly updated. The fifth edition, compiled and edited by Barbara J. White and Edward J. Madara, with 700 listings arranged by area of concern, may be ordered directly from The American Self-Help Clearinghouse.

In the annual *World Almanac and Book of Facts* (Mahwah, NJ: Funk &Wagnalls) there are sections on where to get help as well as associations and organizations. Available in book form and a CD-ROM version.

The *Encyclopedia of Associations*, updated annually, published by Gale Research Inc. (P.O. Box 33477, Detroit, MI 48232-5477) is a comprehensive listing of 90,000+ membership associations and organizations (including some 23,000 national) plus international, regional, state, and local groups. Available in the reference section of most libraries in a three-volume hardcover edition as well in a CD-ROM version and online through GaleNet.

REFERENCES

There is a wealth of excellent material available about all aspects of friendship, encompassing sociology, psychology, social psychology, anthropology, history, communication, philosophy, literature, women's studies, men's studies, child development, psychiatry, family studies, and gerontology. This section contains complete bibliographical information for references cited in the text; selected additional sources are also included. However, this bibliography is not intended as a definitive guide; exclusion does not diminish the worth of a particular omitted work. The references for the friendship writings of Aristotle, Cicero, Emerson, Bacon, Thoreau, and Montaigne are listed in their entirety. There are now also two popular anthologies that contain excerpts from these and numerous other friendship-related writings: see the listings below for *The Norton Book of Friendship*, edited by Welty and Sharp, and *The Oxford Book of Friendship*, edited by Enright and Rawlinson. For 693 sources on friendship and related topics up to 1984, see J.L. Barkas (a/k/a Jan Yager), *Friendship:A Selected, Annotated Bibliography*.

BOOKS AND REPORTS

Adams, Margaret. *Single Blessedness: Observations on the Single Status in Married Society*. NY: Penguin, 1978.

Allan, Graham A. *A Sociology of Friendship and Kinship*. London:

George Allen & Unwin, 1979.

Aries, Philippe. *Centuries of Childhood.* Trans. by Robert Baldick. NY: Vintage, 1962.

_____. *Western Attitudes Toward Death.* Trans. by Patricia M. Ranum. Baltimore: John Hopkins University Press, 1974.

Aristotle. *Aristotle in Twenty-Three Volumes/Vol. 1,. The Nicomachean Ethics.* Trans. by H. Rackham. Books 8 & 9. Cambridge, MA: Harvard University Press, 1968.

Asher, Steve and John Gottman, ed. *The Development of Children's Friendships.* Cambridge, MA: Cambridge University Press, 1981.

Auchincloss, Louis. *Love Without Wings: Some Friends in Literature and Politics.* Boston: Houghton Mifflin, 1991.

Axtell, Roger E., ed., compiled by The Parker Pen Company. *Do's and Taboos Around the World.* 2nd ed. NY: Wiley, 1990.

Bachrach, Leona L. *Marital Status and Mental Disorder: An Analytical Review.* U.S. Department of Health, Education, and Welfare. Washington, D.C.: U.S. Government Printing Office, 1975.

Bank, Stephen P. and Michael D. Kahn. *The Sibling Bond.* NY: Basic Books, 1982.

Barkas, J.L. (Janet Lee). See Yager, Jan.

Barkley, Nella and Eric Sandburg. *The Crystal-Barkley Guide to Taking Charge of Your Career.* NY: Workman, 1995.

Begleiter, Steve. *Fathers & Sons.* NY: Abbeville Press, 1989.

Bell, Robert R. *Worlds of Friendship.* Beverly Hills, CA: Sage, 1981.

Berger, Peter L. and Hansfried Kellner. *Sociology Reinterpreted.* Garden City, NY: Anchor Press/Doubleday, 1981.

Blau, Peter M. *Exchange and Power in Social Life.* NY: Wiley, 1964.

Blau, Zena Smith. *Old Age in a Changing Society.* NY: Franklin Watts, 1973.

Blieszner, Rosemary and Rebecca G. Adams. *Adult Friendship.* Thousand Oaks, CA: Sage, 1992.

Block, Joel. *Friendship.* NY: Macmillan, 1980.

Bloom, Allan. *Love & Friendship.* NY: Simon & Schuster, 1993.

Bly, Robert. *Iron John: A Book About Men.* NY: Vintage, 1990.

_____. *The Sibling Society.* Reading, MA: Addison-Wesley, 1996.

Bode, Janet. *Trust & Betrayal.* NY: Delacorte Press, 1995.

Bok, Sissela. *Secrets.* NY: Vintage, 1984.

Brain, Robert. *Friends and Lovers.* NY: Basic Books, 1976.

Brenton, Myron. *Friendship.* NY: Stein and Day, 1975.

California Department of Mental Health. *Friends Can Be Good*

Medicine. San Francisco: Pacificon Productions, 1981.

Callanan, Maggie and Patricia Kelley. *Final Gifts: Understanding the Special Awareness, Needs, and Communications of the Dying*. NY: Bantam Books, 1992.

Carnegie, Dale. *How to Win Friends and Influence People*. NY: Pocket Books, 1940 (1936).

Cicero. *On Old Age and on Friendship*. Trans. by Frank O. Copley. Ann Arbor: University of Michigan Press, 1967.

Coser, Lewis. *The Functions of Social Conflict*. NY: Free Press, 1956.

Cott, Nancy. *The Bonds of Womanhood*. New Haven, CT: Yale University Press, 1977.

Covey, Stephen R. *The 7 Habits of Highly Effective People*. NY: Simon & Schuster, 1990.

Davis, Murray S. *Intimate Relations*. NY: Free Press, 1973.

Degler, Carl N. *At Odds: Women and the Family in America from the Revolution to the Present*. NY: Oxford University Press, 1980.

DeMonte, Boye Lafayette. *Japanese Etiquette & Ethics in Business*. 6th ed. Lincolnwood, IL: NTC Business Books, 1994.

Douvan, Elizabeth and Joseph Adelson. *The Adolescent Experience*. NY: Wiley, 1966.

Dowling, Colette. *The Cinderella Complex*. NY: Simon & Schuster, 1981.

Duck, Steve. *Friends, for Life: The Psychology of Close Relationships*. Brighton, England: The Harvester Press Limited, 1983.

_____. *Personal Relationships and Personal Constructs: A Study of Friendship Formation*. NY: Wiley, 1973.

_____. *The Study of Acquaintance*. Hampshire, England: Gower, 1977.

Duck, Steve, ed. *Dynamics of Relationships*. Thousand Oaks, CA: Sage, 1994.

_____. *Personal Relationships 4: Dissolving Personal Relationships*. London: Academic Press, 1982.

_____. *Personal Relationships 5: Repairing Personal Relationships*. London: Academic Press, 1984.

_____ and Robin Gilmour, eds. *Personal Relationships 1: Studying Personal Relationships*. NY: Academic Press, 1981.

_____. *Personal Relationships 2: Developing Personal Relationships*. NY: Academic Press, 1981.

_____. *Personal Relationships 3: Personal Relationships in Disorder*. NY: Academic Press, 1981.

Duck, Steve and Julia T. Wood, eds. *Confronting Relationship Challenges*. Thousand Oaks, CA: Sage, 1995.

Durkheim, Emile. *Suicide: A Study in Sociology*. Trans. by John A. Spauldin and George Simpson. Ed. by G. Simpson. London: Routledge & Kegan Paul, 1952.

Enright, D.J. and David Rawlinson, eds. *The Oxford Book of Friendship*. NY: Oxford University Press, 1992.

Erikson, Erik H. *Childhood and Society*. 2nd ed. NY: Norton, 1950.

Faber, Adele and Elaine Mazlish. *Siblings Without Rivalry*. NY: Avon, 1987.

Feinberg, Paul. *Friends*. NY: Quick Fox, 1980.

Foot, H.C., A.J. Chapman, and J.R. Smith, eds. *Friends and Social Relations in Children*. London: Wiley, 1980.

Freud, Anna. *The Ego and the Mechanisms of Defense*. Rev. ed. NY: International Universities Press, 1966.

Freudenberger, Herbert with Geraldine Richelson. *Burn Out*. Garden City, NY: Doubleday, 1980.

Friday, Nancy. *My Mother/Myself*. NY: Delacorte Press, 1977.

_____. *Jealousy*. NY: Bantam Books, 1985.

Fromm, Erich. *The Art of Loving*. NY: Harper & Row, 1956, 1974.

Glazer-Melbin, Nona, ed. *Old Family/New Family: Interpersonal Relationships*. NY: Van Nostrand, 1975.

Goffman, Erving. *Stigma: Notes on the Management of Spoiled Identity*. Englewood Cliffs, N. J.: Prentice-Hall, 1963.

Goode, William J. *After Divorce*. Glencoe, IL: Free Press, 1956.

Gray, John. *Men Are from Mars, Women Are from Venus*. NY: HarperCollins, 1992.

_____. *Men, Women and Relationships*. Rev. 2nd ed. Hillsboro, OR: Beyond Words Publishing, Inc., 1993.

Greeley, Andrew M. *The Friendship Game*. Garden City, NY: Doubleday, 1971.

Gurdin, J. Barry. *Amitie/Friendship: An Investigation into Cross-Cultural Styles in Canada and the United States*. San Francisco: Austin & Winfield, 1996.

Hall, Edward T. *The Dance of Life: The Other Dimension of Time*. Garden City, NY: Doubleday, 1983.

_____. *The Silent Language*. Garden City, NY: Doubleday, 1959.

Haskins, James. *Street Gangs: Yesterday and Today*. NY: Hastings House, 1974.

Homans, George. *The Human Group*. NY: Harcourt, 1950.

Hymer, Sharon. *Confessions and Psychotherapy*. NY: Gardner Press, 1988.

James, Muriel and Louis M. Savary. *The Heart of Friendship*. NY: Harper & Row, 1976.

Jourard, Sidney M. *The Transparent Self*. NY: Van Nostrand, 1975.

Kadushin, Charles. *Why People Go to Psychiatrists*. NY: Atherton, 1969.

Krantzler, Mel. *Creative Divorce*. NY: New American Library, 1973.

Kubler-Ross, Elisabeth. *On Death and Dying*. NY: Macmillan, 1976.

Leefeldt, Christine and Ernest Callenbach. *The Art of Friendship*. NY: Berkley, 1980.

Levinson, Daniel J. with Charlotte N. Darrow, Edward B. Klein, Maria H. Levinson, and Braxton McKee. *The Seasons of a Man's Life*. NY: Ballantine, 1978.

Lewis, Michael and Leonard A. Rosenblum, eds. *Friendship and Peer Relations*. NY: Wiley, 1975.

Liebow, Elliot. *Tally's Corner*. Boston: Little, Brown, 1967.

Lindsey, Karen. *Friends as Family*. Boston: Beacon Press, 1981.

Lopata, Helena. *Women as Widows*. NY: Elsevier Nort Holand, 1979.

Lopate, Phillip. *Against Joie de Vivre*. NY: Simon & Schuster, Poseidon Press, 1989.

Lynch, James J. *The Broken Heart: The Medical Consequences of Loneliness*. NY: Basic Books, 1979.

Margolies, Eva. *The Best of Friends, the Worst of Enemies: Women's Hidden Power over Women*. Garden City, NY: Doubleday, 1985.

McCall, George, et al. *Social Relationships*. Chicago: Aldine, 1970.

McDermott, Patti. *Sisters and Brothers: Resolving Your Adult Sibling Relationships*. Los Angeles: Lowell House, 1992.

Miller, Stuart. *Men & Friendship*. Boston: Houghton Mifflin, 1983.

Nardi, Peter M., ed. *Men's Friendships*. Newbury Park, CA: Sage, 1992.

Newman, Mildred and Bernard Berkowitz with Jean Owen. *How to Be Your Own Best Friend*. NY: Ballantine Books, 1971.

Perlman, Dan and Letitia Anne Peplau, eds. *Loneliness*. NY: Wiley-Interscience, 1982.

Plato. *Lysis, or Friendship* in *The Works of Plato*, ed. by Irwin Edman. NY: Modern Library, 1928.

Pogrebin, Letty Cottin. *Among Friends*. NY: McGraw Hill, 1985.

_____. *Getting Over Getting Older*. NY: Little, Brown, 1996.

Rawlings, Steve and Arlene Saluter. *Household and Family*

Characteristics: March 1994. Washington, D.C.: Bureau of the Census, U.S. Department of Commerce, Sept. 1995.

Resnick, Jane Parker, ed. *Love and Friendship*. Stamford, CT: Longmeadow Press, 1992.

Riverside Mothers Group. *Don't Forget the Rubber Ducky!* NY: Pocket Books, 1995.

_____. *Entertain Me!* NY: Pocket Books, 1993.

Robinson, Rita. *The Friendship Book: The Art of Making and Keeping Friends*. North Hollywood, CA: Newcastle, 1992.

Rowland, Diana. *Japanese Business Etiquette*. NY: Warner Books, 1985.

Rubin, Lillian Breslow. *Intimate Strangers*. NY: Harper & Row, 1983.

_____. *Just Friends*. NY: Harper & Row, 1985.

Rubin, Zick. *Children's Friendships*. Cambridge, MA: Harvard University Press, 1980.

Saluter, Arlene. *Marital Status and Living Arrangements: March 1994*. Washington, D.C.: Bureau of the Census, U.S. Department of Commerce, Feb. 1996.

Schutz, Susan Polis. *To My Daughter with Love*. Boulder, CO: Blue Mountain Arts, 1986.

Secunda, Victoria. *When You and Your Mother Can't Be Friends*. NY: Delacorte, 1990.

_____ . *Women and Their Fathers: The Sexual and Romantic Impact of the First Man in Your Life*. NY: Dell, 1992.

Selman, Robert L. *The Growth of Interpersonal Understanding*. NY: Academic Press, 1980.

_____ and Lynn Hickey Schultz. *Making a Friend in Youth: Developmental Theory and Pair Therapy*. Chicago: University of Chicago Press, n.d.

Shain, Merle. *Some Men Are More Perfect Than Others*. NY: Charterhouse, 1973.

_____. *When Lovers Are Friends*. Philadelphia: Lippincott, 1978.

Sheehy, Gail. *Passages*. NY: Bantam, 1977.

Siegel, Paula M. *See* Riverside Mothers Group.

Simmel, Geoge. *The Sociology of George Simmel*. Trans. by Kurt H. Wolff. NY: Fress Press, 1950.

Stein, Peter J. *Single*. Englewood Cliffs, N.J.: Prentice-Hall, 1976.

Stocking, S. Holly, Diana Arezzo, and Shelley Leavitt in cooperation with the Boys Town Center. *Helping Kids Makes Friends*. Allen, TX: Argus Communications, n.d.

Sullivan, Harry Stack. *The Interpersonal Theory of Psychiatry.* NY: Norton, 1953.

Tannen, Deborah. *Conversational Style: Analyzing Talk Among Friends.* Norwood, NJ: Ablex, 1984.

_____. *You Just Don't Understand: Women and Men in Conversation.* NY: Ballantine Books, 1990.

Tennov, Dorothy. *Love and Limerance.* NY: Stein and Day, 1979.

Thoreau, Henry David. *The Portable Thoreau.* NY: Viking, 1964.

Vanzetti, Nelly and Steve Duck, eds. *A Lifetime of Relationships.* Pacific Grove, CA: Brooks/Cole, 1996.

Vaughan, Diane. *Uncoupling: Turning Points in Intimate Relationships.* NY: Oxford University Press, 1986 (Vintage Books ed., Random House, 1990).

Wallach, Anne Tolstoi. *Women's Work.* NY: New American Library, 1981.

Weiss, Robert S. ed. *Loneliness: The Experience of Emotional and Social Isolation.* Foreword by David Riesman. Cambridge, MA: MIT Press, 1973.

_____. *Marital Separation.* NY: Basic Books, 1975.

Welty, Eudora and Ronald A. Sharp, eds. *The Norton Book of Friendship.* NY: Norton, 1991.

Wheelis, Allen. *How People Change.* NY: Harper, 1975.

Whyte, William Foote. *Street Corner Society.* Chicago: University of Chicago Press, 1955.

Wyse, Lois. *Women Make the Best Friends.* NY: Simon & Schuster, 1995.

Yager, Jan (a/k/a J.L. Barkas). *Business Protocol: How to Survive & Succeed in Business.* NY: Wiley, 1991.

_____. *Creative Time Management.* Englewood Cliffs, N.J.: Prentice-Hall, 1984.

_____. *Friendship: A Selected, Annotated Bibliography.* NY: Garland, 1985.

_____. *The Help Book.* NY: Scribner's, 1979.

_____. *Making the Office Work for You.* NY: Doubleday, 1989.

_____. *Single in America.* NY: Atheneum, 1980.

_____. *The Vegetable Passion: The History of the Vegetarian State of Mind.* NY: Scribner's, 1978.

_____. *Victims.* NY: Scribner's, 1978.

Youniss, James. *Parents and Peers in Social Development.* Chicago: University of Chicago Press, 1980.

Zey, Michael G. *The Mentor Connection.* Homewood, IL: Dow Jones-Irwin, 1984.

ARTICLES IN JOURNALS, MAGAZINES, AND NEWSPAPERS AND CHAPTERS IN BOOKS

Adams, Margaret. "The Single Woman in Today's Society: A Reappraisal." *American Journal of Orthopsychiatry* 41 (October 1971):776-786.

Albert, S. and S. Kessler. "Ending Social Encounters." *Journal of Experimental Social Psychology* 14 (1978): 541-553.

Allan, Graham. "Class Variation in Friendship Patterns." *British Journal of Sociology* 28 (September 1977):389-393.

Bacon, Sir Francis. "Of Friendship" (1625) in *Classic Essays in English.* Ed. by Josephine Miles. Boston: Little, Brown, 1965.

Bahr, Robert. "Passionate Friendships Between Men." *MGF (Men's Guide to Fashion),* Dec. 1987, pp. 18-20.

Berger, Joseph."For 200 in the Tenzer Family, Grandpa's Circle Is Unbroken." *New York Times,* Oct. 7, 1991, pp. 1, B5.

Berger, Peter L. and Hansfried Kellner. "Marriage and the Construction of Reality: An Exercise in the Microsociology of Knowledge." *Diogenes* 46 (1964):1-25.

Berkman, Lisa F. and Leonard Syme. "Social Networks, Host Resistance, and Mortality: A Nine-Year Follow-up Study of Alameda County Residents." *American Journal of Epidemiology* 109 (1979):186-204.

Berman, Ellen. "How to Get Along with Your Parents Now That You're an Adult." *Bottom Line Personal,* Sept. 30, 1988, pp. 9-10.

"Best Friends Commit Suicide." *The Evening Bulletin* (Gladstone, MO), March 26, 1980, p. C4.

Bigelow, Brian J. "Children's Friendship Expectations." *Child Development* 48 (March 1977):246-253.

Bird, Laura. "Lazarus' IBM Coup Was All About Relationships." *Wall Street Journal,* May 26, 1994, pp. B1, B10.

Bombeck, Erma. "Please Don't Try to Cheer Me Up." *The Advocate* (Stamford, CT), Dec. 7, 1993, p. B7.

_____. "The Very Best Friendships Are Blind." *The Advocate* (Stamford, CT), Oct. 16, 1993, p. B9.

Booth, Alan. "Sex and Social Participation." *American Sociological*

Review 37 (April 1972):183-192.

_____ and Elaine Hess. "Cross-Sex Friendship." *Journal of Marriage and the Family,* Feb. 1974, pp. 38-47.

Brain, Robert. "Somebody Else Should Be Your Own Best Friend." *Psychology Today*, Oct. 1977, pp. 83-84, 120.

Brody, Jane E. "Personal Health: To Avoid Loneliness, Both Emotional and Social Attachments Are Necessary." *New York Times*, April 6, 1983, p. C10.

_____. "Personal Health: Maintaining Friendships for the Sake of Your Health." *New York Times*, Feb. 5, 1992, p. C12.

Broyard, Anatole. "Whistling in the Dark," review of *Friends and Lovers* by Robert Brain. *The New York Times*, Oct. 5, 1976, p. 43.

Burke, Sarah. "In the Presence of Animals: Health Professionals No Longer Scoff at the Therapeutic Effects of Pets." *U.S. News & World Report*, Feb. 24, 1992, pp. 64-65.

Carter, Richard G. "Some Friends Are Worth the Trouble." *Daily News*, Nov. 23, 1989, p. 41.

Cavanaugh, Katherine. "Netgirl: Digital 'Dear Abby.'" *New York Post*, April 4, 1996, p. 34.

Challman, Robert C. "Factors Influencing Friendships Among Preschool Children." *Child Development* 3 (1932):146-158.

Collins, Clare. "Friendships Built on Bytes and Fibers." *New York Times*, Jan. 5, 1992, p. 32.

Corsaro, William A. "'We're Friends, Right?' Children's Use of Access Rituals in Nursery School." *Language in Society* 8 (1979):315-336.

Crispell, Diane. "People Patterns: In Friends, Many See Reflection of Themselves." *Wall Street Journal*, June 30, 1993, p. B1.

Denny, Alma. "Recalling What the Family Never Knew." *New York Times*, June 24, 1981, p. C16.

Dickens, Wenda J. and Daniel Perlman. "Friendship over the Life-cycle" in *Developing Personal Relationships*, chapter 4. Ed. by S. Duck and R. Gilmour. NY: Academic Press, 1981.

Duncan, Lois. "How Not to Lose Friends over Money." *Woman's Day*, March 25, 1986, pp. 20, 22, 25.

Eckerman, Carol O. and Judith L. Whatley. "Toys and Social Interaction Between Infant Peers." *Child Development* 48 (1977):1645-1656.

Eder, Donna and Maureen T. Hallinan. "Sex Differences in Children's Friendships." *American Sociological Review* 43 (April 1978):237-250.

Emerson, Ralph Waldo. "Love" and "Friendship" in *Essays by Ralph Waldo Emerson*, pages 121-156. NY: Harper & Row, 1951.

Enfield, Susan. "The New Buddy System.." *MINC*, August 1991, pp. 86-90.

Fine, Gary Alan. "Social Components of Children's Gossip." *Journal of Communication* 27 (Winter 1977):181-185.

Fischer, Lucy Rose. "Transitions in the Mother-Daughter Relationship." *Journal of Marriage and the Family*, August 1981, pp. 613-622.

Freud, Sigmund. "Certain Neurotic Mechanisms in Jealousy, Paranoia and Homosexuality." *Collected Papers of Sigmund Freud,* vol. 2. Ed. by Ernest Jones. NY: Basic Books, 1959.

Gaines, Stanley O., Jr. "Exchange of Respect-Denying Behaviors Among Male-Female Friendships." *Journal of Social and Personal Relationships* 11 (1994):5-24.

Genasci, Lisa. "Love & the Bottom Line." *The Advocate* (Stamford, CT), Feb. 12, 1995, Sect. F, pp. F1- F2.

Goleman, Daniel. "As Sex Roles Change, Men Turn to Therapy to Cope with Stress." *New York Times*, August 21, 1984, pp. C1, C5.

_____. "Emotional Support Has Its Destructive Side." *New York Times*, August 27, 1985, pp. C1, C3.

_____."Stress and Isolation Tied to a Reduced Life Span." *New York Times*, Dec. 7, 1993, p. C5.

_____. "Therapy Groups Yield Surprising Benefits for Cancer Patients." *New York Times*, Nov. 23, 1989, p. B15.

Goode, William J. "A Theory of Role Strain." *American Sociological Review* 25 (1960):483-496.

Gove, Walter R. "Sex, Marital Status, and Mortality." *American Journal of Sociology* 79 (July 1973):45-67.

Green, Elise Hart. "Friendships and Quarrels Among Preschool Children." *Child Development* 4 (1933):237-252.

Hacker, Helen Mayer. "Blabbermouths and Clams: Sex Differences in Self-Disclosure in Same-Sex and Cross-Sex Friendship Dyads." *Psychology of Women Quarterly* 5 (April 1981):385-401.

Hallinan, Maureen T. "Classroom Racial Composition and Children's Friendships." *Social Forces* 61 (September 1982):56-72.

Halpern, Howard. "You *Can* Establish a Friendship with Your Adult Children." *Bottom Line Personal*, July 30, 1986, pp. 13-14.

Hare, A. Paul. *Handbook of Small Group Research*, adapted and reprinted in Donald Light Jr. and Suzanne Keller, *Sociology,* 2nd ed. NY: Knopf, 1979, p. 185.

Hartup, Willard W. "Children and Their Friends" in *Issues in Childhood Social Development*, chapter 5, pp. 130-170. Ed. by H. McGurk. London: Methuen, 1978.

_____. "The Company They Keep: Friendships and Their Developmental Significance." *Child Development* 67 (1996):1-13.

Hess, Beth B. "Friendship and Gender Roles over the Life Course" in *Single Life*, pp. 104-115. Ed. by Peter J. Stein. NY: St. Martin's Press, 1981.

Hoffer, William. "Friends in High Places." *Writer's Digest,* October 1986, pp. 42-44.

Honig, Alice Sterling and Carl DiPerna. "Research Review: Peer Relations of Infants and Toddlers." *Day Care and Early Education*, Spring 1983, pp. 36-39.

Hughes, Michael and Walter R. Gove. "Living Alone, Social Integration, and Mental Health." *American Journal of Sociology* 87 (July 1981):48-74.

Irby, Christopher. "You Know You Shouldn't Lend Money to a Friend, but…" *Woman*, Sept. 1989, pp. 82-83.

Irish, Donald P. "Sibling Interaction: A Neglected Aspect in Family Life Research." *Social Forces* 42 (March 1964):279-288.

Jacklin, Carol Nagy and Eleanor E. Maccoby. "Social Behavior at Thirty-three Months in Same-Sex and Mixed-Sex Dyads." *Child Development* 49 (1978):557-569.

Jacobson, David. "'Fair-weather Friend: Label and Context in Middle-Class Friendships." *Journal of Anthropological Research* 31 (1975):225-234.

Jecker, Jon and David Landy. "Liking a Person as a Function of Doing Him a Favor." *Human Relations* 22 (1969):371-378.

Kadushin, Charles. "The Friends and Supporters of Psychotherapy: On Social Circles in Urban Life." *American Sociological Review* 31 (1968):786-802.

Karr, Albert R. "It's Who You Know." *The Wall Street Journal,* Oct. 16, 1990, p.1.

Kellogg, Mary Alice. "When True-Blue Turns Green." *Savvy*, May 1986, p. 28.

Kelly, Michael. "A President-Elect with a Way with People." *New York Times,* November 4, 1992, pp. 1, B2.

Knupfer, Genevieve, Walter Clark, and Robin Room. "The Mental Health of the Unmarried." *American Journal of Psychiatry* (Feb. 1966):841-851.

Kobrin, Frances E. and Gerry E. Hendershot. "Do Family Ties Reduce Mortality? Evidence from the United States, 1966-1968." *Journal of Marriage and the Family* 39 (Nov. 1977):737-745.

Kwitney, Ziva. "Bosom Buddies." *Seattle Post-Intelligencer*, Feb. 15, 1981, pp. 3, 10-11.

La Gaipa, John J. "Children's Friendships" in *Developing Personal Relationships,* pp. 159-183. Ed. by Steve Duck and Robin Gilmour. NY: Academic Press, 1981.

Lazarsfeld, Paul F. and Robert K. Merton. "Friendship as Social Process: A Substantive and Methodological Analysis." In *Freedom and Control in Modern Society*, pp. 18-66. Ed. by M. Berger, T. Abel, and C. Page. NY: Van Nostrand, 1954.

Leonard, John. "Private Lives: On Losing a Friend Your Private World Can Least Afford." *New York Times*, March 2, 1977, p. C14.

Lever, Janet. "Sex Differences in the Games Children Play." *Social Problems* 23 (1976):478-487.

Lewis, Robert A. "Emotional Intimacy Among Men." *Journal of Social Issues* 34 (1978):108-121.

Linscott, Judith. "Play Group Success Story." *Parents*, Nov. 1992, pp. 124, 126, 129.

Litwak, Eugene and Ivan Szelenyi. "Primary Group Structures and Their Functions: Kin, Neighbors, and Friends." *American Sociological Review* 34 (August 1969):465-481.

Lopate, Philip. "What Friends Are For." *Utne Reader*, Sept./Oct. 1993, pp. 78-85.

Louv, Richard. "A Place for Neighbors." *Parents*, Nov. 1992, pp. 93-95.

Lowenthal, Marjorie Fisk. "Social Isolation and Mental Illness in Old Age." *American Sociological Review* 29 (1964):54-70.

Margolis, Susan. "Some of My Best Friends Are Men." *Working Woman Weekends,* June 1988, pp. 146-147.

Miller, Leslie. "Sexual Abuse Survivors Find Strength to Speak in Numbers." *USA Today*, Aug. 27, 1992, p. 6D.

Montaigne. "Of Friendship" in *The Complete Essays of Montaigne,* pp. 135-144. Ed. and trans. by Donald M. Frame. Stanford, CA: Stanford University Press, 1958.

Murphy, Ann Pleshette. "Friends for Life." *Parents,* 1989, p. 9.

Naegele, Kaspar D. "Friendship and Acquaintances: An Exploration of Some Social Distinctions." *Harvard Educational Review* 28 (1958):232-252.

Nardi, Peter M. "That's What Friends Are For." In *Modern Homosexualities*, Ken Plummer, ed., pp. 108-120. NY: Routledge, 1992."

_____ and Drury Sherrod. "Friendship in the Lives of Gay Men and Lesbians." *Journal of Social and Personal Relationships.* 11 (1994):185-199.

Nelson, Sara. "The Day AIDS Hit Home." *Self,* Jan. 1988, pp. 117-119.

Nemy, Enid. "Lunch for Women: Food and Ideas." *New York Times,* April 6, 1983, p. C8.

Newcomb, Theodore M. "The Prediction of Interpersonal Attraction." *The American Psychologist* 11 (Nov. 1956):575-586.

Oden, Sherri and Steven R. Asher. "Coaching Children in Social Skills for Friendship Making." *Child Development* 48 (1977):495-506.

Olds, Sally Wendkos. "How to Stay Close in Love Without Losing Your Salf." *Redbook*, April 1978, pp. 107, 164, 166, 168.

Ornish, Dean. "Isolation...and Your Heart." *Bottom Line Personal,* July 15, 1992, pp. 11-13.

Paine, Robert. "In Search of Friendship: An Exploratory Analysis in 'Middle-Class' Culture." *Man,* new series 4 (Dec. 1969):505-524.

Parlee, Mary Brown and *Psychology Today* editors. "The Friendship Bond: PT's Survey Report." *Psychology Today*, Oct. 1979, pp. 43-54, 113.

Pearlin, Leonard I. and Joyce B. Johnson. "Marital Status, Life-Strains and Depression." *American Sociological Review* 42 (Oct. 1977):704-715.

Plath, David W. "Contours of Consociation: Lessons from a Japanese Narrative" in *Life-Span Development and Behavior*, vol. 3, pp. 287-305. NY: Academic Press, 1981.

Pleck, Joseph H. "Man to Man: Is Brotherhood Possible?" in Nona Glazer-Malbin, ed.*Old Family/New Family*. NY: D. Van Nostrand, 1975, pp. 229-244.

Plummer, William and Sandra Gurvis. "After 58 Years, a Round-Robin Letter Keeps on Delivering." *People*, 1988, pp. 99-100.

Pogrebin, Letty Cottin. "The Times of Your Life: Marriage, Children, More." *Family Circle*, May 14, 1996, pp. 50, 52.

_____. "When Friends Come Before Family." *Family Circle*, June 28, 1994, pp. 54, 56,+.

Pollitt, Katha. "Hers: Why Are Women Psychotherapy's Best Customers?" *New York Times*, Jan. 9, 1986, p. C2.

Pool, Ithiel de Sola and Manfred Kochen. "Contacts and Influence." *Social Network* 1 (1978):5-51.

Powers, Edward A. and Gordon L. Bultena. "Sex Differences in Intimate Friendships of Old Age." *Journal of Marriage and the Family* (Nov. 976):739-747.

Prose, Francine. "Living with Choices: The Home-versus-Work Decision puts a Strain on Mothers—and Their Friendships." *Parents*, May 1989, pp. 131-133.

Reina, Ruben E. "Two Patterns of Friendship in a Guatemalan Community" in *Society and Self.* Bartlett H. Stoodley, ed. Glencoe, IL: Free Press, 1962, pp. 215-222.

Rosen, Norma. "Hers: Fraud by Friendship." *New York Times Magazine*, Aug. 26, 1990, Sec. 6, pp. 24, 65.

Rosenblatt, Roger. "Friends and Countrymen." *Time*, July 21, 1980, pp. 50-51.

Sapadin, Linda A. "Friendship and Gender: Perspectives of Professional Men and Women." *Journal of Social and Personal Relationships* 5 (1988):387-403.

Schwartz, Barry. "The Social Psychology of the Gift." *American Journal of Sociology* 73 (July 1967):1-11.

Secunda, Victoria. "The *New Woman* Friend." *New Woman*, August 1992, pp. 72-75.

Seiden, Anne M. and Pauline B. Bart. "Woman to Woman: Is Sisterhood Powerful?" in *Old Family/New Family*, pp. 189-228. NY: Van Nostrand, 1975.

Selman, Robert L. and Anne P. Selman. "Children's Ideas About Friendship: A New Theory." *Psychology Today*, Oct. 1979, pp. 71-72, 74, 79-80, 114.

Sharpe, Anita. "How to Find Guys to Hang Around and Do Stuff With." *Wall Street Journal*, May 9, 1994, pp. 1, A6.

Shotland, R. Lance and Jane M. Craig. "Can Men and Women Differentiate Between Friendly and Sexually Interested Behavior?" *Social Psychology Quarterly* 51 (1988): 66-73.

Shulman, Norman. "Life-Cycle Variations in Patterns of Close Relationships." *Journal of Marriage and the Family* 37 (Nov. 1975):813-821.

Simmel, Georg. "Friendship, Love and Secrecy." Trans. by Albion Small. *American Journal of Sociology* 11 (1906):457-466.

Simon, Rita James, Gail Crotts, and Linda Mahan. "An Empirical Note About Married Women and Their Friends." *Social Forces* 48 (June

1970):520-525.

Slade, Margot. "Marriage of a Friend: Mixed Blessing." *New York Times*, Dec. 31, 1984, p. 18.

Smith-Rosenberg, Carroll. "The Female World of Love and Ritual: Relations Between Women in Nineteenth Century America." *Signs* 1 (August 1975):1-29.

Sobel, Dava. "Freud's Fragmented Legacy." *New York Times Magazine*, Oct. 26, 1980, pp. 28-31, 102, 104, 106-108.

Stein, Harry. "Just Good Friends." *Esquire,* August 1980, pp. 21-23.

Stern, Barbara Land. "Your Well-Being: Improve a Life-long Relationship: Make Friends with Your Parents." *Vogue*, June 1983, p. 114.

Sutcliffe, J.L. and B.D. Crabbe. "Incidence and Degrees of Friendship in Urban and Rural Areas." *Social Forces* 42 (Oct. 1963):60-67.

Suttles, Gerald. "Friendship as a Social Institution" in *Social Relationships*, ed. by G.J. McCall, et al. Chicago: Aldine, 1970.

Tognoli, Jerome. "Male Friendship and Intimacy Across the Life Span." *Family Relations* 29 (July 1980):273-79.

Vaughan, Diane. "Uncoupling: The Social Construction of Divorce" in *Social Interaction*, pp. 323-338. NY: St. Martin's Press, 1979.

Verbrugge, Lois M. "Marital Status and Health." *Journal of Marriage and the Family* 41 (May 1979): 267-285.

_____. "The Structure of Adult Friendship Choices." *Social Forces* 56 (Dec. 1977):576-597.

Weinraub, Bernard. "Bush Urges Youngsters to Help Friends on Drugs." *New York Times*, Sept. 13, 1989, p.A24.

Weiss, Robert S. "The Emotional Impact of Marital Separation." *Journal of Social Issues* 32 (1976):135-145.

Weissman, Myrna M. and Eugene S. Paykel. "Moving and Depression in Women." *Society* 9 (July/August 1972):24-28.

Williams, Robin M. "Friendship and Social Values in a Suburban Community." *Pacific Sociological Review* 2 (1959):3-10.

Wolfe, Linda. "Friendship in the City." *New York* July 18, 1983, pp. 20-28.

Yager, Jan. "The Dual-Career Couple: Making Time for Each Other." *Modern Bride,* Oct./Nov. 1989, p. 150.

_____. "The Friendship Factor in Marriage." *American Baby*, March 1988, pp. 65, 78+.

_____. "Marriage and Friendship." *Modern Bride,* Feb/March 1987, pp. 500, 502.

_____. "What to Do If You're Fired." *Parade,* May 31, 1992, p. 16.

_____. "Why New Mothers Need New Friends." *McCall's,* Jan. 1988, p. 41.

_____. "Working with Your Husband: Blessing or Curse?" *Modern Bride,* Dec./Jan. 1981, pp. 20, 28, 30.

MISCELLANEOUS MATERIALS AND FILMS

Barkas, J.L. See Jan Yager

Bigelow, Brian J. "Disengagement and Development of Social Concepts: Toward a Theory of Friendship." Paper presented at the First International Conference on Personal Relationships, Madison, WI, July 1982.

Boys Town Center. "Helping Friendless Children." Boys Town, NE: The Boys Town Center, booklet, n.d. (received Feb. 1983).

"Break the Silence: Kids Against Child Abuse." Written and directed by Melissa Jo Peltier. Executive Producer, Arthur Shapiro. Produced by Brenda Reiswerg. Aired on CBS-TV, May 31, 1994.

Columbia University Press. *The Columbia Dictionary of Quotations.* NY: Columbia University Press, 1993, 1995. (CD-ROM version in *Microsoft Bookshelf,* 1996 edition.)

Davidson, Lynn and Lucile Duberman. "Same-Sex Friendships: A Gender Comparison of Dyads." Unpublished manuscript, 1979.

Fischer, Claude S. and Stacey J. Oliker. "Friendship, Sex, and the Life Cycle." Berkeley: Institute of Urban and Regional Development, University of California, March 1980.

Gurdin, J. Barry. "Some of My Best Friends Are...The Relationship of Ethnicity to Close Friendship." Paper prepared for the XI International Congress of Anthropological and Ethnological Science, 1983.

Hacker, Helen Mayer. "The Influence of Gender Roles on Reciprocal Ratings in Same-Sex and Cross-Sex Friendship Dyads." Paper presented at the IXth World Congress of Sociology, I.S.A. Uppsala, Sweden, August 14-19, 1978.

Hartup, Willard W. and Nan Stevens. "Friendships and adaptation in the life course." Manuscript received June 1996 (in press, *Psychological Bulletin*).

"It's a Wonderful Life." Directed by Frank Capra. Written by Frank Capra, Frances Goodrich, Albert Hackett, and Jo Swerling (1946).

deJong-Gierveld, Jenny. "Loneliness and the Degree of Intimacy in Personal Relationships." Paper presented at the First International Conference on Personal Relationships, Madison, WI, July 1982.

Stein, Peter J. "Understanding Single Adulthood." Paper presented at the National Council on Family Relations annual meeting, Aug. 14-18, 1979, Boston, MA.

"Thelma & Louise." Directed by Ridley Scott. Written by Callie Khouri. (1991).

Tuchman, Gaye. "Kaddish for an American Family." Unpublished essay.

Yager, Jan. "Friendship Patterns Among Young Urban Single Women." Doctoral dissertation, City University of New York, 1983.

____. "Single and Jewish: Conversations with Unaffiliated Jewish Singles." NY: American Jewish Committee, Oct. 1985.

Yale School of Medicine, Office of Public Information. "Emotional Support Predicts Survival After Heart Attacks," *Yale Medical News.* Press release, Dec. 14, 1992 (about Dr. Lisa F. Berkman's *Annals of Internal Medicine* epidemiology study reported in the Dec. 15th issue).

Acknowledgments

First and foremost, to my very best friend, mentor, and husband, Fred Yager, I say, "Thanks." Fred has been hearing about this book and reading its various drafts since our first date more than a decade ago. He is my biggest fan, and I thank him for his love and collaborative support. I also want to thank our two sons for their patience and understanding for the extended periods of time when I was preoccupied with researching, writing, contemplating, and rewriting this book.

There are others who have been there for me, through thick and thin: my parents, the late Dr. William Barkas, and his beloved wife, my mother, Gladys Barkas; my exceptional and wonderful sister Eileen Hoffman, my sister-in-law Karen, and my devoted close friends: Joyce Guy-Patton, Mary Tierney, Judy Cohn, Nona Aguilar, Sharon Fisher, Marcia Hoffenberg, Mitzi Lyman, Gail Tuchman, Cathy Sebor, Elia Schneider, Ginny Mugavero, Jennifer Ash, Joyce Bronstein, Lucy Freeman, Lucy Hedrick, Pramila Poddar, and Rhonda Ginsberg; my niece Vanessa, my nephews Sky Lobovits and Ariel; Trish; my great-nephew, Seth; Carrie; my mother-in-law, Mary Yager; my sisters-in-law Becky, Mary, Karen, and Lisa; my brother-in-laws Dick, Billy, and Joel; all my aunts (Peggy Silver, Grace Barkas, the late Evelyn Hodes), uncles (Irving Silver, Arthur Barkas, Sye Hodes), and the rest of my extended family; my cousins whom I consider friends: Carol Ann Finkelstein and Morris Shoretz, Phyllis Silver Henkel, Daryl Shulman, Keith and Arlene Silver, Stu and Fran Silver, Pnina and Harriet Klein, Leila and Milt Posner, Suzanne, Allan and Benjamin Katz, Karen and David Walant, and all their children; Val Smith, a special person who, from the moment we all met her, has helped my family feel at home in the Connecticut town we relocated to; Dr. David Leeds; and my parents' friends Charlotte and Hank Greene, and Dave and Lil Schaeffer.

Next, I want to thank all those I have interviewed, or who filled out a questionnaire, over the years, named or anonymous, whether or not your comments or quotes were actually printed in this book. Your cooperation, and trust, have been pivotal to the original research upon which this book is based. I especially want to thank those I interviewed for my dissertation, reports and book on singles, booklet about friendship over the life cycle, articles about marriage and friendship, study of work and friendship, and study of the adult survivors of childhood sexual abuse.

A special thanks to Kathron Compton at the Society of Human Resource Management, who was kind enough to provide me with the randomly generated labels of members that enabled me to ultimately analyze surveys from 257 male and female SHRM members. Those surveys, and follow-up interviews, helped provide me many of the insights into work and friendship shared in this book. I also want to especially thank Dr. Steve Duck of the University of Iowa, whom I first met at a conference on interpersonal relationships at the University of Wisconsin in 1982. Dr. Duck is a well-known name in the field of interpersonal relationships; he has always been enthusiastic and helpful to my research. Researchers in interpersonal relationships owe Dr. Duck a special thanks for all he has done over the years bringing together so many from diverse disciplines at the International Network on Personal Relationships. Outplacement expert Laurence J. Stybel, Ed.D., was kind enough to read a draft of the manuscript and to provide valuable feedback and reactions. There are others who read some or all of various drafts of this book and provided welcome comments: Bill Daniels, Harry Levinson, Dan Perlman, Zick Rubin, Nella Barkley, Willard W. Hartup, Beverely Cuthbertson-Johnson, James M. Shuart, Lucy Freeman, Mike DeSola, Vicky Secunda, Jonathan G. Harris, Georgina Coombs, Mitch Davis, Stephen R. Covey, Albert Ellis, Gary Alan Fine, Elaine Hatfield, Barbara Church-Katten, Lucy H. Hedrick, Jane Pollak, Frances Horowitz, and John G. Murphy. (Since this list is still expanding, forgive me if your name does not appear here.)

I also want to thank sociologist and criminologist Richard Quinney, who was familiar with my book *Victims* and, in 1978, encouraged me to go back to school for my doctorate. Helaine Patterson in the Office of Public Information at Yale School of Medicine has been very generous with her time and in sending me press releases and other materials. Marilyn and Tom Ross, co- founders of SPAN (co-authors of *The Complete Guide to Self-Publishing*, Cincinnati, OH: Writer's Digest Books, 3rd edition, 1994), Dan Poynter (*The Self-Publishing Manual*, Santa Barbara, CA: Para Publishing, 1995), Jan Nathan and Terry Nathan of Publishers Marketing Association (PMA), Pat Dolson, and especially Tim Ward, Bob Kreger, and account executive David Saunders of BookCrafters have been very helpful to me as I made the leap from author to publisher, as I learned how to typeset this book, design its interior and its cover, and master dozens of other technical and practical concerns and details. *Book $elling 101* by Art and Jean Heine (Virginia Beach, VA: J-Mart Press, 1995) and Avery Cardoza's *The Complete Guide to Successful Publishing* (NY: Cardoza Publishing, 1995) have also been helpful as well as several organizations, in addition to PMA and SPAN: AAP (Association of American Publishers Inc.), ABA (American Booksellers Association), Women's National Book Association, New York City chapter; NEBA (New England Booksellers Association); Irwin Zucker of Book Publicists of Southern California. A very warm thanks to my friend and colleague, Sally Wendkos Olds, who placed the very first order for this book.

I also want to express my appreciation of cartoonist Tom Cheney, whose work I first became familiar with through a holiday card that I received from the *National Business Employment Weekly*, for granting me permission to reprint his illustrations; as well as Johnny Hart and Perri Hart for permission to reprint Hart's *B.C.* cartoon.

There are so many others who have offered friendship and help over the years. The list that follows may seem extensive but, over 17 years, there are lots of thanks to convey. (As extensive as this list is, I am sure I have unintentionally left out someone. Forgive my unintentional oversight!) A special thanks also to: Nancy Creshkoff, Mary Claycomb, and Barney Rosset, my bosses in publishing; Janice E. Hayman, Tia and Dick Denenberg, Dieter Hagenbach, Charles and Ann Rucker, Sharon Giese, Carole Addabbo and Larry Moskowitz, Patti Zimmer, Priscilla Orr, Jody Rosengarten, Marilyn Horowitz, Barry Meadow, Dick and Judy Delson, Doug Cheek, AWED, Janet Siegenthaler, Lindsey Pollak, Cammie Morgan, Bob Stein, Nancy Trent, Sharon Hymer, Janet and Edgar Grana, Milt and Barbara Haynes, Candy, Eddie, and Mollie Craven, Val San Antonio, Judge Jack and Evelyn Weinstein, Karen McMahon, Cathy Gavin, Helen Kistler, Jerry Hackman, Jose Novoa, John Beaulieu, Randy Rogers, Steve Herzfeld, Jacqueline Murphy, David Friedrichs, John Glass, Jan Fritz, Dan Chekki, Peter Nardi, the late Alfred McClung Lee, Elizabeth Lee, Marshall Clinard, the late John Clausen, Lucille Duberman, Claude Fisher, William J. Goode, Ted Huston, Mike Brown, the late Ed Sagarin, Judith Stein, Nicholas Babchuk, P.H. Wright, Stanley O. Gaines, Jr., Anne Peplau, David Sills, Steve Buff, Janet Billson, Stephen Steele, Bogdan Denitsch, Kenneth Rubin, Bradford Smart, Art Shostak, David J. Kallen,, Peter J. Stein, Ralph Stavitz (who helped distribute my survey at St. John's University), Richard Harris, Betty Sung, Patricia Kendall, Cynthia Fuchs Epstein, the late David

Caplovitz, Elizabeth Clark, the late Michael Wubnig, Stephen P. Bank, my dissertation advisor Charles Kadushin, Andrew H. Greeley, Linda Sapadin, Herbert J. Freudenberger, Joan Blumenfeld, Trish Dayan, Steven R. Asher, Penelope Leach, Burton White, T. Berry Brazelton, David Plath, Clark E. Cunningham, Michelle Landberg, Tovah Klein, Rebecca Renwick, Jeffrey Brenner, Joseph Giordano, H.I. Day, Alice Honig, Harold Burson, Charles Peebler, J. Douglas Phillips, Andrew Sherwood, Stanley P. Heilbronn, Christopher Forbes, Debbie Harkins, Polly Bergen, Beverly Garland, Neal Sherman, Paulette Ensign, Stephanie Winston, Sandy Bernstein, Stephanie Culp, Letitia Baldrige, Dorothea Johnson, Barbara Babcock Chizmas, Randi Freidig, Doe Lang, Camille Lavington, Diana Rowland, John Lutz, the late Thomas Chastain, Betty Yarmon, Letty Cottin Pogrebin, Rosemary Corriere, Tal Dean McAbian, Irene Cohen, Marilyn Howard, Charlie Matthau, David Carradine, Estelle Parsons, Julie Phelan, Elizabeth Guber, Joel Simon, Murem Sharpe, Phyllis Beckerman, Marti Harding, Jim Mugavero, Mark Goines, John Sturges, Nana Greller, Mardi Harding, Dori Olds, Sheldon Cherry, Gil Cates, Jill Wood, Rabbi Irwin Isaacson.Suzanne Timel, Michael Korda, Gay Talese, Ernest Callenbach, Martin Poll, Bob Plunkett, MaryAnne Kasica, Dan Kadlec, Arlyn Greenbaum, Mitch Davis, Bill Daniels, Mary Claycomb, Barney Rosset, Andrea Plate, John Ware, Carol of Kreative Kids, the late Harold and Miriam Hoffman, Rev. Dorothy Payne, Lynn Mullins, Judy Rothstein, Eve Siegal, Dina Merrill; my outstanding teachers over the years—Beatrice Salzman, the late Mr. Smolar, Hayes B. Jacobs, Mrs. Snipes, the late Dr. Pratt, and Howard Siegman.

A heartfelt thanks to my monthly support group of Connecticut writers: Vicky, Janice, Claire, Jennifer, Jane, Elizabeth, and Fran; to members of the American Society of Journalists and Authors (ASJA) including Sally Wendkos Olds, Julian Block, Claire Berman, Joan Detz, Elizabeth S. Lewin, Vicky Secunda, Claire Safran, Janice Papalos, Jane Resnick, Murray Teigh Bloom, Sondra Forsyth, Kelly Good McGee, David Zimmerman, Lynne Alpern, Anne Barry, Barbara Brabec, Shirley Camper Soman, Sherry Suib Cohen, Claudia Caruana, Kay Cassill, the late Isobel Silden, Robert Gannon, Mark Fuerst, Crescent Dragonwagon, Grace Weinstein, Dodie Schultz, Dian Dincin Buchman, Bonnie Remsberg, Ron Engh, Michael Zey, Susan Lapinski, Jacqueline Thompson, Alex Cantor Owens, Kay Cassill, Paula M. Siegel, Marilyn Green, Shari Steiner, Kate Kelly, Dorothy Beach of Dial-a-Writer, Robert Bahr, Catherine Lanham Miller, Shirley Sloan Fader, Glen Evans, Judith Ramsey Ehrlich, Lynne S. Dumas, Claudia Dreifus, Margaret DiCanio, Flora Davis, Margaret

Danbrot, Alan Caruba, Charlotte Libov, Norman M. Lobsenz, Robert Scott Milne, Linda Murray, Nena O'Neill, Paulette Cooper, Joan German-Crapes, Donna Goldfein, Tania Grossinger, the late Mort Weisinger, Bernie Hurwood, Maurice Zolotow, and June Roth; members of the Connecticut Press Club including Lori Moody, Rita Pepazian, Audrey Thompson, Stephanie Dahl, Carolee Ross, Caroline Owens, Doris Skutch; my playgroup friends—Rhonda Ginsberg, Maxine Friedlich, Shelley Kruk, Paula Green, Loralee Granowitz, Barbara Schwartz, Beverly Stein, and the group's founder, Sandy Lada; my neighbors Mugzy, Ann, Joanna, Michelle, Mary, Sue, Eleanore, Laurie, Monica, Ann; Fran Dorf, Rabbi Sharon Sobel, Cantor Marina Belenky, Dorothy S. Fields, Marcia Bick, Fran Schechter, Suellyn Bache, Deborah Finkel, Sally Kelman, Marlene Hacker, Karen Neems, Laura Levine, Katy Myers, Eileen Orlow, and Phyllis Lyons; my magazine, newspaper, and book editors especially my first editor at Scribner's, Patricia Cristol, and my first publicist at Scribner's, Susan Richman, and the late Charles Scribner; Ron Roel, Marty Edelston, Maureen Smith Williams, Mary Ann Cavlin, Cele Lalli, Tony Lee, V.J. Pappas, Toni Gerber Hope, Fran Carpentier, Jean Pascoe, Betty Jane Raphael, Donna Jackson, Rick Greene, Scott DeGarmo, Howard Siner, David Hendin, Sid Goldberg, Paula Reichler Parker, Sara Perl, Susan Tito, Dan Barber, Susan Jarzyk, Peter Goldman, Jim Kennedy, Cynthia Folino, Susan Ginsberg, Mary Kuntz, Susan Hipsley, Kate Kelley, Sam Vaughan, Les Pockell, Howard Epstein, Nancy Evans, Mike Hamilton, Kim Hendrickson, Debbie Wiley, Sally Arteseros, Mark Golin, Jennifer Fairfield, Dariion Dizon, Margaret V. Daly, Don Rauf, Jane Chesnutt, Pat Curtis, and Noelle Ray; Barbara S. Sarason, Kiyoshi Asano, Gabriela Vergara, Georgina Coombs, Jonathan G. Harris, Lora Fountain, Helene Raude, and Fotel/GGX Inc.

I also want to thank my first friends at Public School 31 in Bayside, Queens—Emily Rock, Anita Walsh, Jane Grossinger, Brenda Milchman, Jeanne Muratore; Paula Fins, Roberta Serben, Marsha Groden, and from my block Helene Jarvis, Esme Hochbaum, Barry Goode, Ginny Mugavero, and Arlene Potash, and Linda Zaks from my block and around the corner; Linda Blatt, and, from Francis Lewis High School, Marilyn Marcuson, Margaret Lazarus, Bruce Serlen, Diana Krieg, Ilene Peiser, Janet Chall, Etta Roth, Meredith Maislin, Susan Malkin, Sheila Bayor Conner, Robin Freistadt Fraser, and so many others; Linda Marsa; my camp friends Roz Bindman and Betty Singer; and Francine Martossi from Greenwood Lake.

If I had known then what I know now about *friendshifts*, going to a different middle school than everyone else, going off to college, or selling our summer home would not have ended those friendships; I still treasure the memories of those special relationships.

ABOUT THE AUTHOR

Jan Yager, the former J.L. (Janet Lee) Barkas, has a Ph.D. in sociology from City University in New York (1983), where she was a National Science Foundation Fellow. Her dissertation was on friendship patterns among young urban single women, and she has continued conducting original research on friendship in a variety of settings and with a range of groups—from workers to widows. Dr. Yager has a B.A. in Fine Arts from Hofstra University, where she was named Art Student of the Year (1968). She also has an M.A. in criminal justice from Goddard College Graduate School; prior to that, she did graduate work in psychiatric art therapy at Hahnemann Medical College.

Dr. Yager is the author of 11 highly acclaimed nonfiction books including *Business Protocol: How to Survive & Succeed in Business* (Wiley, 1991); *Making Your Office Work for You* (Doubleday, 1989); *Creative Time Management* (Prentice-Hall, 1985); *Victims* (Scribner's, 1978); *The Help Book* (Scribner's, 1979); *The Vegetable Passion: A History of the Vegetarian State of Mind* (Scribner's, 1975); and *Friendship: A Selected, Annotated Bibliography* (Garland, 1985). *Business Protocol* earned First Place in the 1992 Communications Contest of the National Federation of Press Women (NFPW). There have been British, Dutch, Japanese, and Spanish translations of several of her books.

A former assistant professor in the Department of Behavioral Sciences at New York Institute of Technology, as well as a visiting assistant professor at Penn State, she has also taught at St. John's University, Temple University, and The New School for Social Research. Her 250+ articles have appeared in *Parade, The New York Times, Harper's, Woman's Day, Modern Bride, Boardroom Reports, The National Business Employment Weekly, Redbook,* and *Family Circle.*

A frequent TV and radio talk show guest, workshop leader, and speaker, Dr. Yager resides in Connecticut with her husband and children.

How to Contact the Author

Requests for information about Dr. Yager's workshops or her availability for speaking on *Friendshifts: The Power of Friendship and How It Shapes Our Lives* may be directed to her at the following address:
Jan Yager, Ph.D.
P.O. Box 8038
Stamford, CT 06905-8038

Readers of this book are also invited to share their comments about *Friendshifts* with Dr. Yager, as well as any suggestions for any future revised editions, although there is no assurance of a personal reply.

This book was produced on a Compaq Presario 5528 using the Microsoft® Word 7.0 word processing program for Windows® 95. It was then reformatted using Adobe PageMaker® 6.0 and printed out on a Hewlett Packard LaserJet 5MP printer. Camera ready copy was then supplied to BookCrafters in Fredericksburg, Virginia in order to print hardcover editions of this title using a Cameron Belt press and adhesive case binding with Kivar 7 cloth. The dust jacket was printed via offset lithography using 2 PMS colors and 1 metallic PMS color.

Friendshifts™ was created with Microsoft WordArt (Wave 2).

Index

If you wish to receive a *free* listing of other available publications, drop a note to the publisher at the address below.

You may order additional copies of *Friendshifts: The Power of Friendship and How It Shapes Our Lives* by Jan Yager, Ph.D. through your local bookstore or directly from the publisher at the address below by sending a money order or check for $22.95 plus $5.00 shipping and handling per copy (double the postage for foreign orders). (For books shipped to a CT address, add applicable 6% sales tax.)

Hannacroix Creek Books, Inc.
1127 High Ridge Road, #110
Stamford, CT 06905 USA
(203) 321-8674 (203) 968-0193 (fax)

All orders must be prepaid.
Checks should be made out to "Hannacroix Creek Books, Inc."

Contact the publisher for information on the discount programs the are available for bulk purchases.